D0878477

# Gender Issues in Education

# Gender Issues in Education

**Herbert Grossman**
*San Jose State University*

**Suzanne H. Grossman**
*Gay Austin School*

**Allyn and Bacon**
Boston • London • Toronto • Sydney • Tokyo • Singapore

Series Editor: *Virginia Lanigan*
Editorial Assistant: *Nicole DePalma*
Composition Buyer: *Linda Cox*
Manufacturing Buyer: *Megan Cochran*
Production Coordinator: *Cheryl Ten Eick*
Editorial-Production Service: *Spectrum Publisher Services*

Copyright © 1994 by Allyn and Bacon
A Division of Simon & Schuster, Inc.
160 Gould Street
Needham Heights, Massachusetts 02194

All rights reserved. No part of the material protected by this
copyright notice may be reproduced or utilized in any form or by
any means, electronic or mechanical, including photocopying,
recording, or by any information storage and retrieval system,
without the written permission of the copyright owner.

**Library of Congress Cataloging-in-Publication Data**

Grossman, Herbert, Ph. D.
    Gender issues in education / Herbert Grossman, Suzanne H.
Grossman.
        p. cm.
    Includes bibliographical references and index.
    ISBN 0-205-15039-X
    1. Sex differences in education—United States—Cross-cultural
studies.   2. Sex discrimination in education—United States—Cross-
cultural studies.   3. Educational equalization—United States—
Cross-cultural studies.   I. Grossman, Suzanne H.   II. Title.
LC212.92.G76   1993
370.19'345—dc20                                    93-10049
                                                        CIP

Printed in the United States of America

10  9  8  7  6  5  4  3  2  1      96  95  94  93

*To our children, Bill and Michele*

# Contents

# Preface

Our society is in the process of achieving gender equity and redefining the relationships between males and females in all aspects of public and private life. This text is concerned with one significant area in which this is taking place—the schools. It focuses on three educationally relevant gender issues.

1. The disparate educational outcomes of males and females
2. The gender-biased ways teachers treat students
3. The gender-stereotypical societal role for which schools prepare students

The outcomes of education for female and male students have been the subject of much discussion and research. Although most students attend coeducational schools and classes, males and females have different school experiences and leave school with different skills. Some of these gender differences cut across class and ethnic boundaries. In general, females have a lower dropout rate than males. They also are less likely to get into trouble for behavioral problems, less likely to be disciplined by their teachers or suspended from school, and less likely to be placed in special education programs for the learning disabled, behavior disordered, or emotionally disturbed.

Gender differences vary for students from different socioeconomic classes and ethnic backgrounds. European American females (American females from a European cultural heritage regardless of the number of generations removed from their heritage) score higher than European American males on verbal tasks and basic computational skills, and receive higher grades in English and foreign language courses. However, European American females, especially those from working-class backgrounds, score lower than males on tests involving complex mathematical skills, word problems, and visual-spatial abilities, and they receive lower grades in math and most science courses. Females take fewer advanced math, computer, and science courses—the courses that are so important for college admission and success in many technological and scientific fields. They react less positively than males to difficult and challenging situations and to the possibility of failure. Females are less likely to take risks and are less confident than males in many situations that have been, and are still often, seen as belonging to the *male domain*. They are more likely to attribute their poor performance to lack of ability even when objective evidence indicates that other factors, such as lack of effort or sexist instruction, account for their poor achievement.

The gender differences among African American students do not conform to this pattern. African American females do better than their male peers on tests of verbal, science, and mathematics achievement. They enroll in more advanced math and science courses and do not have less confidence in their abilities in these academic subjects. They do not perceive these subjects as being in the male domain. American Indian, Asian/Pacific Island American, and Hispanic American students also have unique gender differences.

Many factors contribute to these gender, ethnic, and socioeconomic class differences in educational outcomes. Some gender differences apply to most ethnic groups because to a limited degree the genders are biologically predisposed to function differently. More important, society expects and teaches all Americans, regardless of their ethnic and socioeconomic backgrounds to behave in gender-specific ways by modeling gender-specific roles that children can copy and then rewards them for doing so. In addition, society structures the lives of each gender differently, thus reproducing the status quo in each generation.

Many gender differences do not apply to all ethnic groups and socioeconomic classes. Each ethnic group and socioeconomic class also has its own gender-specific behavioral expectations that its members are exposed to and rewarded for fulfilling. In addition, American society structures the lives of males and females in each group differently, thereby reproducing unique gender dissimilarities in each of them.

One purpose of this text is to help teachers to appreciate the contributions these various factors make to gender inequity and to reduce such inequality by employing gender-appropriate educational approaches. Teachers treat students in a gender-biased manner. Research indicates that they have different academic expectations for males and females and encourage them to enroll in different courses and extracurricular activities. Teachers provide males and females with unequal amounts and different kinds of attention. They employ different classroom management techniques with each gender and teach students to act differently. In addition, they use classroom procedures that often involve the separation of students by gender.

A second purpose of this text is to bring these facts to the attention of teachers and to help them discover and eliminate any gender biases they may have.

The third purpose of this text is related to the issue of whether teachers should continue to prepare males and females for different roles. This issue has caused enormous controversy among educators. There are four distinct positions.

**1.** Educators should prepare the genders to fulfill different roles because there are natural, physiological differences between the sexes. They should not relate to students in an androgynous manner.

**2.** Educators should prepare students for the androgynous roles that are increasingly available to them, and they should encourage students to do what is necessary to bring about a less sexist society.

**3.** Educators should decide for themselves whether they want to prepare students to fulfill different gender roles or to encourage students to fill similar roles because the desirability or undesirability of gender roles is something for each professional or group to decide.

**4.** Educators should help students decide for themselves whether or not they wish to conform to any particular gender role and whether or not they prefer to be androgynous.

The authors' purpose is not to convince teachers that any one of these positions is preferable to the others. Rather, it is to help educators to critically examine the rationales underlying these four points of view and their implications for educating students.

The authors believe it is important for readers to compare how they believe they *should* deal with gender issues to how they *actually perform* in a classroom when these issues arise. To that end, self-quizzes and other activities have been included in this volume to enhance readers' insight into their views on gender issues, and if they are experienced teachers, their behavior in class. (Some of these exercises are appropriate for experienced teachers; many others are designed for teachers-in-training.) The authors realize that self-insight alone may not be sufficient to change behavior, especially in an environment structured to make change difficult. But, they believe it is a good way to begin.

The book is divided into two parts. Part 1 examines gender differences in students' school experiences, as well as societal roles and their origins. Chapter 1 begins by describing the current educationally relevant differences between the genders. Special attention is placed on students' emotional responses, interpersonal relationships, moral development, communication styles, and learning styles. The chapter then examines gender differences in students' enrollment in academic and vocational courses, participation in school activities, academic achievement, and behavior in class. Chapter 2 discusses the origins of these differences.

Part 2 discusses the practical concerns of educators—dealing with gender issues in the classroom. Chapter 3 examines various opinions and definitions of gender equity. Chapter 4 deals with approaches for accommodating educational techniques to gender differences. Chapter 5 describes techniques for eliminating gender-specific behavior.

Because we know much more about the role gender plays in the classroom than we knew twenty years ago, there is a heavy emphasis on research throughout the text. This does not mean we now know all there is to know about gender issues. Although we do know a lot about some gender differences, many important issues need to be studied. In addition, all too often, conclusions about all students are derived from the results of studies that are not representative of the geographical, socioeconomic, or ethnic diversity of students. Too many studies include only European American students. Others—working-class students, African Americans, Asian/Pacific Island Americans, Hispanic Americans, and other non-European Americans—are grossly underrepresented in the research on gender. Clearly, the results of studies that include only one ethnic or socioeconomic group cannot be generalized to all students.

Research results also paint a static picture. What was true of a group a number of years ago may not be true today, and even less so tomorrow. Yet, research studies are not commonly replicated every few years. As a result, research data can be misleading. For example, descriptions of the self-concepts of African American female students that were based on research done in the 1950s and 1960s, prior to attempts to increase African American self-pride and before the introduction of Black studies and multicultural education into the school curriculum, no longer apply. Likewise, studies on females' career choices and their plans to enroll in higher education conducted prior to the women's liberation movement can offer misleading guidelines to today's educators. This research indicated that fewer females aspired to professional careers in law, medicine, engineering, and the like, which require university degrees, than is true for contemporary female students.

To avoid the problems just listed, the authors have tried to deal with gender issues in a socioeconomic and ethnic context and to include the results of the most up-to-date research. They believe the text includes the information about gender issues that educators need to be informed consumers of research-based knowledge.

The inclusion of research concerning different ethnic groups is somewhat uneven. This results from the fact that much more is known about gender differences among some ethnic groups such as African Americans and Hispanic Americans than about other groups such as Chinese Americans and Vietnamese Americans. The authors could have supplemented the research by including studies about gender differences among ethnic groups living abroad. However, they believe that such information would provide an inaccurate understanding of the cultural characteristics of Americans from these ethnic backgrounds who live in the United States.

Readers may be uncomfortable with some of the terminology used in the book. This is unavoidable. People use the same term in different ways and different terms for the same concept. Some authors use the terms *sex* and *gender* interchangeably, while others use the term *sex* to refer to biological differences and *gender* when referring to differences that they assume are not biological. The terms *gender stereotypes, gender-typical behavior,* and *gender-specific behavior* all refer to similar concepts. The same applies to *gender bias* and *sexism,* as well as *low income, lower class, working class,* and *poor.*

To some individuals, one term is preferable to the others because of the connotation. What may appear to some as a minor difference in terminology can signify major differences in point of view. It is often the case that no usage will satisfy everyone.

In most cases, the authors have attempted to handle the problem of terminology by using the most current terms, with the understanding that these may change and become dated. When a number of terms are in use and no overwhelming reason exists to prefer one over another, they have used several current terms for the same concept. In a few cases, they have used the term they prefer even though it may not be the one in fashion. The authors hope that readers will look beyond the controversy over terminology to the more substantive issues dealt with in the text.

## ACKNOWLEDGMENTS

We would like to thank the following professors for their valuable comments about earlier drafts of the manuscript: Ji-Mei Chang, Elba Maldonado-Colon, June McCullough, and Pat Millar. Patricia Beard took the wonderful photographs. The following schools and agencies in California permitted her to photograph their students: Adams Middle School, Richmond; Art, Research and Curriculum, Oakland; El Cerrito High School, El Cerrito; Gay Austin School, Berkeley; Oxford Elementary School, Berkeley; Patti's Playhouse, El Cerrito; Prospect School, El Cerrito.

H. Grossman
S. H. Grossman
Berkeley, California

# ▶ Part 1

## Gender Differences and Their Origins

# ► 1

# Gender Differences

In general, females and males experience disparate educational outcomes and fulfill different gender-specific roles both in school and in the larger society. However, these differences do not apply to all students. Although many educators still tend to speak about, and act on, misleading gender stereotypes, no generalization about male-female behavioral differences applies to all males or all females.

All males and all females do not conform to any particular gender-stereotypical behavior pattern. Even in situations in which people tend to behave in a gender-stereotypical manner, their actual behavior cannot be predicted on the basis of their sex alone (1–2). For example, ethnic and socioeconomic factors significantly influence people's behavior. There are also important regional/geographic differences in the way individuals behave. Because of prejudice, some individuals are prevented from fulfilling roles they would prefer. Contextual factors, such as the reactions people expect from others, help to determine whether they will behave in their preferred manner. As a result, generalizations about gender differences among all female and all male students can be highly misleading. In addition, any characterization of *women of color,* African American males, underrepresented minorities, working-class students, or virtually any other ethnic group or socioeconomic class can be equally inaccurate.

This chapter briefly discusses some factors other than gender that help determine students' behavior. Then it describes gender differences in students' educational outcomes and societal roles. It explores gender differences within various ethnic groups and socioeconomic classes, as well as those that cut across ethnic and socioeconomic class lines.

More is known about gender differences among European American middle-class students because research has been focused on them. However,

Many children, especially younger ones, do not
conform to gender stereotypes.

we do know quite a bit about gender differences among non-European
American and working-class students. A statement like the following that
was substantially correct a while ago is much less true today. To act as if it
were still true would be to proceed in ignorance.

> *Given that the general sex literature is based largely upon white middle-
> class children and adults, it offers us limited information with reference to
> the possibilities of differences in patterns of sex differentiation across ethnic
> and cultural groups. (3, p. 140)*

## INFLUENCES ON BEHAVIOR

### *Ethnic and Socioeconomic Class Differences*

Different ethnic groups expect different gender-specific behavior from their members. As a result, students from varied ethnic backgrounds do not behave in the same gender-specific ways. Students brought up in other countries, or by parents who were born in other countries, or by parents who belong to ethnic groups that do not share the values and expectations of European American middle-class parents may learn to behave in the gender-specific ways of their own ethnic group rather than in the ways typical of the European American majority. For example, European American students tend to be exposed to more nontraditional role models (models that run counter to those that were common twenty or more years ago) than do their Hispanic American and Asian/Pacific Island American peers who are brought up in families and communities that have more traditional values, beliefs, and expectations about gender roles.

Subgroups within these larger ethnic groups also differ. Although not all students fit the following generalizations, Mexican American students tend to be exposed to more traditional role models than the Nicaraguan American students who were brought up in the atmosphere of relative equality between the genders that was encouraged by the Sandinistas after their assumption of power. Filipino females tend to grow up in a society in which the roles that the genders fulfill are much more alike than in Vietnam. American Indians who maintain their traditional life-styles live differently than those who have acculturated to the mainstream European American culture. And while students from Italian, Russian, Greek, English, Irish, Scandinavian, Polish, Turkish, Armenian, German, Swiss, Spanish, Portuguese, and other European heritages have some European cultural characteristics in common when compared to African American or Asian Pacific/Island American students, their cultural heritages are also notably different.

There is diversity among students brought up in families with similar ethnic backgrounds. Parents who want their children to maintain their own ethnic identities may encourage and even pressure them to maintain traditional values, attitudes, and behavior patterns to a much greater degree than parents who want to assimilate and acculturate into the American mainstream. For example, Mexican migrant workers and their children who plan to return to Mexico may be less motivated to adopt European American values and behavior patterns than those who intend to settle here permanently.

Students from different socioeconomic backgrounds are also influenced by dissimilar cultural experiences. In addition, the change in attitude toward gender-specific roles that has occurred in the United States during the past twenty or thirty years has been primarily a middle-class phenomenon. As a result, students from working-class backgrounds are more likely to be brought up to fulfill traditional roles than middle-class students.

Even students from the same socioeconomic class may not be equally motivated to maintain their cultural heritage. Students in upwardly mobile low-income families and those who identify with and wish to join or emulate the middle class may be less likely to aspire to, or fulfill, traditional gender roles than students who are content with their economic situation.

There is also a relationship between socioeconomic class and ethnic background that has to do with immigration patterns. For example, immigrants from certain countries such as the Philippines, South Korea, and Taiwan have tended to be predominantly middle class, while those from Mexico, El Salvador, and Haiti have been overwhelmingly from working-class backgrounds. Thus, as a result of immigration patterns, Filipino American, Korean American, and Taiwanese American students are more likely to come from backgrounds that approximate that of European American middle-class students, while Mexican American, Salvadorean American, and Haitian American students' values and life-styles, although different from those of European American students, tend to be more similar to those of working-class rather than middle-class European American students.

## Regional Differences

Regional differences create diversity among ethnic and socioeconomic groups. For example, Mexican American students who live in *border towns* in Texas, New Mexico, and Arizona, and Cuban Americans who live in areas with large Hispanic American populations such as Miami are more likely to be exposed to the traditional Latino cultural life-styles and attitudes than Mexican American and Cuban American students who live in other parts of the country. As a result, they may have more traditional points of view about gender roles. Likewise, students from low-income families growing up in Appalachia have somewhat different experiences and exposure to middle-class values and behavior patterns than students from cities such as New York, Detroit, or Atlanta, and they may be more likely to behave in traditional ways than urban students.

## Prejudice

Students treated in a prejudicial manner are often discouraged from aspiring to certain roles or prevented from fulfilling the roles to which they aspire. For example, racism in employment discourages many working-class African American male students from hoping to fulfill traditional male roles because they know they are less likely than European Americans to have the opportunity to be the *bread winner* of the family and to enjoy the status associated with being the primary source of financial support. Poor parents who can barely afford to have one child attend college may persuade their daughters to sacrifice their desires for higher education so that their brothers can obtain a college or university degree.

Teachers' prejudicial attitudes toward students from certain ethnic and socioeconomic backgrounds often counteract or exacerbate students' gender-specific behavior in school. For example, teachers tend to treat African American females in ways that are likely to cause them to doubt their academic abilities even more than European American females. They manage the behavior of African American males in ways that lead them to behave more disruptively than males in general. (See chapter 2 for a more detailed discussion.)

### Contextual Factors

Whether students will behave in gender-stereotypical ways depends in part on the expectations, attitudes, and actions of the people they are with and the consequences they expect. Males and females behave differently in same-sex and mixed-sex groups. And they conform in some degree to both the expectations of teachers who support and encourage androgynous behavior and those who reward them for fulfilling gender-stereotypical roles. (See the following discussion and chapters 4 and 5.)

## GENDER DIFFERENCES

While generalizations about gender differences can be misleading, it is important to recognize that some gender differences cut across class, ethnic, and geographic boundaries, and certain descriptions of socioeconomic classes or ethnic groups tend to apply to the majority of their members. Such generalizations can be helpful because they can sensitize educators to the possibility that their students may behave in certain gender-specific ways. Educators should never assume, however, that their students will necessarily do so. It is as important to avoid relating to students on the basis of incorrect gender stereotypes as it is to avoid being insensitive to the role gender-specific attitudes and behavior may play in students' lives.

Gender differences do not appear all at once. They develop gradually, each stage influencing the development in subsequent stages to help produce the gender differences we see among adults. A few appear during the infant and toddler stages. Many more appear during the preschool stage. Others occur during elementary and secondary school. For this reason, gender differences discussed in this section are divided into three age groups—infants and toddlers, preschoolers, and school-age children and youth.

For many years, some educators have believed that the age when differences between males' and females' behavior first appear provides a clue about whether the difference is innate (biologically determined) or caused by environmental (psychosocial) influences. "A useful strategy is to assume that the earlier a particular behavioral difference appears in the life cycle, the more likely it is influenced by biological factors" (7, p. 217).

Others are convinced that we can determine the school's role in forming sex-roles by examining the degree to which the sexes come to school already behaving differently or learn to behave differently during their school years. However, it is far from certain that gender differences in infants and toddlers are definitely determined biologically or that gender differences observed in school-age children and youth, but not in infants, toddlers, and preschoolers should be attributed to their school-related experiences. (See chapter 2.)

This section describes the gender differences that have been confirmed by research. These include dissimilarities in emotional, relationship, moral, communication, and learning styles, motivation to avoid success, school participation, academic achievement, and behavior problems.

## Infants and Toddlers

In most respects, male and female infants and toddlers behave similarly, with a few gender differences present during the first year or two of their lives. During the first year of life, although there are many exceptions to the rule, girls appear to be more fearful than boys and to cry more often when they are frightened (6). By the time they are eighteen months old, girls are already quieter and calmer than boys, who exhibit higher levels of excitement (9). By then, girls have started to show fewer angry, frustrated outbursts. Boys do not exhibit a similar decline in the intensity or frequency of angry outbursts (10). By the end of their first year, boys and girls are already demonstrating some sex-stereotypical preferences for toys (4, 5, 8). For example, although the research is limited, it appears that at this age many females prefer cuddly toys and males prefer robots.

For some individuals, the paucity of gender differences at this stage signifies that most of the gender differences seen in older children are learned. Others disagree, believing that many of the differences observed in older children are biologically determined. They claim that some potential differences are not observed until children expand their behavioral repertoires enough for these differences to be reflected in their behavior. (See chapter 2 for a more detailed discussion of this issue.)

## *Preschoolers*

During preschool, the differences between the sexes in what they play with and how, and where they play, are much more striking (11–24). While definitely not true of all children, most boys prefer to play with airplanes, trucks and cars, blocks, water, and sand; girls prefer dolls, beads, cradles, kitchen toys, make-up, dress-up, art, and dance activities. Boys engage in more rough-and-tumble play than girls. They are also more likely to select activities that are loosely structured, self-initiated, and self-organized, with few externally imposed rules or guidelines and few special roles for each child that are interdependent. An example would be everyone running back and forth in a pack pretending to be firefighters putting out a fire. Girls tend to organize more structured activities, such as playing Little Mermaid or Snow White, in which they assign each other specific interdependent roles and follow an established storyline. Boys tend to engage in more exploratory behavior, such as digging in a sandbox and taking clocks apart, and they choose to play outside. While playing or engaged in other activities, boys are also more physically active (25–27).

Gender differences also show up in the way preschoolers relate to others (28–42). Girls tend to be more polite and helpful and less aggressive and assertive than boys. When faced with potential conflicts, girls tend to at-

Preschoolers tend to prefer gender stereotypical activities.

tempt to preserve the existing harmony by compromise and avoidance, while boys are more likely to confront them head on. Boys get their way with others by physical means—pushing, posturing, and demanding. Girls are more likely to use verbal manipulation ("You can't be my friend. I'm not going to invite you to my party"), verbal persuasion, and polite suggestions. While boys may demand and order others ("Give me that," "Tie your shoe," "This is for the shot [injection] I'm gonna give you"), girls are more indirect and mitigate their requests ("Could you give me the doll?" "This is for the shot I'm gonna give you, OK?").

Girls are more likely to join in the activities of their playmates; boys tend to make more independent choices. While girls are responsive to feedback from teachers and peers of either sex, boys are much less oriented toward and responsive to their teachers and appear to lack interest in and ignore feedback from girls. In the presence of boys, girls become more passive than they usually are and acquiesce to their demands; boys tend to interrupt girls more. In general, girls are more responsive to the desires of boys than boys are to the desires of girls.

The way preschool teachers react to these differences during children's formative stages can affect the way students will function both in and out of school. For example, whether teachers choose to accept that girls tend to act passively around boys and acquiesce to their demands or whether they encourage female students to become more assertive may influence a child's future relationships with the opposite gender.

## School-Age Children and Youth

As children mature and advance in school, the gender differences observed in preschoolers continue, often in more pronounced forms, and additional differences appear. As a result, the behavior of male and female students becomes more disparate during their school years.

## Emotional Differences

Both elementary and secondary school-age girls and boys continue to exhibit somewhat different emotional styles (43–55). Although some children do not fit the mold, school-age girls continue to be more fearful and anxious than boys. Until recently, this difference was especially noticeable among European American and Hispanic American females in courses such as science and math, traditionally thought to be in the male domain (46, 51, 52, 55). African American females are no more, and may even be a little less, anxious than African American males in these courses (49, 52). During the past few years, females have become less anxious in these courses, perhaps because these courses are now less likely to be perceived as being in the male domain (47, 50). There is also some evidence that males are more anxious than females in English classes, a course that many males perceive to be in the female domain (51).

Female students are also more willing to express their fears and anxieties. But when boys express emotions, they do so more intensely. Girls are also more likely to experience themselves as sad or depressed. Boys are angry more often than girls.

Teachers tend to pay more attention to the angry and disruptive behavior of boys than to the less disruptive behavior of girls. As a result, anxious, sad, and depressed girls (and boys as well) often do not receive the assistance that their emotional problems warrant (see chapter 2). This may be one reason why boys are overrepresented and girls underrepresented in special education programs for students with emotional problems.

## Relationships

Throughout their school careers, the genders exhibit the same contrasts in the ways they relate to others that are observed in their preschool behavior. In general, boys continue to be more assertive, aggressive, and concerned about dominance (56–69). Although the research is not consistent, most studies have found that girls are more altruistic and helpful, especially when strength is not involved (e.g., moving furniture), and the help required is not seen as being in the male domain (e.g., science and mathematics homework). Girls are more likely to share things like equipment and materials with others and to behave in a more supportive manner when their class-mates face the kinds of challenges, problems, and disappointments that lead them to turn to others (70–79). With many exceptions (80), girls are also less competitive than boys (81–84). (See chapter 4 for a more detailed discussion of this topic.)

Some educators think teachers should encourage males to behave more altruistically and cooperatively and less aggressively and assertively. And some think teachers should encourage females to behave more assertively and competitively, especially if they want to succeed in fields that they believe require such behavior. (See chapter 5 for a more detailed discussion of this topic.)

Females are more likely to share their thoughts and feelings with their peers and parents (86–89). There is some evidence that people who do not share their feelings and experiences with others are more likely to develop emotional problems than those who do so (85, 90). If this is true, males, and, of course, females who do not disclose their feelings to others are at a disadvantage.

Females generally tend to avoid conflicts with others, rather than deal with them openly (66, 69, 91). This can benefit the group by reducing the kinds of quarrels and disagreements that cause rifts among students and reduce the group's efficiency. But it can also impede the group's progress when it is necessary to resolve disagreements among members.

Female students tend to seek the assistance and approval of adults more than boys do (92–95). Educators who believe this reflects greater female sensitivity to, and concern about, the feelings of others view this as a posi-tive characteristic. However, educators who believe this stems from female students' lack of self-confidence and a tendency to be overly dependent on the approval of others consider this a negative personality characteristic. They are also concerned that female dependency on others during their school years may contribute to the fact that adult females tend to feign helplessness as a way of influencing others more than men do (96, 97).

It is unlikely that teachers would consciously encourage students to pretend to be helpless in order to manipulate others. However, teachers who are insensitive to the possibility that they may contribute to their students' learned helplessness may inadvertently do so by providing female students with more assistance than they need.

As they do in preschool, males continue to exercise a dominant role in mixed-sex groups throughout their educational careers (98–102). Boys initi-ate and receive more of the interaction, do more of the talking, and are more influential in the decision-making process than girls, especially girls who are generally acquiescent to others. While girls tend to be equally responsive to the requests of either sex, boys continue to be responsive primarily to other males.

Some evidence, mostly anecdotal, suggests that in comparison to European American females, many of these differences apply to a greater degree to Hispanic American and Asian/Pacific Island American females who are brought up in families that adhere to traditional ideas about gender roles. But they appear less often or not at all in other ethnic groups that do not bring up their children to fulfill these gender-specific roles (103–111). For example, African American females do not relate to others in these gender-specific ways (107, 108). Many African American females do not act passively, allow males to dominate mixed groups, or use learned helplessness as a way of obtaining their aims. Cultural and economic reasons explain why this is true. Culturally, African Americans do not expect the genders to fulfill different roles to the same extent as European Americans do, and so African American parents do not model these different roles to the extent that European Americans do (105, 106, 110, 111). As Lewis explains:

> *The black child, to be sure, distinguishes between male and females, but unlike the white child he is not inculcated with standards which polarize behavioral expectations according to sex. . . . Many of the behaviors which whites see as appropriate to one sex or the other, blacks view as equally appropriate to both sexes, or equally inappropriate to both sexes; and the sex differences that do exist are more in the nature of contrasts than of mutually exclusive traits. (106, p. 228)*

Economic factors also play a part. Research indicates that African American females tend to be brought up to be independent, aggressive, and assertive because racism has so disabled African American males economically that females cannot rely on males to the extent and in the ways that European American females can (108, 109). According to Simpson:

> *The American caste system has historically enforced the underemployment of Black males. Cognizant of this fact, these Black women were taught that they must be economically independent, regardless of their marital status.*
>
> *White oppression of Black people has created a situation in which, compared to Whites, the underemployment and lower income of Black males and the higher incidence of marital disruption makes it difficult for Black women to anticipate an economically dependent full-time homemaking role with equanimity. (108, p. 126–127)*

Some teachers are not troubled by male dominance of mixed-gender situations. Many others perceive it as a problem that needs correcting. (See chapters 4 and 5 for a more detailed discussion of these points of view.)

## *Moral Approach*

For children to grow up to be good citizens, they have to learn how to behave morally toward others. In recent years, there has been a great deal of theorizing and research about moral development (112–136). There are two different perceptions of moral development, one proposed primarily by males such as Kohlberg and Piaget (126, 130), and a second proposed primarily by females (113, 119–122, 129).

The male point of view sees moral development in terms of improvement in two abilities. The first is people's ability to apply abstract, relatively impersonal, and inflexible principles of justice and fairness to evaluating alternative solutions to situations in which the rights of individuals and/or groups are in conflict. The second ability is people's capacity to act in fair and just ways to resolve these conflicts even when they have to sacrifice their own desires and interests to do so.

Gilligan and her female associates have a different perception of moral development. In their view, the male perception of moral development "reflects a limited western male perspective and may therefore be biased against women and other groups whose moral perspectives are somewhat different" (120, p. 13).

They suggest that moral development involves progress in three areas that are not considered by male theorists—people's increasing sensitivity to the feelings and needs of others, their sense of responsibility for others, and their desire and willingness to care for others. According to this view, people act morally when the needs and feelings of another person compel them to respond in a caring, responsible way, even if the other person has no just claim for such a response.

The difference between male and female morality has been explained in the following way.

> *Men evoke the metaphor of "blind justice" and rely on abstract laws and universal principles to adjudicate disputes and conflicts between conflicting claims impersonally, impartially, and fairly. Women reject the strategy of blindness and impartiality. Instead, they argue for an understanding of the . . . needs of individuals . . . and the particular experiences each participant brings to the situation. (113, p. 8)*

Lyons believes that in male morality "issues, especially decisions of conflicting claims between self and others (including society) are resolved by invoking rules, principles, or standards." Men's moral decisions and actions are evaluated by considering "whether values, principles or standards are (were) maintained, especially fairness." In female morality "problems are generally construed as issues of relationships or of response, that is, how to respond to others in their particular terms." They are "resolved through the activity of care." And women evaluate their actions in terms of "maintaining connections of interdependent individuals to one another or promoting the welfare of others or preventing their harm; or relieving the burdens, hurt, or suffering (physical or psychological) of others" (129, p. 136).

She illustrates the difference between female and male morality in terms of two responses to the question, "What does morality mean to you?" A male responded: "Morality is basically having a reason for or a way of knowing what's right, what one ought to do and when you are put into a situation where you have to choose from among alternatives . . . having some reason for choosing among alternatives." A female responded: "Morality is a type of consciousness, I guess, a sensitivity to humanity, that you can affect someone else's life . . . and you have a responsibility not to endanger other people's lives or hurt other people" (129, p. 125).

Although the research about gender differences in moral development and behavior is not completely consistent, it appears to be true that in general, but with many exceptions, males and females tend to perceive and relate to moral dilemmas in the gender-stereotypical ways described by Gilligan and Lyons. Typically, adults believe females behave somewhat more morally than males. For example, in comparison to the way adults describe boys, they describe girls as telling the truth more consistently and following through more often on what they say they are going to do. Adults also see boys as more prone to maintain a double standard (demanding that others behave more morally than they do), less self-critical of their behavior, and more likely to cheat.

Some people believe that some of the differences adults observe between the genders may be more apparent than real—the product of observer bias and preconceived expectations. And there is some support for their skepticism. For example, while research shows that teenage girls do commit less overt aggression than boys, they engage in more covert aggression. Research also suggests that girls may not cheat less than boys when they think they can get away with it. Krebs, in a review of the research on teachers' perceptions of their students' moral characteristics, entitled "Girls—More Moral than Boys or Just Sneakier," claims this:

*Teachers do view girls as more moral than boys, but the teachers' viewpoint is not supported by behavioral evidence. If girls are not more moral than boys, why do teachers persist in thinking that they are? Apparently, girls do look better than boys do when the teacher is present and making demands, but teachers have mistakenly assumed that girls are generally more moral than boys; that they are more moral not only when the teacher is present, but also when she is absent. (127, pp. 61–62)*

Research indicates that with many exceptions, when measured by tests of moral judgment, girls' moral development tends to proceed more rapidly than boys . There is also evidence that females are more empathic than males (112, 117, 123). As noted above, they are also more responsive to the needs of others. And there is some evidence that males are more likely to cheat on tests (115).

## Communication Style

Most of what is known about gender differences in communication styles concerns European Americans. It is an established fact that European American males and females employ somewhat different communication styles (66, 69, 137–150). Sheldon (66) and Tannen (69) have shown that gender differences in communication styles reflect, and are derived from, the different ways males and females relate to others. Following are two examples of this.

One example is the connection between the way girls relate to each other and the way they speak. As noted above, girls tend to avoid conflict, preserve harmony, and organize their relationships with others in nonhierarchical egalitarian ways. The way they communicate serves these ends. In comparison to boys, they speak politely, with few four-letter and forceful words. They tend to suggest and hint rather than command, and they express themselves less directly—("Let's play house, OK?" "Should we do it?" versus "Gimme the hammer." "Don't touch it"). When they enter into ongoing conversations, they do so in a polite, unintrusive manner.

The second example deals with the way females relate to males. Just as preschool and school-age females tend to act passively in the presence of males and acquiesce to their demands, in mixed groups they allow males to dominate the conversation by permitting them to choose the topics of conversation, interrupt, and hold the floor more often.

Maccoby (145) describes the differences in the male and female communication styles as follows.

> *Boys in all-boy groups, compared with girls in all-girl groups, more often interrupt one another, more often use commands, threats, and boasts of authority, more often refuse to comply with another child's demand, more often give information, heckle a speaker, tell jokes or suspenseful stories, "top" someone else's story, or call another child names. Girls in all-girls groups, on the other hand, more often express agreement with what another speaker has just said, pause to give another girl a chance to speak, and acknowledge what another speaker has said when starting a speaking turn. It is clear that speech serves more egoistic functions among boys and more socially binding functions among girls. (145, p. 758)*

Gender differences in communication styles among European Americans continue into adulthood. Females continue to speak less directly than men. For example, Tannen (69) cites the example of a woman who asks her husband, "Would you like to stop for a drink?" Taking the question literally, he responds "no," and they don't stop. She becomes angry because she wanted to stop, and he becomes frustrated and annoyed because, in his opinion, his wife played games with him instead of telling him what she wanted.

European American women also continue to support and maintain the conversation of others. They signal their attention to the person speaking by nodding, saying "uh hum," and so on. They express their agreement with the speaker, ask leading questions, and interrupt less often. Male adults in all-male groups are less likely to talk about themselves or their feelings than females in all-female groups, as they did when they were younger.

There has been very little research on gender differences in communication styles among non-European Americans. We do know that like European American females, African American females use a less confrontational communication style than males (66, 69, 142). For example, African American males issue direct orders, while females tend to suggest rather than order. And males typically accuse their peers directly to their faces, while females attribute their accusations to third parties by saying things like "Lula said you said I was a . . ." or "Rita tol' me what you did with the birthday present I gave you," thereby avoiding direct accusations and direct confrontations. African American females are also more polite than African American males, but less polite than European American females.

Little is known about possible gender differences in communication styles in other ethnic groups. Therefore, we do not know whether the gender differences described in this section apply to other non-European American groups.

## Learning Style

Research conducted in the 1970s indicated that females were better able to delay making a decision or arriving at a conclusion about something until they had all the information they required. They were also better able to wait for a more desirable reward or outcome rather than to settle immediately for something less desirable (151–152). More research is needed to determine whether this is still the case.

Females and males who are less impulsive have an advantage over their more impulsive peers in school. Students who can wait until they know what they are supposed to do and how they are supposed to do it, and who can work on a long-term project for the rewards they will eventually receive

---

**BOX 1–1    Self-Quiz**

*Communication Style*

What is your opinion about gender differences in communication styles? State whether you think teachers should accept, encourage, or discourage each of the following gender differences in communication styles.

1. Girls' language is more polite.
2. Girls tend to suggest rather than command.

3. Girls express themselves less directly.
4. Females support and maintain the conversation of others.
5. Boys interrupt one another more often.
6. Males in all-male groups are less likely than females in all-female groups to talk about themselves or their feelings.
7. Females allow males to dominate the conversation.

---

or the satisfaction they will eventually gain, are likely to experience more success in school than students who cannot do this.

Studies done in the 1950s, 1960s, and 1970s indicated that males were better able to disregard old solutions to problems and find new ones when the old solutions no longer apply (153–157). Since much has changed since then, additional research is required to investigate whether this difference still exists.

This difference favors males. The more flexibility students demonstrate in shifting from inappropriate solutions to alternative approaches that have promise for success, the more rapidly they will arrive at effective ways of dealing with the educational tasks that confront them.

Girls react less positively than boys to difficult and challenging situations. They are less persistent when faced with difficult tasks in school and are less likely to take risks (158–163). And they do not expect to do as well as boys following failure or the threat of failure (163–168).

Gender differences in self-concept and self-esteem have been the focus of a great deal of research (169–190). Although it is not true of African Americans, in most ethnic groups females tend to be less self-confident than males about school, especially in situations that are in the male domain, such as mathematics and science courses, in competitive situations, and when they lack objective information about how well they have done or can do in situations that involve mastery of tasks in the male domain (52, 173, 175, 177, 179, 181, 184, 187, 190). Females are not less self-confident than males in courses such as *reading*, which are not perceived to be in the male domain and in situations that involve their perceived ability to develop friendly relationships with others, to be popular, to resolve conflicts with others, to break bad habits, to gain self-insight, and so on.

It is unclear whether there also are gender differences in students' over-all self-concepts and self-esteem. Some studies have found that males have higher self-concepts and self-esteem (170, 180, 184, 185); some studies have found no differences between the self-concepts and self-esteem of African American, European American, and Indian American males and females (3, 112, 176, 182, 183, 188). One study found that females, especially African Americans, have more positive self-concepts and higher self-esteem than males (189).

Students differ in terms of the extent to which they believe they are in control of, and responsible for, what happens to them in their lives. Some studies have found that females are more likely than males to believe that they are in control of their lives (183, 196). Some studies have found the opposite (189, 195, 200). And some researchers have found no gender differences for either African American or European American students (207, 211). Thus, there is no reason to believe that males and females differ in this respect.

The results of studies that have examined how students explain their school-related experiences (rather than in their personal lives) paint a different picture. While a few researchers have found no gender differences (193, 198, 210), most studies indicate that males and females attribute their academic successes and failures to different factors. Researchers who have compared males' and females' beliefs about whether they or external factors have greater influence over their general school performance have found that in comparison to males, females, especially those from a working-class background, are more likely to attribute their general academic performance to internal factors (192, 199, 209). However, in courses such as math and science, which are thought to be in the male domain, females tend to attribute their poor performance to internal factors such as lack of ability and their success to external factors such as luck, rather than effort or ability (162, 191, 194, 197, 201, 203, 205, 206, 212). Males' attributions are different. They are more likely to attribute their failures to external factors and their success to internal factors across courses and subjects. (202, 204–206, 208)

Females who conform to these gender-specific behavior patterns can have serious difficulty both in and out of school. Students who are appropriately self-confident are more likely to succeed than those who do not believe they have what it takes to succeed. Likewise, students who can attempt to accomplish things that involve the possibility of failure and can bounce back from the unavoidable failures that almost all students experience from time to time will do better over time than those who avoid possible failure and who are too discouraged by failure to try again. Students who avoid difficult and challenging situations deny themselves growth opportunities. Students who attribute their poor performance to imagined inabilities are less likely to attempt to succeed the next time they face a similar challenge. (Chapters 4 and 5 discuss the various approaches educators can take to deal with these problems.)

European American gifted, average, and low-ability females, especially those from working-class backgrounds, prefer cooperative learning environments and may learn better in certain kinds of cooperative situations (see chapter 4). In group settings, they are more oriented toward group rather than individual goals. Boys respond better to competitive and individualistic situations (81–84, 198, 213–218, 221, 223, 225, 226). These gender stereotypes do not apply to the same degree to American Indians and Hispanic Americans, who grow up in a much less competitive environment (220, 222, 224).

These differences have important educational implications. Since some students learn more efficiently in cooperative learning environments while others learn more in competitive settings, students' achievement depends in part on whether their teachers' instructional style matches their cooperative or competitive learning style. (Chapters 4 and 5 discuss the various approaches educators can take to deal with these differences.) In today's schools, students who learn better in competitive situations may have an advantage since competitive environments predominate (219). However, the recent focus on cooperative learning may be shifting the balance somewhat.

The genders are not equally susceptible to the influence of other people (227–232). Although some research indicates the contrary (231), girls are more likely than boys to modify their opinions and attitudes to conform to others and to copy what others model; boys tend to maintain their ideas and opinions despite what others may think or feel.

It is not clear that one learning style is preferable to another. Some situations call for maintaining one's own opinions and attitudes in the face of opposition. But, when others have more experience, knowledge, and training, it may be better to modify one's ideas and opinions accordingly. Students who cannot distinguish between these two situations and those who are too inflexible to adjust to others' opinions as the situation demands are at a distinct disadvantage. Thus, the most helpful approach teachers can use may be to help students learn to function in both ways. (Chapters 4 and 5 discuss this topic at greater length.)

In mixed groups, girls tend to be equally responsive to requests from, and reinforcement by, either sex. However, boys are responsive primarily to other males (233–237). Females are also less likely than males to participate in group discussions and to assume leadership positions (98–102).

Educators who think individuals should be responsive to the demands of others may find fault with the typical male response to the requests of females. And teachers who believe the sexes should relate to each other on an equal basis may object to the way male and female students relate. They may also feel that females are denying themselves important learning opportunities by allowing males to routinely assume the leadership role. On the other hand, individuals who are comfortable when males dominate mixed-groups may not have any trouble with the sex-role differences listed in this section.

Girls, especially young ones, are more adult-oriented than boys. While they seek the help, support, and feedback of their teachers, boys are more responsive to feedback from their peers (238, 240–243, 245). However, boys who lack self-confidence in their abilities also require teacher feedback to perform well (244).

Females achieve more when adults are present than when they are absent (92). There is suggestive evidence that when they are young, females self-esteem is more dependent on feedback from others; males' self-esteem, however, may be more dependent on their ability to master their environment (239). European American girls are also more likely to use learned helplessness when they are older as a way of influencing others (246, 247). (See above discussion that African American females may not use learned helplessness.)

Males and females differ in terms of their preferences for learning environments that involve active manipulation versus more sedentary learning, working with others or alone, working independently or with teachers' guidance and instruction, and using numbers, logic, and computers (94, 213, 218). In comparison to females, males prefer learning environments that involve working independently, actively manipulating materials, and using numbers, logic, and computers. In fact, some males achieve more when working on programmed materials and computers than when they are given direct instruction by their teachers. Females prefer teacher explanations and directions and working with people. (See chapter 4 for a more detailed discussion of this topic.)

The reason why many females seek their teachers' feedback, learn more in their presence, and prefer working with others, but males prefer to function independently, is unclear. Some educators argue that females learn better in interpersonal situations while males learn better in impersonal ones. They believe females' learning is enhanced when they and their teachers are equally involved in the process of examining their experiences together. And they tend to evaluate the female style more favorably than the male style. Other educators attribute the difference to what they believe is female students' inability to function independently, and they feel that females need to develop independent learning skills. (Chapters 4 and 5 discuss in greater detail the advantages and disadvantages of these gender differences and techniques for dealing with them.)

Girls are more sensitive than boys to nonverbal cues (248, 249). This may be an advantage for females. Since people sometimes say things they do not mean and mean things they do not say, students who are sensitive to teach-

Males tend to prefer to work alone; females are more dependent on adults.

ers' nonverbal communication, as well as their verbal communication, may learn more because they perceive more.

In experimental situations, students' gender schema—their perceptions of gender roles—affect their learning and memory. In general, females and males learn and remember better information that is relevant to their gender roles and conforms to their gender stereotypes (250–256). There are exceptions to this. Students who have traditional or stereotypical views about gender roles have difficulty learning and remembering information that does not conform to their stereotypes, such as adults engaged in nontraditional activities. This may indicate that they have difficulty accepting and processing information that runs counter to their preconceived notions about gender roles. More androgynous students do not experience this difficulty, perhaps because they do not have preconceived notions (251, 252, 254–256).

It is unclear whether the findings in experimental situations also occur outside of the laboratory and affect students' learning in other more naturalistic settings, such as school. It is certainly possible that students who view the world in more gender-stereotypical ways may learn less efficiently than more androgynous students whose range of interests and perceptions are not restricted by gender stereotypes. However, more research is needed before any conclusions about the effects of students' perceptions of gender roles (gender schema) on their learning can be drawn.

### Matched and Mismatched Teaching and Learning Styles

As previously mentioned, students whose learning styles match their teachers' teaching styles tend to learn more and experience school more positively than students whose learning styles clash with their teachers' styles of teaching. Since males and females have somewhat different learning styles, teachers who employ the same teaching techniques with all students regardless of gender will be more successful with the gender that has the matching learning style. For this reason, some educators advise teachers to use different teaching styles with each gender, at least with students whose learning styles fit the gender stereotype. But educators who believe one learning style is more desirable than another advise teachers to help students modify their approaches to learning. (Chapter 3 includes a more detailed discussion of whether educators should adapt their teaching styles to their students learning styles or assist students in modifying their gender-

---

**BOX 1–2    Self-Quiz**

*Learning Style*

Do you agree with those who believe that some learning styles are more desirable than others? For each of the following differences, state whether you think one is preferable to the other or whether each has its advantages in certain situations.

1. Females learn more effectively in cooperative situations. Males achieve more in competitive situations.
2. Females tend to modify their opinions and attitudes to conform to others. Males are more likely to stick to their ideas despite what others think or feel.
3. Females model the behavior of others. Males tend to maintain their behavioral styles despite the models to which they are exposed.
4. Females seek the support and feedback of their teachers. Males function more independently.
5. Females achieve more when adults are present. Males sometimes achieve more when working on programmed materials and computers than when they are given direct instruction by their teachers.
6. Females prefer teacher explanations and directions and working with people. Males prefer learning environments that involve working independently, actively manipulating materials, and using numbers, logic, and computers.

stereotypical learning styles. Chapters 4 and 5 describe techniques for accomplishing each of these goals.)

## Motivation to Avoid Success

Although the evidence is somewhat inconsistent, it appears that males and
females have different reactions to success in school (69, 259–261, 263). Many
European American females, especially those from less affluent and working-class backgrounds, have mixed feelings about, and are uncomfortable
with, success in courses or occupations traditionally thought of as being in
the male domain. This applies to a lesser degree to African American females.

Research indicates that there are at least two reasons for this (69, 257–
259, 262, 263). One is that some females are concerned that they may seem
less feminine and be less popular with males if they outperform them in
these areas. An example of this is a study that found that African American
females stories about a successful African American heroine included concerns that she "must not only contend with boyfriends who become upset
and feel inferior, but also with other males in her class who feel they should
not have to compete with a woman. Success also leads to a questioning of
feminine identity in that the heroine fears being seen as a freak ... this
successful girl is seen either as an obnoxious misfit who had nothing better
to do or as one whose greatest dilemma is now finding a man who is her
equal" (259, p. 708).

A second reason why some females are uncomfortable with success is
that success provokes a conflict between their desires to achieve and their
more traditional perception of the ideal female as less oriented to achievement and individualism than to collaboration and egalitarianism. In this
vein, Tannen explains:

> *Appearing better than others is a violation of the girls' egalitarian ethic:*
> *People are supposed to stress their connection and similarity. ... It is no*
> *wonder that girls fear rejection by their peers if they appear too successful*
> *and boys don't. Boys from the earliest age, learn that they can get what they*
> *want—higher status—by displaying superiority. Girls learn that display-*
> *ing superiority will not get them what they want—affiliation with their*
> *peers. For this they have to appear the same as, not better than their friends.*
> *(69, pp. 217–218)*

Males may also be uncomfortable with success in certain situations.
There is some evidence that males may also avoid success if their peer group
devalues school success or if they perceive success in school as a feminine

characteristic (264). (See chapter 4 for a more detailed discussion of this issue.)

It is unfortunate that some students avoid academic success because it is incompatible with their self-image or their desire to be popular or it evokes peer pressure not to succeed. Clearly, this topic deserves much more attention from researchers than the little it has received.

## School Participation

### Academic Courses

In high school, where students have the opportunity to select their courses and activities, males and females make somewhat different choices (265–296). Although females have been enrolling in advanced science and math courses in greater numbers in recent years, their enrollment has not increased as much as males (271, 276). As a result, in most areas of the country, American Indian, Hispanic, and European American females, especially those from working-class backgrounds, still express less interest in, and participate less than boys in, advanced math courses such as intermediate algebra and calculus, and in science courses such as physics and chemistry. This gender gap may be less true of European females who live in areas where gender-stereotypical perceptions of education are not as prevalent (288) and of females who prefer competitive rather than cooperative environments (284).

Females, especially those from working-class backgrounds, also participate less in computer courses, especially in those that involve programming. The situation nationally is typified by a California study (281) that found that although females comprised 42 percent of the students enrolled in all high school courses that involved computer instruction, they represented 86 percent of the students enrolled in word processing courses, but only 37 percent of the students enrolled in computer programming courses.

### Vocational Courses and Career Aspirations

Although there has been some shift since the 1970s, males and females continue to choose different vocational education courses and aspire to different careers and occupations (177, 260, 297–327). Females comprise over 90 percent of the students in cosmetology, clerical, home economics, and health courses and less than 10 percent of the students in courses that deal with agriculture, electrical technology, electronics, appliance repair, auto mechanics, carpentry, welding, and small engine repair.

One reason why males and females select different academic and vocational courses is that they aspire to different careers. Beginning in preschool, males and females tend to aspire to gender-stereotypical occupations and careers. Females are less likely to aspire to mathematics, science, or engineering careers. In comparison to African American, Hispanic American, Southeast Asian American, and working-class European American males, females, including those that are gifted and talented, aspire to less prestigious and lower paying occupations that typically do not require a college degree. This is especially true of females who have more traditional views of gender roles. It is also more likely to be true of younger children because females' career aspirations become less gender stereotypical as they advance from kindergarten through high school (299, 300).

These gender differences appear not to apply to the same extent to females brought up in rural areas, Filipino American females, and middle-class European American females, especially if their mothers have nontraditional high paying jobs (316, 320–323). "The most powerful set of predictors of whether young women are aspiring to nontraditional, high status careers is the socioeconomic background of their family" (323, p. 22).

### Participation in Extracurricular Activities

During the early 1980s, males and females participated very differently in their school's extracurricular programs (264, 328). One group of researchers described these differences in the following terms:

> *Males more often belong to chess, science, and lettermen's clubs and females more often belong to dance teams and aspire to be cheerleaders on the rally squad. Even though both sexes play in the band, they generally play different instruments (girls on the flutes, boys on the tubas) and have different responsibilities (drum majors who lead the band and majorettes who twirl batons). Jobs on school newspapers and in student government are typically sex segregated. Boys are more often sports editors, girls are feature reporters. Boys are more often presidents of student bodies, while girls are often secretaries." (264, p. 40)*

Additional research is needed to determine whether these patterns exist today.

Some see no problem in these gender differences. Others find them undesirable. The major cause of their concern is their belief that the kinds of activities students participate in and the roles they assume in the activities they are involved in affect the career choices they make and their eventual life-styles.

## Academic Achievement

Research has revealed differences between the achievement of male and female students in many areas (329–370). However, many of them do not apply to all ethnic groups and socioeconomic classes and many do not appear to be as significant today as they were even in the early 1980s.

### Verbal, Visual-Spatial, and Mathematics Skills

American Indian, African American, Hispanic American, and European American girls typically develop their verbal skills at an earlier age than boys and achieve higher levels of success on tests of verbal skills in elementary and secondary school (336, 342–344). In the case of gifted students, these differences tend to occur at an earlier age. There is also a gender gap that appears to cut across ethnic and socioeconomic class lines between the lower scores of females and the higher scores of males on visual-spatial tasks (335, 359–70).

In elementary school, the mathematics gender gap favors African American, European American, and Hispanic American females, but not American Indians. In high school, again with the exception of American Indians, girls score higher than boys on tests involving basic computational skills. However, there is no consistent gender gap in advanced mathematics courses and on tests involving complex mathematical skills and word problems. European American males outscore European American females. But African American females outperform African American males. And there is some evidence that, at least in tenth grade mathematics, Asian Pacific/Island American females also outperform males.

To some extent the discrepancy between the math achievement of males and females is situation specific. European American females who attend schools in which the climate does not foster the gender-stereotypical idea that math is in the male domain tend to do better in math (346). And females who do not view math as a male subject perform better than those who do (356).

Many educators suggest that some females who score lower than males on math achievement tests are not less skilled mathematicians. Rather, they score lower because they become anxious when they take such tests and because test items are biased against females (371–83). And some researchers question the validity of female students' scores on standardized math tests because their low scores are poor predictors of their junior high school, high school, and college achievement (384–86). (Chapter 2 includes a more detailed discussion of various points of view regarding the causes of the gender gap on academic achievement tests.)

Individuals who believe mathematics achievement tests are biased against females criticize current assessment instruments for their male-oriented content, overuse of male nouns and pronouns, and stereotypical portrayal of the genders. Studies done in the 1970s and 1980s provide some evidence to support their contention. In the 1970s and 1980s, standardized test items were more likely to use male pronouns such as *he* and *his* than *she* and *hers* and to include more male oriented content (373, 376, 377, 381–83).

Since each gender does better on mathematical word problems that are stereotypically relevant (questions about guns, trains, cars, soldiers, and so on for boys and beads, cooking, jump ropes, bottles of perfume, dolls, pocketbooks, and the like for girls), and on items that include gender-specific pronouns, the overuse of male-oriented content and pronouns penalized female students (371, 380). New studies are needed to determine whether these biases have been corrected.

### Science Skills

There has been a great deal of research regarding possible gender differences in science achievement (387–97). Research indicates that males do not outperform females in elementary school science tests. They begin to outscore females during middle school. In high school they definitely tend to achieve more than females on tests of general science and physical science, but not health science information. The results of studies of gender differences in achievement in chemistry, earth sciences, and the biological sciences are inconsistent.

These generalizations do not apply to the same degree to students from different socioeconomic and ethnic backgrounds (351, 388, 391, 396). Gender differences in science achievement are greater for students from middle and upper socioeconomic backgrounds than for working-class students (388, 391, 396). African American males do not do better than their female peers on science achievement tests nor do they display or report more interest in science subjects (351, 391, 396).

### Computer Skills

Gender comparisons of computer skills consistently favor males. Males outperform females on tests of computer literacy (272, 398). They do so even when both genders have equal exposure to computers and instruction in computer skills.

### Significance of Gender Differences in Visual-Spatial, Verbal, Mathematics, Science, and Computer Skills and Knowledge

In recent years, the gender gap has decreased considerably in many, but not all subject areas (399–410). The difference between males and females on tests of verbal ability has decreased at all levels of achievement except on tests of vocabulary. The gap between European American males and females on standardized math achievement tests has narrowed considerably. This has not been the case for the gender differences in science or visual-spatial skills. Nor has it been true of gifted math students. In fact, the gender gap among gifted/high scoring students on tests of science, math, and vocabulary achievement has actually increased (177, 399, 404, 407–9).

The decreases in the gender gap on verbal and mathematics tests for most students have led some authors to believe the current differences between males and females in these subjects have become insignificant. Others contend that the test score differences, while smaller than in the past, are significant. Few educators are complacent about the increase in the gender gap among gifted students.

What is the practical significance of the gender differences on tests of visual-spatial, mathematical, science, verbal, and computer skills? Halpern asks "Can they be used to explain why we have so few female mathematicians or engineers? Can they help us predict a male's or female's ability to perform a task? Can they be used to justify discrimination?" (403, p. 60).

These issues are discussed in the chapters that follow. However, it is important to note that while there are significant differences in the average scores males and females from some ethnic and socioeconomic backgrounds receive on standardized tests in these subjects, the differences are not very great. In addition, there is a great deal of overlap in their scores and many females exceed the average scores of males on tests in subjects in which males excel and many males exceed the average scores of females on tests in subjects in which females excel. Therefore, the observed differences between large groups of females and males should not be used to arrive at predictions or conclusions about a specific individual in the absence of information about that particular person.

## Behavior Problems

Males, especially African Americans, are much more likely than females to get into trouble, to be disciplined by their teachers, and to be suspended from school for behavioral problems (411–18). One reason for this appears to be differences between male and female behavior patterns. As noted above, beginning in preschool and continuing throughout their educational careers, males are more competitive, assertive, dominant, aggressive, and active. These are the very behaviors that are likely to get them into trouble.

---

**BOX 1–3    Self-Quiz**

*Sex-Role Stereotypical Behavior in School*

Did your behavior and attitudes during your school career fit the gender-stereotypical patterns that are typically observed in students? Does your behavior currently fit the descriptions of gender-specific behavior in any of the following areas?

- Emotional styles
- Interpersonal relationships
- Moral approach
- Communication style
- Learning style
- Enrollment in academic and vocational courses
- Participation in extracurricular activities
- Academic achievement

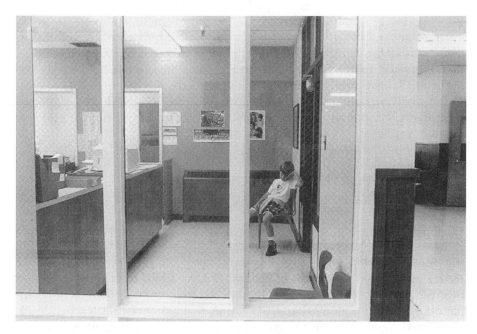

Males are more likely to get into trouble and to spend time in the principal's office.

Males are also much more likely to be enrolled in educational programs for students with behavior disorders and emotional disturbances (419–22). At least three factors contribute to this disparity. One is the difference in male-female behavior patterns noted above. A second cause is teacher intolerance of African American and working-class male behavior patterns (see chapter 2).

A third contributing factor is the fact that teachers tend not to refer females with emotional problems for the special education services they require. Although fewer females are enrolled in programs for students with emotional problems, as noted above, in comparison to male students, they are more fearful and anxious in many school situations and they are more likely to experience sadness or depression.

## SUMMARY

Beginning in infancy, important educationally relevant gender differences begin to appear. These differences include students' emotional responses, interpersonal relationships, moral development, communication styles, learning styles, enrollment in academic and vocational courses, participation in extracurricular activities, academic achievement, and behavior problems. Educators should be sensitive to the possible influence that gender has in the school life of many students. However, different ethnic and socioeconomic groups do not assign males and females the same gender roles. And many students do not conform to the gender-specific patterns that characterize their particular group. Therefore, educators should avoid gender-stereotypical thinking and not assume that all male and female students behave similarly.

## ISSUES FOR FURTHER THOUGHT AND DISCUSSION

1. As noted, generalizations about gender-typical behavior can be helpful if they sensitize educators to their students' possible behavior patterns. But they can be harmful if educators assume they can predict the behavior of individual students in terms of generalizations about their gender. In light of these two possibilities, should teachers be exposed to the kinds of generalizations included in this book? If they should, what should teachers do to avoid basing their educational approaches on overgeneralizations and stereotypes?

2. Some educators believe it is better to emphasize the similarities among ethnic and socioeconomic groups than to stress their differences because focusing on differences can feed into people's prejudices and create hostility and conflicts. Others believe that it is essential to recognize dissimilarities among groups of people because their needs, desires, motives, and goals are different. Do you think educators should use a multicultural approach that requires them to consider the kinds of differences discussed in this text or should they attempt to treat all students the same, regardless of their ethnic and socioeconomic backgrounds? If you believe that educators should take these differences into consideration, how can they do so and avoid creating resentment, hostility, and conflict among their students?

## ACTIVITIES

To deal with gender-role differences in school, you first must be able to identify them when they occur. The following activities are designed to improve your skills in observing gender differences among your students. You will be able to complete activities 1–6 if you have some classroom teaching experience. Activities 7–9 are appropriate for anyone taking courses.

**1.** Compare the way your students interact in single-sex and mixed-sex groups. Do they interact differently in the two situations? Do they interact in a gender-stereotypical manner?

**2.** If you are a preschool teacher, observe the extent to which students select toys and activities that conform to gender stereotypes and the degree to which they attempt to get their way with others in gender-stereotypical ways.

**3.** If you are an elementary or middle school teacher, describe your students' learning styles and decide whether they conform to the gender patterns reported in this chapter.

**4.** If you are a secondary school teacher, obtain the names of the students who are enrolled in higher level science and mathematics, foreign language courses, and so on. Review the list to determine whether the student make-up follows the gender patterns that researchers have reported. Do the same for student enrollment in the various vocational courses available in your school.

**5.** Obtain the names of the presidents, vice-presidents, secretaries, and so on of the various student organizations. Do the roles that males and females have in these organizations conform to the prevailing gender stereotypes?

**6.** Obtain the names of the students who participate in the various student clubs and organizations. Do males and females participate in activities that conform to gender stereotypes?

**7.** Is there a preponderance of males or females in any of your classes? If so, does the disproportionate enrollment conform to current gender-stereotypical career interests and choices?

**8.** Observe the students in your classes. Do males and females volunteer answers equally often? When they work in mixed groups, do males and females fulfill gender-stereotypical roles? When groups give oral reports to the class, do males do most of the reporting?

**9.** Canvas the students in your class regarding their preferred learning styles through an informal questionnaire or one that has been published. Do the results conform to those previously reported for males and females?

## REFERENCES

The contention that sex-linked behavior tends to be situation specific is discussed in the following references.

1. Deaux, K., and Major, B. 1987. Putting gender into context: An interactive model of gender-related behavior. *Psychological Review* 94: 369–89.

2. Maccoby, E. E. 1988. Gender as a social category. *Developmental Psychology* 24 (6): 755–65.

The following reference discusses the fact that gender research is focused primarily on middle-class European American students.

3. Hare, B. R. 1985. "Reexamining the central tendency: Sex differences within race and race differences within sex." In *Black Children: Social, Educational and Parental Environments*, edited by H. P. McAdoo and J. L. McAdoo. Beverly Hills: Sage Publications.

## Gender Differences

### Infants

The following articles deal with gender differences while children are infants and toddlers.

4. Fein, G., Johnson, D., Kosson, N., Stork, L. M., and Wassermen, L. 1975. Sex stereotypes and preferences in the toy choices of 20-month-old boys and girls. *Developmental Psychology* 11: 527–28.
5. Jacklin, C., Maccoby, E. E., and Dick, A. 1973. Barrier behavior and toy preference: Sex differences (and their absence) in the year-old child. *Child Development* 44: 196–200.
6. Jacklin, C. N., Maccoby, E. E., and Doering, C. H. 1983. Neonatal sex-steroid hormones and timidity in 6–18 month-old boys and girls. *Developmental Psychobiology* 16: 163–68.
7. Kagan, J. 1972. The emergence of sex differences. *School Review* 80: 217–27.
8. Kearsley, R. B., and Zelazo, P. R. 1979. *Sex Typed Differences in the Spontaneous Play Behavior of Infants 9½ to 15½ Months of Age*. ERIC ED 168 699.
9. Marcus, J., Maccoby, E. E., Jacklin, C. N., and Doering, C. H. 1985. Individual differences in mood in early childhood: Their relation to gender and neonatal steroid. *Developmental Psychobiology* 18: 327–40.
10. Van Leishout, C. F. M. 1975. Young children's reactions to barriers placed by their mothers. *Child Development* 46: 879–86.

### Preschool

Gender differences in play preferences are discussed in the following references.

11. Cameron, E., Eisenberg, N., and Kelly, T. 1985. The relations between sex-type play and preschoolers' social behavior. *Sex Roles* 12 (5): 601–15.
12. Carpenter, C. J. 1979. *Relation of Children's Sex-Typed Behavior to Classroom and Activity Structure*. ERIC ED 178 173.
13. Charlesworth, W. R., and Dzur, C. 1987. Gender comparisons of preschoolers' behavior and resource utilization in group problem-solving. *Child Development* 58: 191–200.
14. DiPietro, J. A. 1981. Rough and tumble play: A function of gender. *Developmental Psychology* 17 (1): 50–58.
15. Fagot, B. I. 1985. Beyond the reinforcement principle: Another step toward understanding sex roles. *Developmental Psychology* 21: 1097–1104.
16. Giddings, M., and Halverson, C. F. 1981. Young children's use of toys in home environments. *Family Relations* 30: 69–74.
17. Harper, L. W., and Sanders, K. M. 1975. Preschool children's use of space: Sex differences in outdoor play. *Developmental Psychology* 11 (1): 119.

18. Johnson, J. E., and Ershler, J. 1981. Developmental trends in preschool play as a function of classroom program and child gender. *Child Development* 52 (3): 995–1004.

19. Maccoby, E. E. 1988. Gender as a social category. *Developmental Psychology* 24 (6): 755–65.

20. Montemayor, R. 1974. Children's performance in a game and their attraction to it as a function of sex-typed labels. *Child Development* 45: 132–56.

21. O'Brien, M., and Huston, A. C. 1985. Development of sex-typed play behavior in toddlers. *Developmental Psychology* 21 (5): 866–71.

22. Pellegrini, A. D. 1983. *Childrens' Social Cognitive Play Behavior; The Effects of Age, Gender, and Activity Centers.* ERIC ED 245 814.

23. Varma, M. 1980. Sex-stereotyping in block play of preschool children. *Indiana Educational Review* (July): 32–37.

24. Weintraub, M., and Leite, J. 1977. "Gender Labels and Early Sex Role Stereotypes and Sex-Typed Toy Preference." Paper presented at the annual meeting of the Eastern Psychological Association, Boston.

References that indicate that males are the more active sex are as follows.

25. Maccoby, E. E., and Feldman, S. S. 1972. Mother-attachment and stranger-reactions in the third year of life. *Monographs of the Society for Research in Child Development* 37.

26. Pedersen, F. A., and Bell, R. Q. 1970. Sex differences in preschool children without histories of complications of pregnancy and delivery. *Developmental Psychology* 3: 10–15.

27. Smith, P. K., and Connolly, K. 1972. "Patterns of play and social interactions in preschool children." In *Ethological Studies of Child Behavior,* edited by N. Blurton-Jones. Cambridge, England: Cambridge University Press.

Differences in the way the sexes relate to others are the focus of the following articles.

28. Ankeney, M. A., and Goodman, G. 1976. Passive aggression versus active aggression in preschool children. *Child Study Journal* 6 (4): 235–44.

29. Becker, J. A., and Smenner, P. C. 1986. The spontaneous use of "thank you" by preschoolers as a function of sex, socioeconomic status, and listener status. *Language in Society* 15 (4): 37–45.

30. Charlesworth, W. R., and La Frenier, P. 1983. Dominance, friendship utilization and resource utilization in preschool children's groups. *Ethology and Sociobiology* 4: 175–86.

31. Cook, S. A., Fritz, J. J., MacCormack, B. L., and Visperas, C. 1985. Early gender differences in the functional use of language. *Sex Roles* 12 (9): 909–15.

32. Esposito, A. 1979. Sex differences in children's conversation. *Language and Speech* 22 (3): 213–20.

33. Fagot, B. L., and Hagan, R. 1985. Aggression in toddlers: Responses to the assertive acts of boys and girls. *Sex Roles* 12 (3): 341–51.

34. Feldbaum, C. L., Christenson, T. E., and O'Neal, E. D. 1980. An observational study of the assimilation of the newcomer to the preschool. *Child Development* 51: 497–507.

35. Hyde, J. S. 1984. How large are gender differences in aggression? A developmental meta-analysis. *Developmental Psychology* 20: 722–36.

36. Jacklin, C. N., and Maccoby, E. E. 1978. Social behavior at 33 months in same-sex and mixed-sex dyads. *Child Development* 49: 557–69.

37. Jennings, K. D., and Suwalsky, J. T. 1982. Reciprocity in the dyadic play of three-year-olds. In *The Paradox of Play*, edited by J. W. Loy. West Point, New York: Leisure Press.

38. King, L. A., and Barnett, M. A. 1980. *The Effects of Age and Sex on Preschoolers' Helpfulness.* ERIC ED 188 779.

39. Maccoby, E. E., and Jacklin, C. 1980. Sex differences in aggression: A rejoiner and reprise. *Child Development* 51: 964–80.

40. Sachs, J. 1987. "Preschool boys' and girls' language use in pretend play." In *Language, Gender, and Sex in Comparative Perspective*, edited by S. U. Philips, S. Steele, and C. Tanz. Cambridge, England: Cambridge University Press.

41. Serbin, L. A., Sprafkin, C., Elman, M., and Doyle, A. B. 1984. The early development of sex differentiated patterns of social influence. *Canadian Journal of Social Science* 14 (4): 350–63.

42. Walters, J., Pearce, D., and Dahms, L. 1957. Affectional and aggressive behavior of preschool children. *Child Development* 28: 15–26.

## School Age

The following references describe gender differences in emotional reactions.

43. Baron, P., and Perron, L. M. 1986. Sex differences in the Beck Depression Inventory scores of adolescents. *Journal of Youth and Adolescents* 15 (2): 165–71.

44. Brody, L. R. 1984. Sex and age variation in the quality and intensity of children's emotional attributions to hypothetical situations. *Sex Roles* 11 (1): 51–59.

45. Choquet, M., and Menke, H. 1987. Development of self-perceived risk behavior and psychosomatic symptoms in adolescents: A longitudinal approach. *Journal of Adolescence* 10: 291–308.

46. Czerniak, C., and Chiarelotti, L. 1984. *Science Anxiety: An Investigation of Science Achievement, Sex and Grade Level Factors.* ERIC ED 243 672.

47. Hadfield, O. D., and Maddux, C. D. 1988. Cognitive style and mathematics anxiety among high school students. *Psychology in the Schools* 25: 75–83.

48. Harlow, L. L., Newcomb, M. D., and Bentler, P. M. 1986. Depression, self-derogation, substance use and suicide ideation: Lack of purpose in life as mediational factor. *Journal of Clinical Psychology* 42: 353–58.

49. Haynes, N. M., Comer, J. P., and Hamilton-Lee, M. 1988. Gender and achievement status differences on learning factors among black high school students. *Journal of Educational Research* 81 (4): 233–37.

50. Holden, C. 1987. Female math anxiety on the wane. *Science* 236 (4802): 660–61.

51. Marsh, H. W. 1987. *The Content Specificity of Math and English Anxieties: The High School and Beyond Study.* ERIC ED 300 402.

52. Matyas, M. L. 1984. *Science Career Interests, Attitudes, Abilities, and Anxiety Among Secondary School Stu-*

*dents: The Effects of Gender, Race/Ethnicity, and School Type/Location.* ERIC ED 251 309.

53. Reynolds, W. 1984. Depression in children and adolescents. *School Psychology Review* 13: 171–82.

54. Worchel, F., Nolan, B., and Wilson, V. 1987. New perspectives on child and adolescent depression. *Journal of School Psychology* 25 (4): 411–14.

55. Wynstra, S., and Cummings, C. 1990. *Science Anxiety: Relation with Gender, Year in Chemistry Class, Achievement, and Test Anxiety.* ERIC ED 331 837.

Gender differences in aggressiveness, assertiveness, and dominance are discussed in the following articles.

56. Barrett, D. E. 1979. A naturalistic study of sex differences in children's aggression. *Merrill Palmer Quarterly* 25 (3): 193–204.

57. Bender, D. S. 1976. *Psychosocial Dimensions of Sex Differences in the Academic Competence of Adolescents.* ERIC ED 128 695.

58. Block, J. H. 1976. Debatable conclusions about sex differences. *Contemporary Psychology* 21 (8): 517–22.

59. Burdett, K., and Jensen, L. C. (1983). The self-concept and aggressive behavior among elementary school children from two socioeconomic areas and two grade levels. *Psychology in the Schools* 20 (3): 370–75.

60. Eagly, A. H. 1987. *Sex Differences in Social Behavior: A Social Role Interpretation.* Hillsdale, NJ: Erlbaum.

61. Hyde, J. S. 1984. How large are gender differences in aggression? A developmental meta-analysis. *Developmental Psychology* 20: 722–36.

62. Hyde, J. S., and Linn, M. C. 1986. *The Psychology of Gender: Advances*

*through Meta-Analysis.* Baltimore: Johns Hopkins University Press.

63. Maccoby, E. E., and Jacklin, C. N. 1980. Sex differences in aggression: A rejoinder and reprise. *Child Development* 51: 964–80.

64. Olson, S. L. 1984. The effects of sex-role taking on children's responses to aggressive conflict situations. *Sex Roles* 10 (9): 817–23.

65. Parke, R. D., and Slaby, R. G. 1983. "The development of aggression." In *Handbook of Child Psychology: Socialization, Personality and Social Development,* 4th ed., edited by P. H. Mussen & E. M. Hetherington. New York: Wiley.

66. Sheldon, A. 1990. Pickle fights: Gendered talk in preschool disputes. *Discourse Processes* 13: 5–31.

67. Smye, D. M., and Wine, J. D. 1980. A comparison of female and male adolescents' social behaviors and cognitions: A challenge to the assertiveness literature. *Sex Roles* 6 (2): 213–30.

68. Sprafkin, J., and Gadow, K. (1987). An observational study of emotionally disturbed and learning-disabled children in school settings. *Journal of Abnormal Child Psychology* 15 (3): 393–08.

69. Tannen, D. 1990. *You Just Don't Understand.* New York: William Morrow.

References that deal with gender differences in sharing, helpfulness, and other forms of altruistic behavior follow.

70. Barnett, M. A. 1978. *Situational Influences and Sex Differences in Children's Reward Allocation Behavior.* ERIC ED 172 081.

71. Dederick, W. E., Dederick, J. G., and Zalk, S. R. 1977. *Interpersonal*

*Values of Intellectually Gifted Adolescent Females: Single-Sex Co-Education.* ERIC ED 140 523.

72. Harris, M. B., and Siebel, C. E. 1975. Affect, aggression, and altruism. *Developmental Psychology* 11: 623–27.

73. O'Bryant, S. L., and Brophy, J. E. 1976. Sex differences in altruistic behavior. *Developmental Psychology* 12: 554.

74. Radke-Yarrow, M., Zahn-Waxler, C., and Chapman, M. 1983. Children's prosocial dispositions and behavior. In *Handbook of Child Psychology*, 4th ed., vol. 4, edited by E. M. Hetherington. New York: Wiley.

75. Shegetomi, C. 1982. "Children's Altruism." Ph.D. diss., University of Utah.

76. Shegetomi, C., Haitmann, D. P., and Gelfand, D. M. 1981. Sex differences in children's reputation for helpfulness. *Developmental Psychology* 17: 434–37.

77. Skarin, K., and Moely, B. E. 1976. Altruistic behavior: An analysis of age and sex differences. *Child Development* 47 (4): 1159–65.

78. Weissbrod, C. S. 1980. The impact of warmth and instructions on donation. *Child Development* 51: 279–81.

79. Zarbatany, L., Hartmann, D. P., Gelfand, D. M., and Vinciguerra, P. 1985. Gender Differences in altruistic reputations: Are they artifactual? *Developmental Psychology* 21 (1): 97–101.

The references that follow focus on gender differences in competitive and cooperative behavior.

80. DeVoe, M. W. 1977. Cooperation as a function of self-concept, sex and race. *Educational Research Quarterly* 2 (2): 3–8.

81. Kagan, S., and Madsen, M. C. 1972. Rivalry in Anglo-American and Mexican children of two ages. *Journal of Personality and Social Psychology* 24: 214–20.

82. Moely, B. E., Skarin, K., and Weil, S. 1979. Sex differences in competition-cooperation behavior of children at two age levels. *Sex Roles* 5 (31): 329–42.

83. Pepitone, E. A. 1973. *Patterns of Interdependence in Cooperative Work of Elementary School Children.* ERIC ED 091 047.

84. Skarin, K., and Moely B. E. 1974. *Sex Differences in Competition-Cooperation Behavior of Eight-Year-Old Children.* ERIC ED 096 015.

Differences in the extent to which males and females discuss their thoughts and feelings with others is the focus of the following references.

85. Carpenter, B. N. 1987. "The relationship between psychopathology and self-disclosure: An interference/competence model." In *Self Disclosure: Theory, Research and Therapy*, edited by V. J. Derlaga and J. H. Berg. New York: Plenum.

86. Hill, C. T., and Stull, D. E. 1987. "Gender and self disclosure: Strategies for exploring the issue." In *Self Disclosure: Theory, Research and Therapy*, edited by V. J. Derlaga and J. H. Berg. New York: Plenum.

87. Littlefield, R. P. 1990. Self disclosure among some negro, white, and Mexican-American adolescents. *Journal of Consulting Psychology* 21 (2): 133–36.

88. Norrell, J. E. 1984. Self-disclosure: Some implications for the study of parent-adolescent interaction. *Journal of Youth and Adolescence* 13: 163–78.

89. Papini, D. R., Farmer, F. F., Clark, S. M., Micka, J. C., and Barnett, J. K. 1990. Early adolescent age and gender differences in patterns of emotional self-disclosure to parents and friends. *Adolescence* 25 (100): 959–76.

90. Stiles, W. B. 1987. " 'I have to talk to somebody': A fever model of disclosure." In *Self Disclosure: Theory, Research and Therapy,* edited by V. J. Derlaga and J. H. Berg. New York: Plenum.

Gender differences in reactions to conflict is the topic of the following article.

91. Miller, P. M., Danaher, D. L., and Forbes, D. 1986. Sex-related strategies for coping with interpersonal conflict in children aged five and seven. *Developmental Psychology* 22 (4): 543–48.

Gender differences in seeking teacher and adult feedback and approval is the focus of the following references.

92. Caplan, P. 1979. "Beyond the box score: A boundary condition for sex differences in aggression and achievement striving." In *Progress in Experimental Personality Research,* vol. 9, edited by B. Maher. New York: Academic Press.

93. Carpenter, C. J., and Huston-Stein, A. 1980. Activity structure and sex-typed behavior in preschool children. *Child Development* 51: 862–72.

94. Eiszler, C. F. 1982. *Perceptual Preference as an Aspect of Adolescent Learning Styles.* ERIC ED 224 769.

95. Huston, A. C., Carpenter, C. J., Atwater, J. B., and Johnson, L. M. 1986. Gender, adult structuring of activities, and social behavior in middle childhood. *Child Development* 57: 1200–9.

Females' use of helplessness to influence others is the subject of the following articles.

96. Johnson, P. 1976. Women and power: Toward a theory of effectiveness. *Journal of Social Issues* 32 (3): 99–110.

97. Parsons, J. E. 1982. Sex differences in attributions and learned helplessness. *Sex Roles* 8 (4): 421–32.

Gender differences in behavior in mixed-sex groups is treated in the following references.

98. Aires, E. 1976. Interaction patterns and themes of male, female, and mixed groups. *Small Group Behavior* 7 (1): 7–18.

99. Lockheed, M. E. 1977. Cognitive style effects on sex status in student work groups. *Journal of Educational Psychology* 69: 158–65.

100. Lockheed, M. E. 1985. "Sex and social influence: A meta-analysis guided by theory." In *Status, Attributions, and Rewards,* edited by J. Berger and M. Zeldich. San Francisco: Jossey-Bass.

101. Lockheed, M. E., and Hall, K. P. 1976. Conceptualizing sex as a status characteristic: Application to leadership training strategies. *Journal of Social Issues* 32 (3): 111–24.

102. Webb, N. M., and Kinderski, C. M. 1985. "Gender differences in small group interaction and achievement in high- and low-achieving classes." In *Gender Influence in Classroom Interaction,* edited by C. Wilkinson and C. B. Marrett. New York: Academic Press.

The following references deal with ethnic differences in female sex roles.

103. Dao, M. 1987. "From Vietnamese to Vietnamese American." Unpublished manuscript, San Jose, CA: San Jose State University.

104. Grossman, H. 1984. *Educating Hispanic Students: Cultural Implications for Instruction, Classroom Management, Counseling and Assessment.* Springfield, IL: Thomas.

105. Kunkel, P., and Kennard, S. S. 1971. *Sprout Spring: A Black Community.* New York: Holt, Rinehart and Winston.

106. Lewis, D. 1975. The black family: Socialization and Sex Roles. *Phylon* 36 (3): 221–37.

107. Scanzoni, J. H. 1971. *The Black Family in Modern Society.* Boston: Allyn and Bacon.

108. Simpson, G. 1984. The daughters of Charlotte Ray: The career development process during the exploratory and establishment stages of Black women attorneys. *Sex Roles* 11 (1/2): 113–39.

109. Staples, R. 1971. The myth of the impotent Black male. *The Black Scholar* 2 (10): 2–9.

110. TenHouten, W. D. 1970. The black family: Myth and reality. *Psychiatry* 33: 145–73.

111. Young, V. H. 1970. Family and childhood in a southern negro community. *American Anthropologist* 72: 269–88.

The following references deal with gender differences in moral attitudes, judgments, and behavior.

112. Adams, G. R., Schvaneveldt, J. D., and Jenson, G. O. 1979. Sex, age and perceived competency as correlates of empathic ability in adolescents. *Adolescence* 14 (56): 811–18.

113. Belenky, M. F., Clinchy, B. M., Goldberger, N. R., and Tarule, J. M. 1986. *Women's Ways of Knowing: The Development of Self, Voice, and Mind.* New York: Basic Books.

114. Brabeck, M. 1983. Moral judgement: Theory and research on differences between males and females. *Developmental Review* 3: 274–91.

115. Brandes, B. 1986. *Academic Honesty: A Special Study of California Students.* ERIC ED 272 533.

116. Brockman, J., Anderson, T., and Armstrong, S. 1978. *The Developmental Relationship Among Moral Judgement, Moral Conduct and a Rationale for Appropriate Behavior.* ERIC ED 165 051.

117. Feshbach, N. D., and Feshbach, S. 1987. Affective processes and academic achievement. *Child Development* 58: 1335–47.

118. Gibbs, J., Arnold, K. D., and Burkhart, J. E. 1984. Sex differences in the expression of moral judgement. *Child Development* 55 (3): 1040–43.

119. Gilligan, C. 1977. In a different voice: Women's conceptions of the self and of morality. *Harvard Educational Review* 47: 481–517.

120. Gilligan, C. 1982. *In a Different Voice. Psychological Theory and Women's Development.* Cambridge, MA: Harvard University Press.

121. Gilligan, C. 1982. New Maps of development: New Visions of maturity. *American Journal of Orthopsychiatry* 52 (2): 199–212.

122. Gilligan, C., Langdale, S., and Lyons, N. 1982. *The Contribution of Women's Thought to Developmental Theory: The Elimination of Sex-Bias in Moral Developmental Theory and Research.* Final report to the Na-

tional Institute of Education, Washington, D.C. ERIC ED 226 301.

123. Hoffman, M. L. 1977. Sex differences in empathy and related behaviors. *Psychological Bulletin* 84: 712–22.

124. Jordan, V. B., and Watte, D, 1979. *The Effects of Self-Oriented and Other-Oriented Questions on Moral Reasoning.* ERIC ED 181 367.

125. Kitchener, K. S., King, P. M., Davison, M. L., Parker, C. A., and Wood, P. K. 1984. A longitudinal study of moral and ego development in young adults. *Journal of Youth and Adolescence* 13 (3): 197–211.

126. Kohlberg, L. 1981. *The Philosophy of Moral Development: Moral Stages and the Idea of Justice.* San Francisco: Harper and Row.

127. Krebs, R. L. 1977. "Girls—more moral than boys or just sneakier?" In *Sex Bias in the Schools: The Research Evidence,* edited by J. Pottker and A. Fishel. Cranbury, NJ: Associated University Presses.

128. Lepper, M. R. 1973. Dissonance, self-perception, and honesty in children. *Journal of Personality and Social Psychology* 25: 65–74.

129. Lyons, N. P. 1983. Two perspectives: On self, relationships, and morality. *Harvard Educational Review* 53 (2): 125–45.

130. Piaget, J. 1965. *The Moral Judgement of Children.* New York: Free Press.

131. Pottker, J., and Fishel, A., eds. 1977. *Sex Bias in the Schools: The Research Evidence.* Cranbury, NJ: Associated University Presses.

132. Rest, J. R. 1979. *Development in Judging Moral Issues.* Minneapolis: University of Minnesota Press.

133. Rest, J. R. 1983. "Morality." In *Manual of Child Psychology,* vol 4., edited by J. Flavell and E. Markham. New York: Wiley.

134. Smye, D. M., and Wine, J. D. 1980. A comparison of female and male adolescents' social behaviors and cognitions: A challenge to the assertiveness literature. *Sex Roles* 6 (2): 213–30.

135. Socoski, P. M. 1984. *Responses to Sex-Bias Criticism in Cognitive Moral Theory.* ERIC ED 278 881.

136. Tavris, C., and Wade, C. 1984. *The Longest War: Sex Differences in Perspective,* 2d. ed. New York: Harcourt Brace Jovanovich.

References concerning gender differences in communication styles follow.

137. Aires, E. 1976. Interaction patterns and themes of male, female, and mixed groups. *Small Group Behavior* 7 (1): 7–18.

138. Andersen, E. S. 1978. "Learning to Speak with Style: A Study of the Socio-Linguistic Skills of Children." Ph.D. diss., Stanford University.

139. Eakins, B., and Eakins, R. G. 1978. *Sex Differences in Human Communication.* Boston: Houghton Mifflin.

140. Fishman, P. M. 1978. Interaction: The work women do. *Social Problems* 25 (4): 397–406.

141. Goodwin, M. H. 1980. "Directive-response sequences in girls' and boys' task activities." In *Women and Language in Literature and Society,* edited by S. McConnell-Ginet, R. Borker, and M. Furman. New York: Praeger.

142. Goodwin, M. H., and Goodwin, C. 1987. "Children's arguing." In *Language, Gender, and Sex in Com-*

*parative Perspective,* edited by S. U. Philips, S. Steele, and C. Tanz. Cambridge, England: Cambridge University Press.

143. Hall, J. C. 1978. Gender effects in decoding nonverbal cues. *Psychological Bulletin* 85: 845–57.

144. Leet-Pelligrini, H. M. 1980. "Conversational dominance as a function of gender and expertise." In *Language: Social Psychological Perspectives,* edited by H. Giles, W. P. Robinson, and P. M. Smith. Oxford, England: Pergamon.

145. Maccoby, E. E. 1988. Gender as a social category. *Developmental Psychology* 24 (6): 755–65.

146. Rosenthal, R., Hall, J. A., Di Matteo, M. R., Rogers, P. L., and Archer, D. C. 1979. *Sensitivity to Non-Verbal Communication.* Baltimore: Johns Hopkins University Press.

147. Sachs, J. 1982. " 'Don't interrupt': Preschoolers' entry into ongoing conversations." In *Proceedings of the Second International Congress for the Study of Child Language,* edited by C. E. Johnson and C. L. Thew. Lanham, MD: University Press of America.

148. Sachs, J. 1987. "Preschool boys' and girls' language use in pretend play." In *Language, Gender, and Sex in Comparative Perspective,* edited by S. U. Philips, S. Steele and C. Tanz. Cambridge, England: Cambridge University Press.

149. Thorne, B., and Henley, N. 1975. *Language and Sex: Differences and Dominance.* Rowley, MA: Newbury House.

150. Zimmerman, D. H., and West, C. 1975. Sex roles, interruptions and silences in conversation. In *Language and Sex: Differences and Dominance,* edited by B. Thorne and N. Henley. Rowley, MA: Newbury House.

The following references deal with gender differences in ability to delay judgment or gratification.

151. Mischel, W. A., and Underwood, B. 1973. "Instrumental Ideation in Delay of Gratification." Unpublished manuscript, Stanford, CA: Department of Psychology, Stanford University.

152. Staub, E. 1972. Effects of persuasion and modeling on delay of gratification. *Developmental Psychology* 6: 166–77.

Gender differences in ability to change sets is the focus of the following references.

153. Block, J. H. 1976. Debatable conclusions about sex differences. *Contemporary Psychology* 21 (8): 517–22.

154. Cunningham, J. D. 1965. Einstellung rigidity in children. *Journal of Experimental Child Psychology* 2: 237–47.

155. Guetzkow, H. 1951. An analysis of the operation of set in problem-solving behavior. *Journal of General Psychology* 45: 219–44.

156. Nakamura, C. Y. 1958. Conformity and problem solving. *Journal of Abnormal and Social Psychology* 56: 315–20.

157. Sweeny, E. J. 1953. "Sex Differences in Problem Solving." Ph.D. diss., Stanford University.

The focus of the following references is on gender differences in reaction to challenges and risk taking.

158. Ginsburg, H. J., and Miller, S. M. 1982. Sex differences in children's risk-taking behavior. *Child Development* 53 (2): 426–28.

159. Goldman, K. S., and Shipman, V. C. 1972. *Risk-Taking 2: Technical Report 19. Disadvantaged Children and Their First School Experiences. ETS-Head Start Longitudinal Study. Technical Report Series.* Princeton: Educational Testing Service.

160. Harter, S. 1975. Developmental differences in the manifestation of mastery motivation on problem-solving tasks. *Child Development* 46: 370–78.

161. Harter, S. 1975. Mastery motivation and need for approval in older children and their relationship to social desirability responses tendencies. *Developmental Psychology* 11: 186–96.

162. Licht, B. G., Kistner, J. A., Ozkaragoz, T., Shapiro, S., and Clausen, L. 1985. Causal attributions of learning disabled children: Individual differences and their implications for persistence. *Journal of Educational Psychology* 77 (2): 208–16.

163. Licht, B. G., Linden, T. A., Brown, D. A., and Sexton, M. 1984. *Sex Differences in Achievement Orientation: An "A" Student Phenomenon.* ERIC ED 252 783.

Gender differences in reactions to failure are discussed in the following references.

164. Dweck, C. S., and Gilliard, D. 1975. Expectancy statements as determinants of reactions to failure: Sex differences in persistence and expectancy change. *Journal of Personality and Social Psychology* 342: 1077–84.

165. Dweck, C. S., and Goetz, T. E. 1978. Attributions and helplessness. In *New Directions in Attribution Research,* edited by J. H. Harvey, W. Ickes, and R. F. Kidd. Hillsdale, NJ: Erlbaum.

166. Miller, A. 1986. Performance impairment after failure: Mechanisms and sex differences. *Journal of Educational Psychology* 78 (6): 486–91.

167. Nicholls, J. G. 1975. Causal attributions and other achievement-related cognitions: Effects of task outcome, attainment value, and sex. *Journal of Personality and Social Psychology* 31: 379–89.

168. Reyes, L. H. 1984. Affective variables and mathematics education. *Elementary School Journal* 84 (5): 558–81.

Gender differences in students' self-concepts and self-esteem are discussed in the following references.

169. Armstrong, J. M., and Kahl, S. 1980. *A National Assessment of Performance and Participation of Women in Mathematics.* Washington, D.C.: National Institute of Education.

170. Berryman, C., Larkins, A. G., and McKinney, C. W. 1983. *Self Concept and Sex of Rural Children.* ERIC ED 231 585.

171. Brush, L. 1980. *Encouraging Girls in Mathematics: The Problem and the Solution.* Boston: Abt.

172. Eccles (Parsons), J., Adler, T. F., Futterman, R., Goff, S. B., Kaczala, C. M., Meece, J., and Midgley, C. 1983. "Expectations, values, and academic behaviors." In *Perspective on Achievement and Achievement Motivation,* edited by

J. T. Spence. San Francisco: W. H. Freedman.

173. Eccles, J., Adler, T. F., and Meece, J. L. 1984. Sex differences in achievement: A test of alternate theories. *Journal of Personality and Social Psychology* 68: 119–28.

174. Fox, L. H., Brody, L., and Tobin, D., eds. 1980. *Women and the Mathematical Mystique.* Baltimore: Johns Hopkins University Press.

175. Hare, B. R. 1979. *Black Girls: A Comparative Analysis of Self-Perception and Achievement by Race, Sex and Socioeconomic Background.* Report No. 271. ERIC ED 173 503.

176. Harter, S. 1982. The Perceived Competence Scale for Children. *Child Development* 53: 87–97.

177. Hyde, J., and Fennema, E. 1990. "Gender Differences in Mathematics Performance and Affect: Results of Two Meta-Analyses." Paper presented at the annual meeting of the American Educational Research Association, Boston.

178. Lenney, E. 1977. Women's self-confidence in achievement settings. *Psychological Bulletin* 84: 1–13.

179. Levine, G. 1990. "Arithmetic Development: Where are the Gender Differences?" Paper presented at the annual meeting of the American Educational Research Association, Boston.

180. Loeb, R. C., and Horst, L. 1978. *Sex differences in self-and teachers' reports of self-esteem in preadolescents. Sex Roles* 4 (5): 779–88.

181. Meece, J. L., Parsons, J. E., Kaczala, C. M., Goff, B., and Futterman, R. 1982. Sex differences in math achievement: Toward a model of academic choice. *Psychological Bulletin* 91: 324–48.

182. Olszewski, P., Kulieke, M. J., and Willis, G. B. 1987. Changes in the self-perceptions of gifted students who participate in rigorous academic programs. *Journal for the Education of the Gifted* 10 (4): 287–303.

183. Prawat, R. S., Grissom, S., and Parish, T. 1979. Affective development in children, grades 3 through 12. *Journal of Genetic Psychology* 135: 37–49.

184. Richman, C. L., Clark, M. L., and Brown, K. P. 1984. General and specific self-esteem in late adolescent students: Race x gender x SES effects. *Adolescence* 20 (79): 555–66.

185. Robison-Awana, P., Kehle, T. J., and Jenson, W. R. 1986. But what about smart girls? Adolescent self-esteem and sex role perceptions as a function of academic achievement. *Journal of Educational Psychology* 78 (3): 179–83.

186. Sherman, J. 1980. Mathematics, spatial visualization, and related factors: Changes in girls and boys, grades 8–11. *Journal of Educational Psychology* 72: 476–82.

187. Stevenson, H. W., and Newman, R. S. 1986. Long-term prediction of achievement and attitudes in mathematics and reading. *Child Development* 57: 646–59.

188. Sullivan, J. L. 1979. *Perceptions of Students' Self and Ideal Self by Teachers and Students at the Red lake Indian Reservation.* ERIC ED 244 759.

189. Tashakkori, A., and Thompson, V. D. 1990. *Race Differences in Self-Perception and Locus of Control During Adolescence and Early Adulthood.* ERIC ED 327 806.

190. Travis, C. B., McKenzie, B. J., and Wiley, D. L. 1984. *Sex and Achievement Domain: Cognitive Patterns of Success and Failure.* ERIC ED 250 601.

The following references deal with students' perceptions of their ability to exert control over their lives and their attribution of the cause of their successes and failures in school.

191. Dweck, C. S., and Reppucci, N. D. 1973. Learned helplessness and reinforcement responsibility in children. *Journal of Personality and Social Psychology* 25: 109–16.
192. Dyal, J. A. 1984. "Cross-cultural research with the locus of control construct." In *Research with the Locus of Control Construct, vol. 3: Extensions and Limitations*, edited by H. M. Lefcourt. New York: Academic Press.
193. Evans, E. D., and Engleberg, R. A. 1988. *Journal of Research and Development in Education* 21 (2): 45–54.
194. Frey, K. S., and Ruble, D. N. 1987. What children say about classroom performance: Sex and grade differences in perceived competence. *Child Development* 58: 1066–78.
195. Gordon, D. A., Jones, R. H., and Short, N. L. 1977. Task persistence and locus of control in elementary school children. *Child Development* 48: 1716–19.
196. Lao, R. C. 1980. Differential factors affecting male and female academic performance in high school. *Journal of Psychology* 104: 119–27.
197. Lewis, M. A. 1989. *Consistency of Children's Causal Attributions across Content Domains.* ERIC ED 306 488.

198. Lewis, M. A., and Cooney, J. B. 1986. *Attributional and Performance Effects of Competitive and Individualistic Feedback in Computer Assisted Mathematics Instruction.* ERIC ED 271 287.
199. Lopez, C. L. and Harper, M. 1989. The relationship between learner control of CAI and locus of control among Hispanic students. *Educational Technology Research and Development* 37 (4): 19–28.
200. Lykes, M. B., Stewart, A. J., and LaFrance, M. 1981. *Control and Aspirations in Adolescents: A Comparison by Race, Sex and Social Class.* ERIC ED 212 948.
201. McMahan, I. D. 1982. Expectancy of success on sex-linked tasks. *Sex Roles* 8: 949–58.
202. Powers, S., and Wagner, M. J. 1983. *Achievement Locus of Control of Hispanic and Anglo High School Students.* ERIC ED 230 355.
203. Reyes, L. H., and Padilla, M. J. 1985. Science math and gender. *Science Teacher* 52 (6): 46–48.
204. Ryckman, D. B., and Peckman, P. D. 1986. Gender differences in attribution patterns in academic areas for learning disabled students. *Learning Disabilities Research* 1 (2): 83–89.
205. Ryckman, D. B., and Peckman, P. D. 1987. Gender differences in attribution for success and failure. *Journal of Early Adolescence* 7: 47–63.
206. Ryckman, D. B., and Peckman, P. D. 1987. Gender differences in attribution for success and failure across subject areas. *Journal of Educational Research* 81: 120–25.
207. Sewell, T., Farley, F. H., Manni, J., and Hunt, P. 1982. Motivation, social reinforcement, and intelli-

gence as predictors of academic achievement in black adolescents. *Adolescence* 17 (67): 647–56.

208. Stipek, D. J. 1984. Sex differences in children's attributions for success and failure on math and spelling tasks. *Sex Roles* 11 (11–12): 969–81.

209. Turner, R. R. 1978. Locus of control, academic achievement, and follow through in Appalachia. *Contemporary Educational Psychology* 3: 367–75.

210. Wahl, M., and Besag, F. 1986. *Gender, Attributions and Math Performance.* ERIC ED 276 620.

211. Wildstein, A. B., Thompson, D. N., and Holzman, T. G. 1982. *Locus of Control and Expectation Set on Two Aptitude Measures.* ERIC ED 277 739.

212. Willig, A. C., Harnisch, D. L., Hill, K. T., and Maehr, M. L. 1983. Sociocultural and educational correlates of success-failure attributions and evaluation anxiety in the school setting for Black, Hispanic and Anglo children. *American Educational Research Journal,* 20 (3): 385–410.

Gender differences in reactions to competition and cooperation are discussed in the following references.

213. Allen, J. L., O'Mara, J., and Long, K. M. 1987. *The Effects of Communication Avoidance, Learning Styles and Gender upon Classroom Achievement.* ERIC ED 291 111.

214. Alvino, J. 1991. An investigation into the needs of gifted boys. *Roeper Review* 13 (4): 174–80.

215. Dalton, D. W., Hannafin, M. J., and Hooper, S. 1989. Effects of individual and cooperative computer assisted instruction on student performance and attitudes. *Educational Technology Research and Development* 37 (2): 15–34.

216. Englehard, G., Jr., and Monsas, J. A. 1989. Performance, gender and the cooperative attitudes of third, fifth, and seventh graders. *Journal of Research and Development in Education* 22 (2): 13–17.

217. Fennema, E. H. and Peterson, P. L. 1985. "Autonomous learning behavior: A possible explanation of gender-related differences in mathematics." In *Gender Influences in Classroom Interaction,* edited by L. C. Wilkinson and C. B. Marrett. New York: Academic Press.

218. Harpole, S. H. 1987. *The Relationship of Gender and Learning Styles to Achievement and Laboratory Skills in Secondary School Chemistry Students.* ERIC ED 288 728.

219. Johnson, D. W., and Johnson, R. T. 1987. *Learning Together and Alone: Cooperation, Competition and Individualization* 2d ed. Englewood Cliffs, NJ: Prentice-Hall.

220. Kagan, S., Zahn, G. L., and Gealy, J. 1977. Competition and school achievement among Anglo-American and Mexican-American children. *Journal of Educational Psychology* 69 (4): 432–41.

221. Lockheed, M. E., Harris, A. M., and Nemceff, W. P. 1983. Sex and social influence: Does sex function as a status characteristic in mixed-sex groups of children? *Journal of Educational Psychology* 75: 877–88.

222. McClintock, C. 1974. Development of social motives in Anglo-American and Mexican children. *Journal of Personality and Social Psychology* 29: 348–54.

223. Peterson, P., and Fennema, E. 1985. Effective teaching, student engagement in classroom activities, and sex-related differences in learning mathematics. *American Educational Research Journal* 22 (3): 309–34.

224. Strube, M. J. 1981. Meta-analysis and cross-cultural comparison: Sex differences in child competitiveness. *Journal of Cross-Cultural Psychology* 12 (1): 3–20.

225. Webb, N. M., and Kenderski, C. M. 1985. Gender differences in small-group interaction and achievement in high- and low-achieving classes. In *Gender Influences in Classroom Interaction*, edited by L. C. Wilkinson and C. B. Marrett. New York: Academic Press.

226. Wilkinson, L. C., Lindow, J., and Chiang, C. P. 1985. "Sex differences and sex segregation in students' small-group communication." In *Gender Influences in Classroom Interaction*, edited by L. C. Wilkinson and C. B. Marrett. New York: Academic Press.

Sex differences in conformity is the focus of the following articles.

227. Becker, B. J. 1986. Influence again: An examination of reviews and studies of gender differences in social influence. In *The Psychology of Gender*, edited by J. S. Hyde and M. C. Linn. Baltimore: Johns Hopkins University Press.

228. Cooper, H. M. 1979. Statistically combining independent studies: A meta-analysis of sex differences in conformity research. *Journal of Personality and Social Psychology* 37: 131–46.

229. Eagly, A. H. 1978. Sex differences in influenceability. *Psychological Bulletin* 85: 85–116.

230. Eagly, A. H., and Carli, L. L. 1981. Sex of researchers and sex-typed communications as determinants of sex differences in influenceability: A meta-analysis of social influence studies. *Psychological Bulletin* 90: 1–20.

231. Van Hecke, M., Tracy, R. J., Cotter, S., and Ribordy, S. C. 1984. Approval versus achievement motives in seventh-grade girls. *Sex Roles* 11 (1): 33–41.

232. Wulatin, M. L., and Tracy, R. J. 1977. "Sex Differences in Children's Responses to Achievement and Approval." Paper presented at the meeting of the Midwestern Psychological Association, Chicago.

Gender differences in responsiveness to peers' requests and reinforcement is discussed in the following references.

233. Fagot, B. I. 1985. Beyond the reinforcement principle: Another step toward understanding sex roles. *Developmental Psychology* 21: 1097–104.

234. Jacklin, C. N., and Maccoby, E. E. 1978. Social behavior at 33 months in same-sex and mixed-sex dyads. *Child Development* 49: 557–69.

235. Lamb, M. E., Easterbrook, A. M., and Holden, G. W. 1980. Reinforcement and punishment among preschoolers: Characteristics, effects, and correlates. *Child Development* 51: 1230–36.

236. Serbin, L. A., Sprafkin, C., Elman, M., and Doyle, A. B. 1984. The early development of sex differentiated patterns of social influence.

*Canadian Journal of Social Science* 14 (4): 350–63.

237. Wilkinson, L. C., and Marrett, C.B., eds. *Gender Influence in Classroom Interaction.* New York: Academic Press.

Gender differences in seeking teacher help, support, and feedback is the focus of the following references.

238. Borth, A. M. 1975. *Sex Differences in Coping and Defending in Two School Contexts.* ERIC ED 115 528.
239. Brutsaert, H. 1990. Changing sources of self-esteem among girls and boys in secondary school. *Urban Education* 24 (40): 432–39.
240. Dweck, C. S., and Bush, E. S. 1976. Sex differences in learned helplessness: I. Differential debilitation with peer and adult evaluators. *Developmental Psychology* 12: 147–56.
241. Eiszler, C. F. 1982. *Perceptual Preference as an Aspect of Adolescent Learning Styles.* ERIC ED 224 769.
242. Henry, S. E., Medway, F. J., and Scarbro, H. A. 1979. Sex and locus of control as determinants of children's responses to peer versus adult praise. *Journal of Educational Psychology* 71 (5): 604–12.
243. Nelson-LeGall, S., and Glor-Scheib, S. 1983. *Help-Seeking in Elementary Classrooms: An Observational Study.* ERIC ED 230 286.
244. Stewart, M. J., and Corbin, C. B. 1988. Feedback dependence among low confidence preadolescent boys and girls. *Research Quarterly for Exercise and Sport* 59 (2): 160–64.
245. Sullivan, H. J. 1986. Factors that influence continuing motivation.

*Journal of Educational Research* 80 (2): 86–92.

Females' use of helplessness to influence others is the subject of the articles listed next.

246. Johnson, P. 1976. Women and power: Toward a theory of effectiveness. *Journal of Social Issues* 32 (3): 99–110.
247. Parsons, J. E. 1982. Sex differences in attributions and learned helplessness. *Sex Roles* 8 (4): 421–32.

The following studies indicate that females are more sensitive to nonverbal cues.

248. Hall, J. C. 1978. Gender effects in decoding nonverbal cues. *Psychological Bulletin* 85: 845–57.
249. Rosenthal, R., Hall, J. A., DiMatteo, M. R., Rogers, P. L., and Archer, D. C. 1979. *Sensitivity to Non-Verbal Communication.* Baltimore: Johns Hopkins University Press.

These articles focus on the relationship between sex-role stereotypes and learning/remembering information.

250. Koblinsky, S. G., Cruse, D. F., and Sugawara, A. I. 1978. Sex-role stereotypes and children's memory for story content. *Child Development* 49: 452–58.
251. Liben, L. S., and Signorella, M. L. 1980. Gender-related schemata and constructive memory in children. *Child Development* 51: 11–18.
252. Martin, C. L., and Halverson, C. F., Jr. 1983. The effects of sex-typing schemas on young children's memory. *Child Development* 54: 563–74.

253. Meehan, A., and Janik, L. M. 1990. Illusory correlation and the maintenance of sex role stereotypes in children. *Sex Roles* 22 (1/2): 83–95.

254. Signorella, M. L. 1987. Gender schemata: Individual differences and context effects. *New Directions for Child Development* 38: 23–37.

255. Signorella, M. L., and Liben, L. S. 1984. Recall and reconstruction of gender-related pictures: Effects of attitude, task difficulty, and age. *Child Development* 55: 393–405.

256. Signorella, M. L., and Liben, L. S. 1985. "Effects of Labels on Children's Memory for Gender-Related Pictures." Paper presented at the annual meeting of the Society for Research in Child Development, Toronto.

References that deal with gender differences in motivation to avoid success are listed next.

257. Burlew, K. A. 1977. Career educational choices of Black females. *Journal of Black Psychology* 3: 89–106.

258. Crovitz, E. 1980. A decade later: Black-white attitudes toward women's familial roles. *Psychology of Women Quarterly* 5 (2): 170–76.

259. Fleming, J. 1978. Fear of success, achievement related motives and behavior in Black college women. *Journal of Personality* 46: 694–716.

260. George, V. D. 1981. *Occupational Aspirations of Talented Black Adolescent Females.* ERIC ED 206 976.

261. George, V. D. 1986. Talented adolescent women and the motivation to avoid success. *Journal of Multicultural Counseling and Development* 14 (3): 132–39.

262. Horner, M. S. 1972. Toward an understanding of achievement-related conflicts in women. *Journal of Social Issues* 28 (2): 157–75.

263. Roberts, L. R. 1986. *Gender Differences in Patterns of Achievement and Adjustment during Early Adolescence.* ERIC ED 288 134.

264. Stockard, J., Schmuck, P. A., Kemper, K., Williams, P., Edson, S. K., and Smith, M. A. 1980. *Sex Equity in Education.* New York: Academic Press.

The following references deal with gender differences in participation in academic courses and activities.

265. Alspach, P. A. 1988. *Inequities in the Computer Classroom: An Analysis of Two Computer Courses.* ERIC ED 301 180.

266. Becker, J. 1983. *School Use of Microcomputers.* 1–3. Baltimore: Center for Social Organization of Schools, Johns Hopkins University.

267. Bryant, L. 1989. Gifted jr. high students: How do they feel? How can we help? *Gifted Child Today* 12 (6): 7–9.

268. Chen, M. 1986. Gender and computers: The beneficial effects of experience on attitudes. *Journal of Educational Computing Research* 2 (3): 265–82.

269. Christensen, R., Witthuhn, J., and Robertson, C. 1982. *American Indian Women and Mathematics: An Annotated Bibliography of Selected References.* ERIC ED 234 970.

270. Dunteman, G., Wisenbaker, J. A., and Taylor, M. E. 1979. *Race and Sex Differences in College Science Program Participation.* Research Triangle Park, NC: Research Triangle Institute.

271. Educational Testing Service. 1989. *What Americans Study.* Princeton, NJ: Educational Testing Service.

272. Fetler, M. 1985. Sex differences on the California State Assessment of Computer Literacy. *Sex Roles* 13 (3/4): 181–91.

273. Fisher, G. 1984. Access to computers. *The Computing Teacher* 11: 24–27.

274. Goertz, M. 1989. *Course Taking Patterns in the 1980's.* Princeton, NJ: Educational Testing Service.

275. Haertel, G. D., Walberg, H. J., Junker, L. S., and Pascarella, E. T. 1981. Early adolescent sex differences in science learning: Evidence from the National Assessment of Educational Progress. *American Education Research Journal* 18 (3): 329–41.

276. Horn, L. 1990. "Trends in High School Math and Science Course Taking: Effects of Gender and Ethnicity." Paper presented at the annual meeting of the American Educational Research Association, Boston.

277. Klinzing, D. G. 1985. *A Study of the Behavior of Children in a Preschool Equipped with Computers.* ERIC ED 255 320.

278. Lee, V. E., and Ware, N. C. 1986. "When and Why Girls 'Leak' Out of High School Mathematics: A Closer Look." Paper presented at the annual meeting of the American Educational Research Association, San Francisco.

279. Leinhardt, G., Seewald, A., and Engel, M. 1979. Learning what's taught: Sex differences in instruction. *Journal of Educational Psychology* 71 (3): 432–39.

280. Linn, M. C. 1983. *Fostering Equitable Consequences from Computer Learning Environments.* ERIC ED 242 626.

281. Linn, M. C. 1985. Gender equity in computer learning environments. *Computers and the Social Sciences* 1: 19–27.

282. Lockheed, M. E. 1985. Women, girls, and computers: A first look at the evidence. *Sex Roles* 13 (3/4): 115–22.

283. Lockheed, M., and Frakt, S. 1984. Sex Equity: Increasing girls' use of computers. *The Computing Teacher* 11 (8): 16–18.

284. MacCorquodale, P. 1984. *Self-Image, Science and Math: Does the Image of the "Scientist" Keep Girls and Minorities from Pursuing Science and math?* ERIC ED 253 493.

285. Metha, A. A. 1983. Decade since Title IX: Some implications for teacher education. *Action in Teacher Education* 5: 21–27.

286. Miura, I., and Hess, R. 1984. Enrollment differences in computer camps and summer classes. *The Computing Teacher* 11 (8): 22–23.

287. Parsons, J. E. 1984. "Sex differences in mathematics participation." In *Women in Science: Advances in Motivation and Achievement,* vol. 2, edited by M. W. Steinkamp, and M. L. Meehr. Greenwich, CT: JAI Press.

288. Rallis, S. F., and Ahern, S. A. 1986. *Math and Science Education in High Schools: A Question of Sex Equity?* ERIC ED 270 326.

289. Rampy, L. 1984. *We Teach Children: Computer Literacy as a Feminist Issue.* ERIC ED 240 028.

290. Revelle, G., Honey, M., Amsel, E., Schauble, L., and Levine, G. 1984. "Sex Differences in the Use of Computers." Paper presented at the annual conference of the

American Educational Research Association, New Orleans.

291. Rosser, P. 1982. Do schools teach computer anxiety. *Ms* 2: 25.

292. Sells, L. 1980. The mathematics filter and the education of women and minorities. In *Women and the Mathematical Mystique,* edited by L. Fox, L. A. Brody, and D. Tobin. Baltimore: Johns Hopkins University Press.

293. Silvern, S. B., Countermine, T. M., and Williamson, P. A. C. 1982. "Young Children Interacting with a Computer." Paper presented at the annual meeting of the American Educational Research Association, New York.

294. Smail, B., and Kelly, A. 1984. Sex differences in science and technology among 11-year-old school children. II-affective. *Research in Science and Technology Education* 2 (2): 87–106.

295. Stage, E. K., and Kreinberg, N. 1982. "Equal Access to Computers." Paper presented at the semi-annual meeting of the American Educational Research Association Special Interest Group: Research on Women in Education, Philadelphia.

296. Tobin, D., and Fox, L. 1980. Career interests and career education: A key to change. In *Women and the Mathematical Mystique,* edited by L. Fox, L. A. Brody, and D. Tobin. Baltimore: Johns Hopkins University Press.

The following references are concerned with gender differences in vocational training and career aspirations.

297. American College Testing Program. 1989. *State and National Trend Data for Students Who Take the ACT Assessment.* Iowa City: American College Testing Program.

298. Anderson, K. L. 1981. Educational goals of male and female adolescents: The effects of parental characteristics and attitudes. *Youth and Society* 12 (2): 173–88.

299. Archer, C. J. 1984. Children's attitudes toward sex-role division in adult occupational roles. *Sex Roles: A Journal of Research* 10 (1–2): 1–10.

300. Canale, J. R., and Dunlap, L. L. 1987. *Factors Influencing Career Aspirations of Primary and Secondary Grade Students.* ERIC ED 288 164.

301. Crowley, J. E., and Shapiro, D. 1982. Aspirations and expectations of youth in the United States: Part 1. Education and fertility. *Youth and Society* 13 (4): 391–422.

302. Danziger, N. 1983. Sex-related differences in the aspirations of high school students. *Sex Roles* 9 (6): 683–95.

303. Dao, M. 1987. "From Vietnamese to Vietnamese American." Unpublished manuscript, San Jose, CA: San Jose State University.

304. Davidson, J. P. 1980. Urban black youth and career development. *Journal of Non-White Concerns in Personnel and Guidance* 3 (8): 119–40.

305. Falkowski, C. K., and Falk, W. W. 1983. Homemaking as an occupational plan: Evidence from a national longitudinal study. *Journal of Vocational Behavior* 22 (2): 227–42.

306. Farmer, H. S., and Sidney, J. S. 1985. Sex equity in career and vocational education. In *Handbook for Achieving Sex Equity Through*

*Education,* edited by S. Klein. Baltimore, MD: Johns Hopkins University Press.

307. Grady, J. 1987. *Trends in the Selection of Science, Mathematics, or Engineering as Major Fields Among Top Scoring SAT Takers.* Princeton, NJ: Educational Testing Service.

308. Grevious, C. 1985. A comparison of occupational aspirations of urban black college students. *Journal of Negro Education* 54 (1): 35–42.

309. Grossman, H. 1984. *Educating Hispanic Students: Cultural Implications for Instruction, Classroom Management, Counseling and Assessment.* Springfield, IL: Thomas.

310. Gupta, N. 1982. *The Influence of Sex Roles on the Life Plans of Low-SES Adolescents.* ERIC ED 235 434.

311. Hannah, J. S., and Kahn, S. E. 1989. The relationship of socioeconomic status and gender to occupational choices of grade 12 students. *Journal of Vocational Behavior* 34 (2): 161–78.

312. Holmes, B. L., and Esses, L. M. 1988. Factors influencing Canadian high school girls' career motivation. *Psychology of Women Quarterly* 12 (3): 313–28.

313. Jensen, E. L., and Hovey, S. Y. 1982. Bridging the gap from high school to college for talented females. *Peabody Journal of Education* 59 (3): 153–59.

314. Karraker, M. W. 1991. *Predicting Adolescent Females' Plans for Higher Education: Race and Socioeconomic Differences.* ERIC ED 337 517.

315. Kelly, K. R., and Cobb, S. J. 1991. A profile of the career development characteristics of young gifted adolescents: Examining gender and multicultural differences. *Roeper Review* 13 (4): 202–6.

316. Lee, C. C. 1985. An ethnic group-gender comparison of occupational choice among rural adolescents. *Journal of Non-White Concerns* 13 (1): 28–37.

317. Linn, M., and Petersen, A. 1986. A meta-analysis of gender differences in spatial ability: Implications for mathematics and science achievement. In *The Psychology of Gender: Advances Through Meta-Analysis,* edited by J. S. Hyde and M. C. Linn. Baltimore: Johns Hopkins University Press.

318. Miller, M. J., and Stanford, J. T. 1987. Early occupational restriction: An examination of elementary school children's expression of vocational preferences. *Journal of Employment Counseling* 24 (3): 115–21.

319. Miranda and Associates. 1977. *Concerns of Minority Women with Respect to Vocational Education.* ERIC ED 164 633.

320. Odell, K. S. 1989. Gender differences in the educational and occupational expectations of rural Ohio youth. *Research in Rural Education* 5 (3): 37–41.

321. Ohlendof, G. W., and Rafferty, D. M. 1982. *The Educational and Occupational Aspirations of Louisiana Rural High School Students: A Comparative Study.* ERIC ED 218 020.

322. Pido, A. J. A. 1978. *A Cross-Cultural Change of Gender Roles: The Case of Filipino Women Immigrants in Midwest City, U. S. A.* ERIC ED 159 244.

323. Ruhland, D. J., Brittle, M., Norris, S., and Oakes, R. 1978. *Determinants of Career Goals in Junior and*

*Senior High School Women.* ERIC ED 185 356.

324. Smith, E. J. 1981. The career development of young Black females: The forgotten group. *Youth and Society* 12 (3): 277–312.

325. Smith, E. J. 1982. The Black female adolescent: A review of the educational, career, and psychological literature. *Psychology of Women Quarterly* 6: 261–88.

326. Vasquez, M. J. T. 1982. Confronting barriers to the participation of Mexican American women in higher education. *Hispanic Journal of Behavioral Sciences* 4 (2): 147–65.

327. Wells, J. 1983. *Statement of the National Coalition for Women and Girls in Education.* Washington, D.C.: National Coalition for Women and Girls in Education.

Gender differences in extracurricular activities is the topic of the following reference.

328. National Center for Educational Statistics. 1984. *High School Seniors: A Comparative Study of the Classes of 1972 and 1980.* Washington, D.C.: U.S. Government Printing Office.

These references discuss gender differences in verbal and mathematics achievement.

329. Allred, R. A. 1990. Gender differences in spelling achievement in grades 1 through 6. *Journal of Educational Research* 83 (4): 187–93.

330. Armstrong, J. M. 1981. Achievement and participation of women in mathematics. *Journal for Research in Mathematics Education* 12: 356–72.

331. Benbow, C. P., and Stanley, J. C. 1980. Sex differences in mathematics ability: Fact or artifact? *Science* 210: 1262–64.

332. Benbow, C. P., and Stanley, J. C. 1982. Consequences in high school and college of sex differences in mathematical reasoning ability: A longitudinal perspective. *American Educational Research Journal* 19 (4): 598–622.

333. Benbow, C. P., and Stanley, J. C. 1983. Sex differences in mathematical reasoning ability: More facts. *Science* 222: 1029–31.

334. Brandon, P. R., Newton, B. J., and Hammond, O. W. 1987. Children's mathematics achievement in Hawaii: Sex differences favoring girls. *American Educational Research Journal* 24 (3): 437–61.

335. Conner, J. M., and Serbin, L. A. 1980. *Mathematics, Visual-Spatial Ability, and Sex Roles.* Washington, D.C.: National Institute of Education.

336. Eastman, S. T., and Krendl, K. 1987. Computer and gender: Differential effects of electronic search on students' achievement and attitudes. *Journal of Research and Development in Education* 20 (3): 41–48.

337. Fennema, E., and Carpenter, T. 1981. Sex-related differences in mathematics: Results from the national assessment. *Mathematics Teacher* 74 (7): 554–59.

338. Fox, L., Brody, L. A., and Tobin, D., eds. 1980. *Women and the Mathematical Mystique.* Baltimore: Johns Hopkins University Press.

339. Fox, L., and Cohn, S. 1980. Sex differences in the development of precocious mathematical talent. In *Women and the Mathematical*

*Mystique,* edited by L. Fox, L. A. Brody, and D. Tobin. Baltimore: Johns Hopkins University Press.

340. Green, R. 1979. *Math Avoidance: A Barrier to American Indian Science Education and Science Careers.* ERIC ED 170 084.

341. Harris, C. S. 1986. *A Summary of the Language Arts Achievement of Students in a Phase-Elective Mini-Course System as Compared to the Language Arts Achievement of Students in a Traditional Program.* ERIC ED 280 064.

342. Harris, L. J. 1977. Sex differences in the growth and use of language. In *Women: A Psychological Perspective,* edited by E. Donelson and J. Gullahorn. New York: Wiley.

343. Hyde, J. S. 1981. How large are cognitive gender differences? A meta-analysis using w and d. *American Psychologist* 36: 892–901.

344. Koenigsknecht, R. A., and Friedman, P. 1976. Syntax development in boys and girls. *Child Development* 47: 1109–15.

345. Lockheed, M. E., Thorpe, M., Brooks-Gunn, J. Casserly, P., and McAloon, A. 1985. *Understanding Sex/Ethnic Differences in Mathematics, Science and Computers Science for Students in Grades Four to Eight.* Princeton, NJ: Educational Testing Service.

346. Lockheed, M. E., Thorpe, M., Brooks-Gunn, J. Casserly, P., and McAloon, A. 1985. *Sex and Ethnic Differences in Middle School Mathematics, Science and Computer Science: What Do We Know?* ERIC ED 303 353.

347. Maccoby, E. E., and Jacklin, C. N. 1974. *The Psychology of Sex Differences.* Stanford, CA: Stanford University Press.

348. Marshall, S. P. 1984. Sex differences in students' mathematics achievement: Solving computations and story problems. *Journal of Educational Psychology* 76 (2): 194–204.

349. Midgley, C. 1983. Expectations, values, and academic behaviors. In *Achievement and Achievement Motivation,* edited by J. T. Spence. San Francisco: W. H. Freeman.

350. Nelson, K. 1973. Structure and strategy in learning to talk. *Monographs of the Society for Research in Child Development,* No. 38.

351. Scott-Jones, D., and Clark, M. L. 1986. The school experience of Black girls: The interaction of gender, race, and socioeconomic status. *Phi Delta Kappan* 67 (7): 520–26.

352. Sharp, L. M. 1989. *The SAT-M Gap: Looking at Micro Level Data.* ERIC ED 307 292.

353. Sherman, J. 1981. Girls' and boys' enrollment in theoretical math courses: A longitudinal study. *Psychology of Women Quarterly* 5: 681–89.

354. Simmons, W. 1990. "Black Male Achievement: Strategies for Ensuring Success in School." Paper presented at the annual meeting of the National Black Child Development Institute, Washington, D.C.

355. Steel, L., and Wise, L. 1979. "Origins of Sex Differences in High School Math Achievement and Participation." Paper presented at the annual meeting of the American Educational Research Association, San Francisco.

356. Travis, K. J., and McKnight, C. C. 1985. Mathematics achievement in U.S. schools: Preliminary findings from the second IEA Mathe-

matics Study. *Phi Delta Kappa* 66: 407–13.

357. Witting, M. A., and Peterson, A. C., eds. 1979. *Sex-Related Differences in Cognitive Functioning: Developmental Issues.* New York: Academic Press.

358. Yarborough, B. H., and Johnson, R. A. 1980. A six-year study of sex differences in intellectual functioning, reading/language arts achievement, and affective development. *Journal of Psychology* 106 (1): 55–61.

The following references relate to gender differences on visual spatial tasks.

359. Burnett, S. A., and Lane, D. M. 1980. Effects of academic instruction on spatial visualization. *Intelligence* 4: 233–42.

360. Connor, J. M., Schachman, M. E., and Serbin, L. A. 1978. Sex-related differences in response to practice on a visual-spatial test and generalization to a related test. *Child Development* 49: 24–29.

361. Connor, J. M., Serbin, L. A., and Schachman, M. E. 1978. Sex differences in children's response to training on a visual-spatial test. *Developmental Psychology* 3: 293–94.

362. Fennema, E. H., and Carpenter, T. P. 1981. Sex-related differences in mathematics: Results from national assessment. *Mathematics Teacher* 74: 554–59.

363. Harris, L. J. 1981. "Sex-related variations in spatial skill." In *Spatial Representation and Behavior Across the Life Span*, edited by L. S. Liben, A. H. Patterson, and N. Newcombe. New York: Academic Press.

364. Linn, M. C., and Petersen, A. C. 1985. Emergence and characterization of sex differences in spatial ability: A meta-analysis. *Child Development* 56: 1479–98.

365. Linn, M. C., and Petersen, A. C. 1986. "Gender differences in spatial ability." In *The Psychology of Gender: Advances through Meta-Analysis,* edited by J. S. Hyde and M. C. Linn. Baltimore: Johns Hopkins University Press.

366. McGee, M. G. 1979. Human spatial abilities: Psychometric studies and environmental, genetic, hormonal, and neurological influences. *Psychological Bulletin* 86: 889–918.

367. Nash, S. C. 1979. "Sex-role as a mediator of intellectual functioning." In *Sex-Related Differences in Cognitive Functioning: Developmental Issues,* edited by M. A. Witting and A. C. Petersen. New York: Academic Press.

368. Petersen, A. G. 1979. "Hormones and cognitive functioning in normal development." In *Sex-Related Differences in Cognitive Functioning: Developmental Issues,* edited by M. A. Witting and A. C. Petersen. New York: Academic Press.

369. Richmond, P. G. 1980. A limited sex difference in spatial test scores with a preadolescent sample. *Child Development* 51: 601–2.

370. Waber, D. P. 1979. "Cognitive abilities and sex-related variations in the maturation of cerebral cortical functions." In *Sex-Related Differences in Cognitive Functioning: Developmental Issues,* edited by M. A. Witting and A. C. Petersen. New York: Academic Press.

Anti-female bias in standardized testing and female anxiety are the topics of these references.

371. Brown, F. G. 1980. Sex bias in achievement test items: Do they have any effect on performance? *Teaching of Psychology* 7 (1): 24–26.
372. Donlon, T. F. 1971. "Content Factors in Sex Differences on Test Questions." Paper presented at the annual meeting of the New England Educational Research Organization, Boston.
373. Doolittle, A. E. 1986. *Gender-Based Differential Item Performance in Mathematics Achievement Items.* ERIC ED 270 464.
374. Dwyer, C. A. 1979. The role of tests in producing sex-related differences. In *Sex-Related Differences in Cognitive Functioning: Developmental Issues,* edited by M. A. Witting, and A. C. Peterson. New York: Academic Press.
375. Eccles, J., and Jacobs, J. E. 1986. Social forces shape math attitudes and performance. *Signs* 11: 367–89.
376. Ekstrom, R. B., Lockheed, M. E., and Donlon, T. F. 1979. Sex differences and sex bias in test content. *Educational Horizons* 58 (1): 47–52.
377. Faggen-Steckler, J., McCarthy, K. A., and Tittle, C. K. 1974. A quantitative method for measuring sex "bias" in standardized tests. *Journal of Educational Measurement* 11: 151–61.
378. Fox, L. 1977. "The effects of sex-role socialization on mathematics participation and achievement." In *Women and Mathematics: Research Perspectives for Change.* National Institute of Education Papers in Education and Work, no. 8. Department of Health, Education, and Welfare: Washington, D.C.

379. Lips, H. M. 1988. *Sex and Gender: An Introduction.* Mountain View, CA: Mayfield.
380. Christoplos, F., and Borden, J. 1978. Sexism in elementary school mathematics. *Elementary School Journal* 78 (4): 275–77.
381. Plake, B. S., Hoover, H. D., and Loyd, B. H. 1980. An investigation of the Iowa Test of Basic Skills for sex bias: A developmental look. *Psychology in the Schools* 17 (1): 47–52.
382. Tittle, C. K. 1973. Women and educational testing. *Phi Delta Kappan* 54: 118–19.
383. Tittle, C. K. 1974. Sex bias in educational measurement: Fact or fiction? *Measurement and Evaluation in Guidance* 6: 219–26.

These references deal with the predictive validity of females' scores on standardized math tests.

384. Bender, D. S. 1976. *Psychosocial Dimensions of Sex Differences in the Academic Competence of Adolescents.* ERIC ED 128 695.
385. Fox, L., and Cohn, S. 1980. Sex differences in the development of precocious mathematical talent. In *Women and the Mathematical Mystique,* edited by L. Fox, L. A. Brody, and D. Tobin. Baltimore: Johns Hopkins University Press.
386. Slack, W., and Porter, D. 1980. Training, validity, and the issue of aptitude: A reply to Jackson. *Harvard Educational Review* 50 (3): 392–401.

Gender differences in science achievement are the focus of the following references.

387. Becker, B. J. 1989. Gender and science achievement: A reanalysis of

studies from two meta-analyses. *Journal of Research in Science Teaching* 26 (2): 141–69.

388. Haertel, G. D., Walberg, H. J., Junker, L., and Pascarella, E. T. 1981. Early adolescent sex differences in science learning: Evidence from the National Assessment of Educational Progress. *American Educational Research Journal* 18 (3): 329–41.

389. Hueftle, S. J., Rakow, S. J., and Welch, W. W. 1983. *Images of Science*. Minneapolis: University of Minnesota Press.

390. Hyde, J. S., and Linn, M. C. 1986. *The Psychology of Gender: Advances through Meta-Analysis*. Baltimore: Johns Hopkins University Press.

391. Maehr, M. L., and Steinkamp, M. 1983. *A Synthesis of Findings on Sex Differences in Science Education Research*. ERIC ED 229 226.

392. Malone, M. R., and Fleming, M. L. 1983. The relationship of student characteristics and student performance in science as viewed by meta-analysis research. *Journal of Research in Science Teaching* 20: 481–95.

393. Shaw, E. L., Jr., and Doan, R. L. 1990. An investigation of the differences in attitude and achievement between male and female second and fifth grade science students. *Journal of Elementary Science Education* 2 (1): 10–15.

394. Smith, S. E., and Walker, W. J. 1985. *High School Physics: A Male Domain?* ERIC ED 262 972.

395. Steinkamp, M. W., and Maehr, M. L. 1983. Affect, ability, and science achievement: A quantitative synthesis of correlational research. *Review of Educational Research* 53: 369–96.

396. Steinkamp, M. W., and Maehr, M. L. 1984. Gender differences in motivational orientations toward achievement in school science: A quantitative synthesis. *American Educational Research Journal* 21 (1): 39–59.

397. Zerega, M. E., Haertel, G. D., Tsai, S., and Walberg, H. J. 1986. Late adolescent sex differences in science learning. *Science Education* 70 (4): 447–60.

The following reference documents the fact that males outperform females on tests of computer literacy.

398. Hawkins, J. 1985. Computers and girls: Rethinking the issue. *Sex Roles* 13 (3/4): 165–80.

References that deal with recent changes in the gender gap in academic ability and achievement are listed next.

399. Becker, C., and Forsyth, R. 1990. "Gender differences in Grades 3 Through 12: A Longitudinal Analysis." Paper presented at the annual meeting of the American Educational Research Association, Boston.

400. Coladarci, T., and Lancaster, L. N. 1989. *Gender and Mathematics Achievement: Data from High School and Beyond*. ERIC ED 308 207. Educational Testing Service 1989. *The Gender Gap*. ERIC ED 314 431.

401. Feingold, A. 1988. Cognitive gender differences are disappearing. *American Psychologist* 43: 95–103.

402. Hall, C. W., and Hoff, C. 1988. Gender differences in mathematical performance. *Educational Studies in Mathematics* 19 (3): 395–401.

403. Halpern, D. F. 1986. *Sex Differences in Cognitive Abilities*. Hillsdale, NJ: Erlbaum Associates.

404. Halpern, D. F. 1989. The disappearance of cognitive gender dif-

ferences: What you see depends on where you look. *American Psychologist* 44: 455–64.

405. Hyde, J. S., and Linn, M. C. 1988. Gender differences in verbal abilities: A meta-analysis. *Psychological Bulletin* 104 (1): 53–69.

406. Leder, G. C. 1990. Gender differences in mathematics: An overview. In *Mathematics and Gender,* edited by E. Fennema and G. C. Leder. New York: Teachers College Press.

407. Lynn, M., and Hyde, J. 1989. Gender, mathematics, and science. *Educational Researcher* 14: 51–71.

408. Martin, D., and Hoover, H. 1987. Sex differences in educational achievement: A longitudinal study. *Journal of Early Adolescence* 7: 65–83.

409. Mullis, I., and Jenkins, L. 1988. *The Science Report Card: Elements of Risk and Recovery.* Princeton: Educational Testing Service.

410. Rosenthal, R., and Rubin, C. B. 1982. Further meta-analytic procedures for assessing cognitive gender differences. *Journal of Educational Psychology* 74 (5): 708–12.

References that indicate that males exhibit more behavior problems and get into more trouble in school than females follow.

411. Center, D. B., and Wascom, A. M. 1987. Teacher perceptions of social behavior in behaviorally disordered and socially normal children and youth. *Behavior Disorders* 12 (3): 200–6.

412. Duke, D. L. 1978. Why don't girls misbehave more than boys in school? *Journal of Youth and Adolescence* 7 (2): 141–57.

413. Eme, R. F. 1979. Sex differences in childhood psychopathology: A review. *Psychological Bulletin* 86: 574–95.

414. Epstein, M. H., Cullinan, D., and Bursuck, W. D. 1985. Prevalence of behavior problems among learning disabled and nonhandicapped students. *Mental Retardation and Learning Disability Bulletin* 13: 30–39.

415. Ludwig, G., and Cullinan, D. 1984. Behavior problems of gifted and nongifted elementary school girls and boys. *Gifted Child Quarterly* 28 (1): 37–39.

416. National Black Child Development Institute. 1990. *The Status of African American Children: Twentieth Anniversary Report.* Washington, D.C.

417. Wadsworth, M. 1979. *Roots of Delinquency: Infancy, Adolescence and Crime.* New York: Barnes and Noble.

418. Werry, J. S., and Quay, H. C. 1971. The prevalence of behavior symptoms in younger elementary school children. *American Journal of Orthopsychiatry* 41: 136–43.

These references discuss gender differences in special education enrollment.

419. DBS Corp. 1986. *Elementary and Secondary School Civil Rights Survey, 1984. National Summaries.* ERIC ED 271 543.

420. DBS Corp. 1987. *Elementary and Secondary School Civil Rights Survey, 1986. National Summaries.* ERIC ED 304 485.

421. Gillespie, P. H., and Fink, A. H. 1974. The influence of sexism on the education of handicapped children. *Exceptional Children* 41 (3): 155–62.

422. Messick, S. 1984. Assessment in context: Appraising student performance in relation to instructional quality. *Educational Researcher* 13 (3): 3–8.

# ▶ 2

## Origins of Gender Differences

Why do males and females have such different experiences and fulfill such different roles both in and out of school? Many factors contribute to these differences. This chapter examines the contributions five of these factors make to the development and maintenance of the gender differences in school outcomes and societal roles described in chapter 1.

## BIOLOGICAL FACTORS

Differences in male and female hormonal systems and the lateralization and specialization of their right-brains and left-brains contribute to a number of the reported gender differences. This section examines the role of these physiological factors.

### *Hormonal Differences*

Some researchers propose that the higher levels of male hormones such as testosterone have both a direct and indirect effect on gender differences. They directly affect gender differences in activity level, assertive/aggressive behavior, and emotional reactions by predisposing males and females to act differently in these areas (1, 3, 4, 7–9, 16–18, 21–23, 25, 32). And, they indirectly affect many of the other male-female differences reported in chapter 1.

The indirect effect of hormonal factors is as follows. First, gender differences in activity level, assertiveness, and emotional reactions predispose males and females to prefer and to engage in activities compatible with their different biological make-ups. Because the genders engage in somewhat different activities, they have different rates of practice with the skills these activities involve. This causes them to excel in some skills and do poorly in others. In turn, this results in many of the other gender behavioral differences described in chapter 1. The following are examples of how this process is presumed to cause gender differences in visual-spatial abilities, cooperative behavior, and levels of independence (35–40).

According to the theory, hormonal differences in activity needs predispose males to select toys such as blocks, vehicles, and so on, as well as outside sports and games that coincidentally provide more opportunity for them to practice visual-spatial skills. The time that males spend as preschoolers playing with these toys and engaging in activities that develop these skills results in their higher scores on tests of visual-spatial relations. Being more active, they tend to prefer loosely structured play activities. These less-structured activities foster independent, creative skills in boys because they provide fewer guidelines for, and restrictions on, boys' behavior. The biologically determined low activity level of girls, on the other hand, causes them to prefer highly structured activities, which affords them practice in cooperative and conforming skills, but little exposure to practicing independent skills. Adults then reward males and females for functioning in these dissimilar ways, thereby reinforcing the indirect effects of their biological predispositions.

Research indicates that hormonal factors do contribute to some of the gender differences described in chapter 1. Males and females do have different levels of testosterone and this does affect their levels of activity and aggression and their emotional reactions (1, 3, 4, 7–9, 16–18, 21–23, 25). It is not clear, however, whether the higher levels of testosterone observed in males *cause* them to behave more assertively and aggressively than females or merely *predispose* them to do so when environmental conditions encourage them to behave in these ways.

Research also lends some support to the idea that hormonal factors exert an indirect influence on gender differences through behavioral compatibility and practice. For example, toddlers and preschool children actually select gender appropriate toys before they are aware of their own gender or the gender appropriateness of the toys they choose. (See chapter 1.) Furthermore, when asked why they choose to engage in certain activities or play with certain toys, they respond that they do so because they enjoy them, not because the activities and toys are gender appropriate or because they are pressured to engage in them (35). However, in general, very little research has been conducted to link biology to the many gender differences described in the previous chapter.

The indirect effects of biological predispositions may indeed occur in the ways they are described above. However, more research is needed to determine how frequently it occurs and how strong an influence it exerts on students' behavior. Biology may well be an important indirect contributing factor to some of these behavioral differences, but the extent of its influence has not yet been clearly established. Until more evidence becomes available, the notion that it is the higher levels of testosterone in males that causes them to function more independently than females, exceed females in visual-spatial skills, dominate conversations, assume leadership roles, control access to toys and equipment in mixed-sex groups, and so on must be considered highly speculative.

## Brain Lateralization/Specialization

A number of researchers believe that male-female differences in verbal, visual-spatial, and mathematics achievement are largely due to differences in the age at which, and the extent to which, their brain's right hemisphere and left hemisphere become specialized in mathematical and verbal functioning (5, 16, 27, 31). Two of the many different ideas about exactly how cerebral specialization may cause these gender differences are more widely accepted than others.

One idea is based on the fact that hemispherical specialization in certain functions such as verbal, visual-spatial, and mathematical reasoning occurs earlier in females than in males, and it proposes that early development of females' brains and their greater hemispheric specialization provides them with a head start that improves their verbal functioning. But because visual-spatial and higher level mathematical abilities develop later than verbal skills, early hemispheric specialization occurs too soon in females for them to develop these other skills to their full potential. A second explanation is that the greater and earlier specialization in females enhances verbal skills that require specialization but weakens skills such as visual-spatial abilities that require more bilateral functioning.

Although research results regarding gender differences in hemispheric specialization are not entirely consistent, on balance, considerable evidence of differences in cerebral lateralization between males and females exists (2, 5, 10–15, 19, 20, 24, 26, 28–30, 33, 34). Researchers have found that hemispheric specialization in females begins earlier, perhaps as early as three months of age, and develops to a greater degree. However, as reviewers of the research have repeatedly concluded, the research does not support any particular one of the many current explanations of how gender differences in cerebral specialization influence students' verbal and visual-spatial functioning (5, 6). In addition, research has not yet established a direct causal relationship between these physiological differences and the ages at which the genders acquire initial language skills or their scores on tests of verbal, mathematical, or visual-spatial skills. Thus, more research is needed before we can consider the biological explanation for gender disparities in these areas as proven. Until we know a great deal more, the following statement will continue to reflect the state of our knowledge about the influence that physiological factors have on the development of gender differences in behavior: "Nature and nurture are like Siamese twins who share a common heart and nervous system. The technology has not yet been developed that will allow them to be separated" (5, p. 4).

The authors also believe that as society and the education it provides students become less sexist, male-female differences in students' attitudes, behavior, career choices, and academic achievement will decrease. And as we learn more about non-European American and nonmiddle-class students, we will find that many of the male-female differences observed among European American middle-class students do not apply to other ethnic and socioeconomic groups. As a result, the need to question whether biological factors contribute to gender differences will diminish. (See chapter 5 for a more detailed discussion of this idea.)

## Predisposition versus Determinism

Educators disagree about the extent to which biological factors determine gender differences. Some think that biological factors *cause* gender differences in behavior and learning. Many others view biology not as a complete determiner of how individuals behave, but as one of several interacting influences. In this view, aptly expressed by Maccoby and Jacklin in 1974, behavioral differences that have a biological base can still be modified by environmental events.

> *We suggest that societies have the option of minimizing, rather than maximizing, sex differences through their socialization practices. A society could, for example, devote its energies more toward moderating male aggression than toward preparing women to submit to male aggression, or toward encouraging rather than discouraging male nurturance activities. In our view, social institutions and social practices are not merely reflections of the biologically inevitable. A variety of social institutions are viable within the framework set by biology. It is up to human beings to select those that foster the life styles they most value. (16, p. 374)*

Although research since 1974 has provided considerable information about the possible biological bases of gender differences, we still are relatively ignorant about which gender differences have a biological component. In addition, very little research has been conducted to determine the extent to which biological factors *cause* versus merely *predispose* males and females to function differently, whether some biological predispositions are more resistant to change than others, and the psychological costs, if any, people pay when they behave in ways that contradict their biological predispositions. Therefore, when educators try to change students' gender-specific behaviors that may have a biological component, they have little to guide them regarding either the extent to which such behavior can be changed or the possible costs involved in attempting to completely eliminate the behavior rather than to modify it. (See chapters 3 and 4 for more detailed discussions of this issue.)

## DIFFERENTIAL REINFORCEMENT

Everyday life experiences confirm that males and females learn gender-stereotypical roles in part because they tend to be positively reinforced for behaving differently—playing with different toys, communicating in different styles, settling arguments differently, enrolling in different courses, participating in different sports, and so on, and negatively reinforced for behaving similarly—boys crying about bruises and scrapes, girls playing in an active, boisterous manner, and the like. In addition, considerable research supports this explanation. While different ethnic and socioeconomic groups may not all share the same ideas about the sex-roles children should learn (see chapter 1), parents tend to reward their children for behaving in ways that they feel are gender-appropriate and punish them for behaving in ways that they feel are gender-inappropriate (16, 41–44). Teachers also use rewards and punishments to modify their students' behavior although they differ about the kinds of behavior they want students to exhibit. (See the section later in this chapter entitled School's Role, as well as chapters 4 and 5.)

Children, even toddlers and preschoolers, also reinforce each other for behaving in gender-stereotypical fashion (45–48). Children in general, and males in particular, reward each other for playing with the right toys, in the right way, and with the right sex; for choosing the correct games and activities; and for relating to each of the sexes in acceptable ways (see chapter 4). Fagot describes the behavior of youngsters between twenty and twenty-five months in a number of her studies:

> Both boys and girls received more positive feedback when they played with members of their own sex. Boys also received a different kind of negative feedback when they engaged in female-typical behaviors, which very directly told them that such behavior is inappropriate. Boys' peer groups gave two kinds of feedback: stay away from certain behaviors and play with others like you. . . . We see that the male peer group starts defining what is not male very early, and that the behaviors that are defined as not male

*drop out of the boy's repertoire. . . . We even see in these young children what might be called the tyranny of the male group, if one is not enthralled with the consequences, or the beginnings of the male bonding process, if one is. (46, p. 1102)*

Differential reinforcement is not as effective as many parents and teachers would like it to be. Ask a group of parents about the effectiveness of their efforts to shape their children's behavior to conform to their wishes and you will get mixed reports. Some will claim that they enjoyed considerable, but not complete success. Others will tell you their children engaged in active rebellion against their wishes, starting during the toddler stage and accelerating during adolescence. Such anecdotal information supports the notion that parental reinforcement is only one of several factors that determine children's behavior styles.

The results of research on teachers' ability to modify students behavior indicates that their efforts also have only limited success. In general, research reveals that teachers have some effect on female students' behavior, attitudes, and opinions but very little, if any, effect on the behavior of males. Research also indicates that much of the effect of teachers' interventions is confined to the classroom; students often revert to their original behavior patterns once they leave their teacher's presence (see chapter 5). Differential reinforcement contributes to the development and maintenance of gender differences, but it is not the sole contributing factor.

## CONSTRUCTIVISM: COGNITIVE AWARENESS AND MODELING

Children voluntarily adopt some gender-stereotypical ways of behaving without having to be rewarded (49–70). They become aware of, and identify

---

**BOX 2–1    Overheard at School**

- "George is playing with a doll."
- "Go away, trucks are for boys."
- "You can't be a superhero. You're not a boy, you're a girl."
- "Don't vote for Linda. Girls can't be presidents."
- "We don't want any stupid girls in our group. "

- "Uh oh! He touched you. Hurry, wipe the poison off."
- "Why does he have to play? Boys can't play jump rope."
- "Girls should play outfield. They could get hurt in the infield if the ball hits them."
- "This is the girls' table."

Students often learn gender stereotypical
behavior at home.

with, their gender, and then copy behavior they believe is appropriate for
their gender. In fact, as their conceptual abilities develop, they construct
increasingly more elaborate schemes of appropriate behavior for their gender and proceed to match their behavior to their constructs.

Maccoby and Jacklin describe the process in the following way: "A child
gradually develops concepts of 'masculinity' and 'femininity,' and when he
has understood what his own sex is, he attempts to match his behavior to
his conceptions. His ideas may be drawn only very minimally from observing his own parents. The generalizations he constructs do not represent acts
of imitation, but are organizations of information distilled from a wide
variety of sources" (16, pp. 365–66).

There is ample evidence that adults, including parents, model gender-specific behavior and communicate gender-specific expectations to children and youth, which children tend to copy (16, 49–70). In some situations, children will not only copy adult behavior, they will also change their attitudes, self-concept, and choice of academic subjects to conform to their parents' and teachers' gender expectations, even when objective evidence would lead them to think differently about themselves and select other subjects (60–70). For example, many girls' evaluation of their mathematical abilities and their decision whether or not to take advanced mathematics courses are more influenced by their parents' and teachers' opinions of their abilities and expectations of how they will fare in these courses than by their actual mathematics grades (63–65, 67).

Some parents, however, do not conform to gender stereotypes.

The effects of parental expectations on females' academic self-concepts and expectations are stronger and more influential for middle-class families than working-class families (60). This may reflect the fact that middle-class and working-class mothers do not have the same academic expectations for their daughters. Unlike middle-class mothers, working-class mothers do not expect females to earn lower grades than males in courses such as mathematics (65, 66). (Also see the section later in this chapter entitled Teacher Attention, Feedback, and Expectations.)

Adult models and expectations do not completely shape children's behavior. Although children may copy the attitudes and behavior of significant adults in their lives, they do not accept their elders' expectations un-critically nor emulate them completely. And many of them even act the opposite of how they see adults behave, especially during the rebellious times of adolescence (see chapter 5).

Considerable evidence also suggests that children as young as two and three years of age develop constructs of appropriate male and female behavior and tend to bring their behavior into line with these constructs (46, 49). Fagot's study, cited above, in which toddlers between the ages of twenty and twenty-four months reinforced their peers for behaving in gender-typical ways is an excellent example of this phenomenon.

The fact that students may adopt the behavior, attitudes, and opinions that their teachers model has important implications. Educators who want to influence the way students behave should not only reward students for behaving in the manner they wish to encourage, they should also model the behavior themselves. Educators who advise students to behave one way and even reward students for behaving that way, but then do not themselves model the behavior may find their attempts to influence students' sex-role behavior ineffective.

The same caveat applies to the gender-related information teachers expose students to in the materials they assign, the language they use, and the expectations they communicate. All this information can influence the gender constructs students form during their school years.

## STRUCTURED REPRODUCTION

One of the schools' many missions is to perpetuate the values, ideas, and attitudes of the societies they serve. Since American society does not completely live up to the high ideals it espouses, much of what is transmitted from generation to generation is what actually *is,* rather than what *should be.* This applies to gender issues as well as to many other aspects of American life. Because many of the prevailing societal views about gender are extremely biased, students are exposed to an educational structure that tends to reproduce gender disparities in outcomes and gender-stereotypical roles. Students are rarely exposed to an educational system that is structured in ways that foster gender equity (71–88).

Some educators with a neo-Marxist perspective see purpose behind the gender bias in the schools' structure. They believe it is only one of many biased structures that European American middle- and upper-class males have set up throughout society to maintain their economic and social power and position. That is, they believe that those who exercise control and power in our society—middle- and upper-class European American males—structure its institutions, including schools, to maintain their special positions by reproducing the inequality that serves their interests (71, 76, 77, 82–87). Thus, they use schools to maintain an ethnic, class, and gender division of labor. According to these theorists, schools provide females, non-European Americans, and working-class students with the kinds of educational experiences that maintain them as a source of cheap, though well-prepared, labor for their enterprises, while more affluent male students are trained to be the leaders of society. And at the same time, schools teach female, working-class, and non-European American students to accept the status quo—their economic and social inferiority.

Giroux has described three ways in which schools could be said to reproduce inequality:

> *First, schools provided different classes and social groups with knowledge and skills they needed to occupy their respective places in a labor force stratified by class, race, and gender. Second, schools were seen as reproductive in the cultural sense, functioning in part to distribute and legitimate forms of knowledge, value, language, and modes of style that constitute the dominant culture and its interests. Third, schools were viewed as part of a state apparatus that produced and legitimated the economic and ideological imperatives that underlie the state's political power. (80, p. 258)*

Grant and Sleeter claim this:

> *School plays a major role in the culture students develop. Like the family and neighborhood, school affects how students understand and pursue their life chances. It provides an institutional ideology, socializing agents, and an experiential context within which students define and shape the way they think about their personal dreams. The school context, containing social relations defined by race, social class, and gender, can produce a student culture in which young people accept and live out their parents' place in a stratified society, in spite of the school's espoused mission as equalizer and escalator to a better life. (82, p. 19)*

Reproduction theorists initially focused on the harm they believed the educational system causes working-class and non-European males. They criticized the schools for the disparity between the lower level of funding for schools that serve students from working-class neighborhoods (89–99), the use of tracking and ability grouping to separate European middle-class students from other students (100–114), and the use of the community college system to prevent working-class and minority students from enrolling in four year colleges (115–20). In recent years, they have paid increasing attention to the schools' sexist effect on females, suggesting that females, especially minority and working-class females, are exposed to two separate but related forces in the schools—those designed to maintain middle- and upper-class hegemony over the working-class and those designed to maintain male hegemony over females. The following quotation is an example of their point of view. Although it focuses on American Indian females' educational experiences in government run schools, it exemplifies what they think about the education many non-European women receive.

> *The governments' master plan for Indian women has been to generate an endless stream of domestics, and to a lesser extent, secretaries. The vocational choices for native children in boarding schools have always been sexist: boys do woodworking, car repair, house painting or farmwork; while girls do domestic or secretarial work . . . When we look at the occupations of native women in this country today, it should come as no surprise to find us locked into the nations' female work ghetto employees; it was designed that way. (86, pp. 47– 48)*

## RESISTANCE, PRODUCTION, AND TRANSFORMATION

Neo-Marxist reproduction theorists also suggest that while students are being exposed to gender and class biases in school and society-at-large, they are also being exposed to ideas and experiences that contradict these biases. They note that nonsexist perceptions of males and females are increasingly available in the media and in the materials students read in school. In addition, many teachers and parents share neither the prevailing gender-stereotypical expectations for children and youth nor the current class and ethnic biases. Thus, bombarded by conflicting messages, students do not passively accept the biases presented to them. Instead, they are constantly involved in a process of accommodating to some messages and resisting others (121– 42).

According to reproduction theorists, especially those with a neo-Marxist perspective, students are alienated, distrustful, angry, and disillusioned about the problems inherent in attending schools that are structured to maintain gender inequality, but many of them also realize that schools are merely one aspect of a society structured against them. And these theorists believe that many students also know that even if they do well in school, a society stratified along gender lines will not afford them the same benefits that males, especially European American upper-class males, receive from succeeding in school. Therefore, instead of acquiescing to the educational system for payoffs they do not believe will be forthcoming, they battle against the system to maintain their own sense of identity.

There are significant gender, ethnic, and socioeconomic differences in the way students resolve these contradictions (122, 128, 141, 142). This makes sense when one considers the fact that male and female students, and students from different ethnic and socioeconomic backgrounds, are exposed to somewhat different expectations about gender roles, and they also have different options available to them for resolving the contradictory pressures they experience.

Some students accommodate more than they resist; others actively resist the biased education they receive and the inferior position it threatens to place them in. Some defy schools' gender and socioeconomic biases in nonconstructive ways. They purposefully misbehave in aggressive or sexual ways, tune out their teachers, refuse to do their homework, come late to school, drop out before graduating, decide not to participate in higher education, and so on (123, 125, 132–35, 137, 138, 142).

Other students battle the same forces in constructive ways. They reject the biased ideas to which they are exposed. Instead, they assert their own experiences, heighten their own sense of self-identity, and leave school transformed into a new person with a new understanding of their gender and class and with the knowledge, skills, value, and self-awareness they require to contribute to transforming society (85, 128–30). Thus, for some students, schools reproduce the gender stereotypes prevalent in society, while in other cases schools actually help students to reject these stereotypes.

We currently lack the knowledge to predict which students will accommodate to the prevailing biases more than they resist them and which will resist more than accommodate. And we certainly cannot predict the forms their resistance will take.

One may agree that European American middle- and upper-class males purposely structure schools in ways that reproduce their power in society ("schools provided different classes and social groups with knowledge and skills they needed to occupy their respective places in a labor force stratified by class, race, and gender" [80, p. 258]). One may also believe that schools simply reflect the biases that permeate society, ("education does not create the sexual division of labour, nor the kinds of work available in the labour market, nor the class relationships of society, but it rarely does anything to undermine them" [77, p. 20]). It is clear though, that despite the progress that has occurred in providing equal educational opportunities to all students, the educational system both perpetuates gender inequity in school and in the larger society, and causes many students to misbehave, tune out, and drop out. (The following section describes many gender-biased educational structures to which students are exposed.)

Educators disagree about whether or not teachers should encourage and assist students to actively resist the gender stereotypes they are exposed to (see chapter 5). For example, neo-Marxist reproductive theorists believe that while it is important to eliminate class, cultural, and gender inequities in the schools, their goal is to transform the very nature of the public schools. Neo-Marxists want teachers to prepare students to resist the reproductive forces of society in more constructive ways, and above all to change both the schools and the social and economic structure of the society they serve, instead of preparing students to fit into the capitalist status quo (85, 132, 143, 144).

> *The ultimate purpose of radical pedagogy is not simply one of changing people's consciousness or restructuring schools along more democratic principles; the latter aims are important but are reformist in nature and incomplete when viewed within a radical problematic. At the core of any radical pedagogy must be the aim of empowering people to recognize and work for a change in the social, political, and economic structure that constitutes the ultimate source of class-based power and domination. (78, p. 427)*

Whether educators agree with this position or not, it is unlikely that many of them believe that misbehaving, tuning out, and dropping out of school are acceptable ways of resisting gender bias in school. Part 2 of this text is designed to assist teachers and students in adopting more constructive approaches to eliminating such bias.

## CONCLUSIONS

Biology, differential reinforcement, modeling, cognitive awareness, and structured reproduction interact with each other in, as yet, undetermined ways to lead a given individual to behave in a particular way in a specific situation (145–47). These factors can contribute to gender differences; however, they do not make male and female students behave differently. Physiological factors only predispose or incline the genders to act in dissimilar ways. Students can modify and channel their biological predispositions. Differential reinforcement, cognitive awareness and modeling, and educational structures *reproduce* gender stereotypes, but they can also *produce* students with new perspectives on gender issues.

Thus, the effects of school on students' gender-typical behavior are not predetermined. Educators can encourage gender differences by reflecting society's gender stereotypes and biases or discourage them by presenting alternative models and helping students examine existing stereotypes and biases in the schools and society-at-large. Educators who want to produce students with new views of gender, as well as those who wish to reproduce the prevailing points of view, should take all these factors into consideration when they deal with gender issues in their classrooms.

## SCHOOL'S ROLE

Teachers exert a major influence on how children learn to behave. Teachers reward behavior they want to encourage and punish behavior of which they disapprove. They consciously expose students to certain information and models of behavior through the articles, short stories, and books they assign to students, the topics they select for class discussion, the guest speakers they invite, the behavior they choose to model, and so forth. They also do the same thing inadvertently, without consciously planning to do so. Because teachers exert such a strong influence over their students, especially in the lower grades, it is important to examine the role teachers play in the development of the gender differences described in the preceding section. This section examines the school's role in the creation and maintainance of gender differences in students' school participation and achievement. Chapter 5 discusses the ways in which teachers can discourage such differences.

### *Administrative Imbalance*

While females comprise a majority of classroom teachers, they are grossly underrepresented in administrative positions (148–51). In 1990, 83 percent of the nation's school principals and superintendents were male and a majority of these, 75 percent, were European American males (151). Thus, the current situation, especially in elementary schools, is no different than the situation described by Frazier and Sadker in 1973: "Elementary school is a woman's world, but a male captain heads the ship" (149, p. 96).

What message does this situation communicate? Many authors believe that it teaches students that males, especially European American males, are, and should be, the authorities. (1148–51). For example, Jacobson suggests that to the American majority culture, the role of the principal and superintendent is that of "leader." Our notion of leader is still very much tied to the image of the white middle-aged male, and that is exactly who the average school administrator tends to be" (151, p. 23). And Lockheed states that "for most students . . . the norm of male preeminence is established early on by the staffing of the school" (150, pp. 121–22).

### *Curriculum Materials*

Many of the curriculum materials such as textbooks, readers, and biographies that students use also introduce society's gender biases into the school structure. Materials currently available (162–73) are not as sexist as the materials used in classes in the 1960s and 1970s (152–61). For example, the disparity in the number of pictures of males and females has been reduced. The stereotypical portrayal of females as nurses and secretaries has been largely eliminated, and working females are engaged in many more occupations. The preponderance of male characters in basal readers has been reduced by eliminating male characters from many stories and replacing them with nonhuman characters such as talking trees or animals without sex-roles.

However, many problems still exist. For example, authors and publishers still use male pronouns to describe individuals whose gender is unknown and *man* for all people. The use of nonhuman characters in basal readers avoids the appearance of sexism, but it does not increase the number of stories with female characters. In fact, stories about males still greatly outnumber stories about females in some students' readers in the higher grades and in the biographies found in school libraries. In most of the material students read, fathers still work and mothers still stay home. When they are at home, mothers do domestic chores such as taking care of children and cooking; fathers build and repair things. When parents work outside the home they are still described as being involved in gender stereotypical jobs, but to a lesser degree. Males are engaged in three times as many different occupations as females, and it is fathers who are the executives, professionals, scientists, firefighters, and police officers. Males participate in a variety of different athletic activities while females continue to be depicted as involved primarily in traditional female sports.

Females are described as overemotional, dependent, concerned about their appearance, and observers rather than participants. Males are actively involved in solving problems and doing adventurous things. Females are still portrayed as receiving help and males as providing help.

In math books, boys learn to count by driving cars, flying planes, and engineering trains, while girls learn to count by jumping rope, measuring cloth, and following cooking recipes. Males are still the scientists in science materials. Although the number of pictures of males and females is about equal in history textbooks, only 5 percent of the text deals with female experiences. Commenting on the status of women in history books, Tetreault concludes "the disparity between the percentage of the total copy devoted to women and the visuals that depict women suggests cosmetic changes distorting the extent to which women have been incorporated" (169, p. 47).

And when females' roles in history are included in the 5 percent of the text devoted to female experiences, women whose contributions fulfill the more acceptable traditional female role are described almost to the exclusion of feminists or those who were involved in feminist issues. Thus, while changes have occurred, curriculum materials are still quite sexist. This situation continues to prevail even though exposing students to such messages increases their gender-stereotypical thinking (174–76).

In the past, some authors claimed that the content of the materials students read at the elementary grade level appealed to the interests of females, and the materials they were exposed to at the secondary level appealed more to male interests. (149, 159) The following two quotations, which discuss the biases found in primary school readers and secondary school history textbooks respectively, are representative of these points of view.

> *Content of textbooks may more often be geared to the major interests of girls than of boys. Boys' interests in outdoor activities such as fishing, vacations and excursions, swimming, horseback riding, and bicycle riding are seldom reflected in first grade readers; nor is there much content dealing with joint activities of father and son. (152, pp. 227–33)*

> *Often, pages will be devoted to discussing the details of various battles in various wars, but intellectual, cultural, and social achievements in which women have traditionally been involved will be totally excluded or glossed over or tagged onto a chapter's end almost as an afterthought. (149, p. 115)*

Because the research on this issue was done quite some time ago, more information is needed to determine the extent to which, if any, such bias has been corrected in recent years.

Bias against females similar to those found in reading materials also occurs in many test items (see chapter 1). The same criticisms have been made about the software available for computers. As Woodill puts it: "Much of computer software has been designed by males for males, as shown by the predominance of male figures in programs, computer ads, and on the software packaging" (173, p. 55).

## Teacher Attention, Feedback, and Expectations

Through the attention and feedback they give students and the expectations they communicate to students, teachers tend to create and maintain gender differences in school in several ways. They reinforce males and females for behaving in different ways, model sexist behavior that students can copy, and provide students with information that can contribute to the cognitive gender stereotypes students form.

Beginning in preschool, boys receive more attention and a different kind of attention from their teachers (16, 177–202). One reason boys receive more attention is that teachers spend more time disciplining them for misbehaving (193, 201, 220). Much of the difference, however, is due to the fact that teachers demonstrate a clear bias in favor of male participation in their classes. Teachers are more likely to call on a male volunteer when students are asked to recite; this is also true when they call on nonvolunteers. When students recite, teachers are also more likely to listen to and talk to males. They also use more of their ideas in classroom discussions and respond to them in more helpful ways (195).

The pattern of giving more attention to males is especially clear in science and mathematics classes. Beginning in preschool, teachers ask males more questions and give them more individual instruction, acknowledgment, praise, encouragement, corrective feedback, opportunities to answer questions correctly, and social interaction (177, 189, 190, 192, 198, 202). In mathematics classes, they wait longer for males to answer questions before calling on someone else, reward females for performing computational skills and males for higher level cognitive skills, demonstrate more concern about giving males remedial help, and expect males to be more interested and proficient in math (190, 191).

Gender differences do not favor males in all subjects. In reading, a course traditionally seen as in the female domain, teachers tend to spend more time instructing and attending to girls (192, 197).

How do females interpret their teachers' apparent disinterest in them? No one knows for sure. However, the authors are concerned that Boudreau's conclusion about the probable interpretation students put on the message teachers give them may be correct. "The idea conveyed to girls is, although subtle, quite clear. What boys do matters more to teachers than what girls do" (182, p. 68).

Teachers also provide males and females different kinds of attention. And again the differential treatment favors males. Teachers tend to give boys more positive feedback than girls (185, 199). They give boys more praise and attention for high levels of achievement and correct responses (183, 184, 186, 188, 202, 205). In fact, teachers give high achieving girls the least amount of attention, praise, and supportive feedback and the largest number of disparaging statements, when compared to low achieving girls and all boys (168, 205). They praise girls more for neatness, following instructions exactly, and raising their hands. Even when they give the wrong answer, girls are often praised for raising their hands and volunteering (204, 208). Many teachers appear to avoid criticizing girls' responses even when they are wrong (208). This can be problematic since there is some evidence that girls learn better when they receive corrective feedback (206). While the above descriptions fit many teachers, there is some evidence that they are more characteristic of European Americans than African Americans (209). This may be one more example of the fact that "Blacks are less gender-typed and more egalitarian than whites" (207, p. 61).

What are teachers inadvertently telling their female students by relating to them in these ways? Are they communicating that they do not expect their female students to be able to perform well in academic areas? Are they implying that they do not believe they can respond correctly? Are they saying that females are too fragile to be criticized? Any and all of these explanations are possible in the absence of research data.

How do female students interpret their teachers' behavior? Again, one cannot be sure. A probable answer is that with the exception of courses in the "female domain," they are still getting the message that teachers do not expect them to do as well as boys.

There are subtle gender differences in teachers' expectations of students academic roles and achievement (178, 210–18). While teachers do not expect males and females to have different achievement levels in school, they view high achievement as a masculine characteristic and low achievement as feminine. They believe that courses such as physics are more appropriate for students with masculine characteristics. And in mathematics classes, they assign females to lower ability groups than their achievement would warrant. These differences can affect students' self-confidence about their academic ability and their motivation to succeed in school.

The message African American females receive is even more destructive (219–22). Teachers, especially European American teachers, perceive and treat African American females in an even more biased manner than European American females (219, 221, 222). They evaluate European American females higher than they evaluate African American females in the areas of responsibility, compliance, persistence, performance, ability, and relationships with others. When they do encourage females, they encourage European American female students in intellectual and academic areas, while they encourage and praise African American students in areas involving social skills. And when female students misbehave, teachers treat African Americans more harshly than European Americans. Grant (219) describes the effect this can have on African American females' perception of the role that is most suitable for them in the following way:

*The emphasis on black girls' social rather than academic skills, which occurs particularly in white-teacher classrooms, might point to a hidden cost of desegregation for black girls. . . . While such skills assuredly are helpful in high-status adult roles, the lesser attention to black girls' work might diminish motivation for gaining credentials to enter such positions. Black girls' everyday schooling experiences seem more likely to nudge them toward stereotypical roles of black women than toward alternatives. (219, p. 109)*

Thus, it appears that African American females receive somewhat different messages at home and in school. In school, their teachers seem to be telling them that all they are good for is the stereotypical roles European Americans have historically assigned to African American females—housekeepers, maids, child care persons, and so on. At home and in their communities, they are being told that they have to gain access to careers and vocations that provide more financial rewards and security because racism prevents African American males from taking care of them.

---

### BOX 2–2   Self-Quiz

*Teacher Attention, Feedback, and Expectations*

Your answers to the questions in this and the following self-quizzes will help you determine if you treat male and female students the same or differently and also evaluate the ways you deal with gender differences in your classroom. You may answer the questions yourself, but it would probably be more helpful to pair up with a colleague and observe one another in your classrooms.

1. Do I provide the same amount and kind of help to all students regardless of their gender?
2. Do I coach males more than females by asking guiding or probing questions when their answers are not correct?
3. Do I praise boys and girls equally for their intellectual/academic accomplishments?
4. When male and female students raise their hands, do I call on them with equal frequency?
5. Do I expect males to answer more questions correctly?
6. Do I expect boys to do better in math and science and girls to do better in language arts, music, and art?
7. Do I criticize girls' and boys' academic work with the same degree of objectivity and frankness?
8. Am I more likely to ask girls easy questions and questions that require factual answers and to reserve the really difficult ones and those that involve critical thinking for boys?
9. Do I attribute the cause of students' poor performance accurately, or am I more likely to attribute boys' poor performance to lack of interest or effort and girls' poor performance to lack of ability?
10. Am I more likely to stand nearer or touch students of my sex than students of the opposite sex or to engage them in conversations unrelated to school?
11. Do I make eye contact more with males than females?

Gender and ethnic differences in teacher attention, feedback, and expectations can have other negative effects on students besides their adverse effect on females' self-concepts and their performance in school (223–28). They may help explain why girls are more likely than boys to react poorly to failure or the threat of failure and to attribute poor performance to lack of ability rather than lack of effort. (See the section on learning styles in chapter 1.) They may also contribute to females' high anxiety during testing situations. (See the section on emotional differences in chapter 1). And they may be one reason why European American females think such subjects as mathematics and science are less important to them and enroll in fewer courses.

## Courses and Activities

While society in general has certain stereotypes about whether certain courses are more appropriate for males or females, teachers and counselors also contribute to the fact that many students believe certain courses belong in the male domain and others in the female domain (156, 227). For example, teachers and counselors tend to reward boys more than girls for learning

Throughout their school careers, males and females are often encouraged to, and rewarded for, engaging in stereotypical activities.

math. They also encourage boys to enroll in math and science-related courses and discourage girls from taking advanced courses such as calculus and physics and boys from enrolling in such *feminine* courses as languages and home economics. Teachers and counselors also have stereotypical views that higher education and certain careers and occupations are more appropriate for one sex or another, and vocational education teachers often harass female students enrolled in nontraditional vocational courses (229–31, 233).

Students receive sexist messages about participation in physical education activities as well. Schools tend to provide different sports experiences for males and females (232–35). Many schools, especially at the middle and high school level, still have separate physical education classes for boys and girls. The schedule for female teams' practice is often determined by when males are not using the facilities and coaches of male teams are paid more than those coaching female teams. Girls are almost routinely excluded from contact sports such as football, rugby, and soccer, and boys are discouraged from participating in girls' activities like dancing, skipping rope, and using the balance beam. When students persist in pursuing activities reserved for the opposite sex they are often labeled *tomboys* or *sissies.*

Although not as frequently as before, boys and girls still tend to be separated for physical education activities in some schools.

## *Gender Segregation/Separation*

Studies done in the late 1970s and middle 1980s revealed that some teachers discourage male-female interaction. Instead of encouraging mixed gender groups some teachers assign different chores to boys and girls. For example, the girls put things in order while boys move furniture. They separate boys and girls when assigning seats or areas to hang up clothes and when forming study and work groups and committees (156, 236, 237). Lockheed and Harris report a particularly pernicious management approach: "In class-

---

**BOX 2–3    Self-Quiz**

*Courses and Activities*

1. Are you likely to encourage boys more than girls to go to college?
2. Do you believe that women should be equally concerned, more concerned, or less concerned about marriage and childbearing than they are about academic and professional success?
3. Do you think of some careers and vocational choices as more appropriate for one sex?

---

**BOX 2–4   Self-Quiz**

*Gender Segregation/Separation*

**1.** Do you segregate boys and girls for some activities?

**2.** Do you sometimes make a special effort to insure that students do not sit, play, or work in same-sex groups, even if they appear to prefer them?

**3.** Do you think that some topics are better dealt with in single-sex groups?

**4.** Do you sometimes assign students to single-sex groups in order to protect female students from being dominated or inhibited by male students or in order to allow boys to deal with certain topics in a male way?

---

rooms, assignment to mixed-sex seating adjacencies or groups often is used as a punishment designed to reduce student interaction instead of as a learning technique designed to foster cooperative interaction" (237, p. 276).

It is unclear how many teachers engaged in these practices in the past and whether teachers continue to do so now. Research is needed to determine if these practices continue and if they are widespread.

## Encouragement of Behavioral Differences

Although all teachers want their students to be well behaved, according to research that was conducted in the 1970s to mid-1980s they appear to have different standards for males and females. Beginning in preschool, teachers tend to encourage gender-stereotypical behavior (199, 238 45). Teachers praise boys more than girls for creative behavior and girls more than boys for conforming behavior. Boys are rewarded for functioning independently while girls are rewarded for being obedient and compliant. Two researchers have described the situation: "The pattern of reinforcement that young girls receive may lead them to stake their sense of self-worth more on conforming than personal competency" (238, p. 73). "Elementary schools reinforce girls' training for obedience, social and emotional dependence, and docility" (244, p. 53). To the extent that their conclusions are correct and still current, the prevailing situation can certainly cause problems for girls in situations that require creativity, assertiveness, or independence.

There is also evidence that teachers accept different kinds of inappropriate behavior from males and females without disciplining them for misbehaving. Huffine, Silvern, and Brooks found that kindergarten teachers discipline males and females for different kinds of misbehavior. They report that "aggression in boys is acceptable while in girls it is not. The reverse seems to be true of disruptive talking. Teachers expect and/or accept talking

---

**BOX 2–5   Self-Quiz**

*Encouragement of Behavioral Differences*

1. Do you ever encourage girls to wear dresses?
2. Do you ask boys to do the physical work such as move furniture and girls to decorate the room, organize the bulletin board, clean up, or other traditional female chores?
3. Do you praise male students, but not female students, for being strong or athletic?
4. Do you appreciate boys who are *all boy?*
5. Do you believe that girls should act like ladies and boys like gentlemen?

6. When males are dominating the group by monopolizing the conversation, making most of the suggestions and decisions, and so on, do you intervene on the females' behalf or encourage them to take a more active role in the group?
7. Do you encourage females not to allow males to dominate them?
8. Do you attempt to encourage female students who are passive or docile to be more assertive and competitive and to take more risks?
9. Do you encourage boys to be less competitive and assertive and more cooperative?
10. Are you put off by boys who do not express their feelings?

---

from girls, at least much more so than from boys. Thus, the stereotypic behaviors, aggressiveness and loquacity, may be acquired and/or maintained by the differential teacher responses to these behaviors" (241, p. 34).

## Intolerance of Male Behavior Patterns

As noted above, beginning in preschool and continuing throughout their educational careers, males and females behave somewhat differently. Males are more competitive, assertive, aggressive, and active. These are the very behaviors that educators, especially female educators, tend to be less tolerant of, more likely to punish, and more likely to punish severely (238, 243, 247, 248, 249). (Also see the sections in chapter 4 on same-sex teaching for references that indicate that male teachers are more tolerant of these behaviors than female teachers. Since these are *male-typical* behaviors, males are more likely than females to be punished for misbehaving.)

Just as some individuals believe females are not less moral than males, just sneakier, some do not think females misbehave less often than males, they just do so less obviously. For example, Marshall describes the differences this way: "Boys misbehave more visibly than girls and in a more disruptive way; therefore, a lot of boys are frequently criticized for their behavior. Girls are seldom seen to misbehave (when they do, it is more discreet) so their behavior is more often praised—and, incidentally, used as a standard of decorum against which boys are measured: 'can't you boys shut up a moment, look at the girls—they're nice and ready to hear what I have to say' " (248, p. 132).

As long as boys get into trouble and are punished more than girls, the result is the same whether the perceived differences between males' and females' behavior actually occur.

African American males are especially likely to suffer the consequences of teachers' intolerance of male behavior because some African American behavior styles are especially unacceptable to teachers. Many African American males and females, as well, express their emotions more intensely than most European Americans. When European American teachers observe African American males behaving aggressively and assertively, they tend to assume that the students are much angrier or upset than they actually are. In attributing a level of anger to African American students that would be correct for European American students who behaved in a similar way, the teachers become uncomfortable, even anxious, and concerned about what they incorrectly anticipate will happen next. As a result, they intervene when no intervention is necessary. Dent explains that "most teachers are unprepared to accept the active, aggressive behavior of Black boys. The aggressive behavior of a Black child is immediately interpreted as hostile. . . . The next step in the process is that the teacher will make futile attempts to control the aggressive, active behavior, but abandons those efforts very quickly and concludes that the child is unmanageable" (246, pp. 78–79).

If teachers appreciated the cultural context of African American males' seemingly aggressive behavior toward others and understood that such behavior is unlikely to cause the physical fight or whatever else they expect to occur between African American students, they would be less likely to have to intervene to make themselves feel more at ease in the situation. This, in turn, would lessen the likelihood that African American males would get into trouble needlessly. (See chapter 3 for a more detailed discussion of this topic.)

## *Classroom Management Techniques*

Being less tolerant of male-typical behavior, teachers tend to reprimand males more often and differently than females (199, 238, 241, 249–51). They tend to speak briefly, softly, and privately to girls but publicly and harshly to boys. And with younger children they tend to use physical methods like poking, slapping, grabbing, pushing, squeezing, and so on with boys and negative comments or disapproving gestures and other forms of nonverbal communication with girls (241). Teachers are more likely to use even harsher

Males are more likely than females to be disciplined publicly.

disciplinary techniques, especially corporal punishment and suspension, with working-class, African American, and Hispanic American males than with middle-class European American males (241, 249, 252–56).

This is unfortunate because public and harsh reprimands and physical forms of discipline and severe punishments can cause students to react rebelliously to punishments that they feel are too harsh for their *crimes.* This may help explain why males get into trouble in school much more often than females and working-class and minority males get into even more trouble than European American middle-class students (257–63).

## Conclusions

The data presented above clearly indicate that schools play an important role in the formation and maintenance of students' stereotypical views of gender roles. As Meece puts it:

*Schools have been slow in adapting to recent changes in the social roles of men and women. As a result, schools may be exposing children to mascu-*

---

**BOX 2–6  Self-Quiz**

*Approaches to Classroom Management and Behavior Problems*

1. Do you want students to behave in a conforming, quiet manner?
2. Do you prefer students to relate cooperatively rather than competitively to their peers?
3. Are you as concerned about the behavior of students who appear to be passive, inhibited, quiet, withdrawn, timid, or overdependent as you are about the behavior of active, assertive, aggressive students?
4. Are you equally comfortable with students who are assertive and with students who are passive?
5. Are you equally comfortable with students who are competitive and with those who are cooperative?
6. Are you equally comfortable with students who prefer to work alone and with those who like to work in groups?
7. If there is a conflict between students, do you feel as comfortable when they face it head on as when they "sweep it under the carpet"?

8. Are you equally comfortable whether students try to find a compromise solution to disagreements or stand up for their rights as they see them?
9. Do you monitor males more closely than females because you expect them to misbehave more often?
10. Are you more likely to believe girls than boys because you think girls are more honest?
11. Are you more likely to punish boys than girls for the same behavior?
12. Do you use a sterner tone of voice with boys than girls?
13. Do you believe that severe forms of punishment are more appropriate for males than females?
14. Are you more likely to reprimand girls privately and calmly and to reprimand boys harshly and publicly?
15. Do you use the same rewards for male and female students or attempt to select rewards that are gender appropriate?

---

*line and feminine images that are even more rigid and more polarized than those currently held in the wider society. Furthermore, the school setting does not seem to provide children with many opportunities to perform behaviors not associated with their gender. Therefore, schools seem to play an important role in reinforcing rigid gender distinctions. (207, p. 67)*

## FOSTERING ETHNIC AND SOCIOECONOMIC CLASS BIAS

The previous section described how educators foster gender differences among their students in general by treating males and females differently.

As was also noted above, though, teachers do not treat students from different ethnic and socioeconomic groups the same. Since all students belong to an ethnic group and a socioeconomic class as well as a gender group, bias against students in school occurs as a result of the interplay between the ways in which teachers relate to students of different genders, socioeconomic classes, and ethnic groups. In some cases, the different treatment students from varying backgrounds receive from teachers increases gender differences—for example, their tendency to use especially harsh discipline techniques with African American males and to to be especially inattentive to the academic needs and achievements of African American females. In other cases, it helps lessen, eliminate, and occasionally even reverse gender differences. Some examples of the ways teachers relate differently to students on the basis of their ethnic and socioeconomic backgrounds were presented earlier in this chapter; this section expands on them.

## Teachers' Expectations

Research conducted in the 1970s and early 1980s indicates that beginning in preschool and continuing through college, teachers and education majors tend to attribute higher intellectual ability to European American middle-class students and expect them to do better in school than African American students (219, 264, 266, 267, 272, 280), Hispanic American students (268, 271, 274, 275, 280), and European American working class students (265, 267, 272, 276–79). This is true even when students' achievement test scores, grades, and school histories suggest the opposite. Teachers' academic expectations are especially low for African American and Hispanic American students who are also working-class, and for minority males as opposed to minority females (272, 273). As stated above, negative expectations for students can have a harmful effect on both their self-confidence and motivation. If this teacher bias toward African American, Hispanic American, and working-class students is still prevalent it could certainly be an important contributing factor to the difference between their participation and achievement in school and that of European American middle-class students.

## Teachers' Evaluations

Research that was done primarily in the 1970s revealed that teachers tend to evaluate African American, Hispanic American, and working-class students' behavior and academic performance in a biased manner (274, 278, 281–91). For example, when assigning students to ability groups, teachers sometimes assign minority and working-class students to lower ability groups than such objective data as test scores would warrant.

Teachers also tend to allow their judgments about the content of students' work to be influenced by whether students express themselves in Black English (the English dialect many African Americans speak, especially, but not exclusively, those from working-class backgrounds), a working-class dialect (a variety of nonstandard dialects spoken by individuals from working-class backgrounds), or standard English (the English used in textbooks, newspapers, television news programs, grammar books, and typically used by most middle- and upper-class European Americans). Even when students' work is identical or of equal quality, teachers tend to judge the oral work of students who speak Black English or a working-class dialect to be poorer than students who speak standard English. In fact, African American students who speak Black English are rated lower than African American students who speak more standard English. And teachers judge students' essays in a similarly biased manner.

At one point, some educators may not have perceived this as a prejudicial approach to evaluation. In the 1960s and early 1970s, researchers typically used European American middle-class students' scores on tests prepared in standard English as the norm to which they compared the scores of students who spoke nonstandard English. As a result, they concluded that Black English and working-class English were inferior to standard English (292–99).

By the mid-1970s, the results of research that did not make that methodological error led most authors to conclude that these varieties of English are actually equally effective and valid forms of communication (300–304). And many scholars, especially those from African American backgrounds, were encouraging schools to incorporate Black English into the curriculum, rather than attempt to eradicate it.

> *Black children must be educated to learn and believe that deviation from the normative pattern of standard English is not an indication that they are abnormal. . . . Whites should not become reference points for how Black children are to speak and behave. One's family and community and how one measures up to one's peers should provide some of these reference points. Black children's encounter with the white world should be filtered through a Black frame of reference, which includes the use of Black English. (301, p. 215)*

Apparently, many teachers still believe that standard English is superior to other forms of English. That is, instead of correctly viewing Black English and working-class dialects as *different* forms of English, they view them as *deficient* forms of English. And they continue to allow their beliefs to prejudice their evaluations of students.

## Teacher-Student Interactions

Many teachers treat non-European students in biased ways. Some of the prejudicial ways they commonly treat African American, American Indian, and Hispanic American students are summarized here. (209, 219, 220, 241, 249, 252–56, 305, 306, 308, 309, 311–16).

Teachers tend to praise African American students less and criticize them more than European American students. When they praise African Americans, the praise they give is more likely to be routine rather than feedback for a particular achievement or behavior. When they do praise African American students for a specific behavior, it is more likely to be qualified ("Your work is almost good enough to be put on the board"), and in the case of females, it is more likely to be for good behavior than for academic work, as noted previously. Since routine and qualified praise are less effective than sincere, unqualified praise for particular activities and accomplishments, the praise African American students receive, even when it is for academic work, is likely to be less effective than the praise European American students receive.

Teachers interact less with African American, and American Indian students than with European American students. Although teachers are especially likely to respond to the questions of male students in general, they are less likely to respond to male African American and American Indian students' questions or direct questions to them. European American females are more likely to receive trusted lieutenant duties and special high prestige assignments, while African American female students' duties typically involve social responsibilities. As reported above, unlike the preferential treatment many teachers give their brightest European American students, they give bright African American females the least attention. And while European American teachers typically demonstrate considerable concern and interest in European American females' academic work, they pay less attention to African American female students' academic work than to their social behavior.

Educators tend to use different classroom management techniques with African American and European American students. Teachers with high percentages of African American students in their classes are more likely to be authoritarian and less likely to use an open classroom approach. Teachers expect African American males to be more disruptive and deviant than European Americans. They spend more time on the lookout for possible misbehavior by African American males. And, as reported, when students misbehave, educators are especially prone to criticize the behavior of African American males and respond more severely to them using corporal punishment and suspension.

Less hard data exists about the kind of treatment Hispanic Americans receive in school. The available research suggests that they fare no better than African American students. Teachers praise them less, give them less encouragement, accept their ideas less often, and direct fewer questions to them than to their European American students.

Working-class European American students also receive unfair treatment in school (278, 305, 307, 310, 314). Beginning in primary school, teachers give them less attention and fewer rewards compared to middle-class students. Educators provide working-class students, especially males, fewer social and instructional contacts, but more disciplinary and control contacts. Teachers in schools that serve predominantly working-class students are more likely to endorse or use corporal punishment, verbal punishment, or suspension than teachers in middle-class schools.

## *Apparent and Real Lack of Bias*

Anecdotal evidence suggests that most teachers would claim they do not treat minority and working-class students differently than they treat European American middle-class students. Undoubtedly some are correct. Not all European American teachers treat non-European American students and working-class students unfairly. African American teachers tend to be less prejudiced than European American teachers toward African American students (209, 219).

At least in some cases, however, the lack of bias against students who belong to a different ethnic group may be more apparent than real (209, 315, 317). Many European American and African American teachers are not aware of their biases. In order to hide their true feelings and attitudes from themselves, some European American and African American teachers unconsciously give students a double message. They consciously praise students who belong to a different ethnic group more than they do students who share their ethnic background, but they unknowingly treat them negatively by giving them less nonverbal positive attention, maintaining a greater distance from them, and touching them less often.

European American teachers exhibit more unconscious prejudice than African American teachers do. In addition to the negative nonverbal communication just mentioned, they also give African American students less positive feedback when they answer questions correctly and fewer helpful hints when they call on them to answer questions. This conforms to the double messages European Americans give African Americans in other areas of their relations with them outside of school (318, 319). As Simpson and Erickson (1983) suggest: "Naturalistic observational studies in the classroom may show overcompensatory behavior on the part of black and white teachers. However, the nonverbal behaviors may indicate a natural preference or comfortableness with students of one's own race" (209, p. 185).

## Students' Reactions

How do African American, American Indian, Hispanic American, and working-class students react to the prejudicial treatment they receive in school? It has already been suggested that it affects their self-confidence, motivation, participation, and achievement. As noted above, other educators believe that teacher bias against these groups of students has a much more harmful effect (121, 127, 133, 135, 136, 138, 139, 141, 275, 276). To their way of thinking, prejudice in school causes these students to become distrustful, angry, and disillusioned about the problems inherent in attending schools that are staffed by insensitive or prejudiced teachers and designed for European American middle-class students. They suggest that because students feel the way they do and believe what they do, many actively resist their teachers in ways described earlier—by purposefully misbehaving, tuning them out, disrupting their lessons, refusing to do homework, coming late to school, and dropping out before graduating. (See the previous section entitled Resistance, Production, and Transformation.)

If these educators are correct, then much of the disruptive behavior, inadequate motivation, lack of participation, poor achievement, and so on that teachers expect from these students are caused, at least in part, by the teachers themselves. Thus, the problem will not be solved until teachers correct their biased attitudes, beliefs, and treatment of non-European American and working-class students. (See the following chapters for a more detailed discussion of this topic.)

---

### BOX 2–7    Self-Quiz

*Ethnic and Socioeconomic Bias*
Are your expectations for non-European American and working-class students accurate or biased? Do you expect them to achieve less or misbehave more than their test scores, grades, and previous performance would indicate? Do you evaluate their work objectively, or does their ethnic or socioeconomic background influence your conclusions?

Ask a colleague to observe your interactions with your students. Specific issues a colleague might examine are: Do you praise and criticize all students equally? Do you provide all students with the same amount and kinds of attention? Do you use appropriate classroom management techniques with students regardless of their ethnic or socioeconomic backgrounds?

---

**BOX 2–8   Self-Quiz**

*Critical Incidents*

It is not always easy to apply a set of principles to real life situations when some of the principles that apply to a specific situation appear to lead to somewhat contradictory solutions. Describe how you think teachers should handle each of the following critical incidents.

**1.** After raising her hand repeatedly to volunteer answers to her teacher's questions without being called on, a fifth-grade student complains that her teacher is unfair because the teacher always calls on the boys to answer the difficult questions. The teacher does not believe she is correct.

**2.** An African American tenth grade male in a predominantly work-ing-class neighborhood school tells his teacher in no uncertain terms to get off his case and stop telling him about the value of a high school diploma. He insists that a high school diploma does not help African Americans. The teacher tells the student he is wrong. The next day the student brings in some articles that confirm that African American males who graduate high school do not earn significantly more than those who do not.

**3.** A teacher overhears two seniors say they plan to protest the prejudice they experienced in school by wearing some outlandish clothes to the graduation ceremony rather than the conservative clothes and cap and gown prescribed by the school administration.

---

## SUMMARY

Many factors contribute to the gender differences observed in school. Males and females are biologically predisposed to function differently. They are reinforced when behaving differently, and they learn different roles by observing adults behaving in gender-stereotypical ways. Further, they are exposed to gender-biased information. And society is structured in ways that promote gender differences. For the present, we are unable to determine which combination of factors contribute to a particular gender difference, how these factors interact to produce the differences, and the relative amount of influence each factor exercises in the case of any particular difference. We also do not know the reasons why some individuals conform to these gender stereotypes and others do not. Much more research is needed before scientific answers can be provided to these important questions.

Schools play a significant role in creating and maintaining gender differences. Gender bias exists in the textbooks that students use, the unequal amounts of attention and different kinds of feedback and encouragement they receive from their teachers, the gender segregation they experience, and so on. Although these factors tend to reproduce gender differences, substantial numbers of students resist their influences to varying degrees.

Students belong to ethnic groups, socioeconomic classes, and gender groups. Bias against students in school occurs as a result of the interplay between the ways teachers relate to students in terms of these three characteristics. Bias against any group of students for any reason is undesirable and should be eliminated.

## ISSUES FOR FURTHER THOUGHT AND DISCUSSION

**1.** Our scientific knowledge of the causes of the gender dissimilarities discussed in this text is extremely limited. There is evidence that biology, differential reinforcement, modeling, cognitive awareness, and structured reproduction contribute to these differences. But we do understand how they interact with each other to lead a given individual to behave in a particular way in a specific situation. As a result, we can neither base our intervention approaches on clear scientific principles of causality nor predict how effective they will be with a particular student or group of students. In the absence of hard scientific data, should teachers take educated guesses about the relative importance of these various contributing factors or should they hold off making assumptions about the causes of gender differences among their students?

**2.** While the evidence that schools help to reproduce the gender inequities found in society-at-large is considerable, there is little to support or refute the neo-Marxist idea that this is done purposely by middle- and upper-class European American males. Does it make a difference whether the reproductive forces in schools and society are purposely created to accomplish a mission or exist today merely because they have existed for a long time? Is there a conflict between the perceived need to restructure society and the schools' mission to perpetuate society's values? Do teachers have the right or obligation to encourage and prepare students to participate in their efforts to change society?

**3.** If self-insight alone is not sufficient to change people's prejudices, what, if anything, should teachers and school administrators do to reduce the gender, ethnic, and socioeconomic class bias that pervades our schools?

**4.** Curriculum materials are excluded from the regulations of Title IX. Some say this is to avoid a possible conflict between its provisions and the right to free speech guaranteed by the Constitution. What role, if any, should teachers play in the elimination of bias in curriculum materials in light of the fact that such bias is not illegal and the possibility that certain interventions may create a conflict between two principles of American democracy?

## ACTIVITIES

As in the previous chapter, some of these exercises are appropriate for experienced teachers while others do not require teaching experience.

**1.** Compare the way you relate to different groups of students by studying your behavior during a few ten minute periods at convenient times during the day. You can study almost any aspect of your teaching. For example, count the number of times you call on students who volunteer, the number of times you assign students to particular chores, the number of times you praise students' work, and so on. Then compare the results for different groups of students, such as males and females, European Americans and non-European Americans, and working-class and middle-class students.

**2.** If you teach multiple subjects (first through eighth grade), determine whether you relate to the genders differently during different subjects such as English or science.

**3.** Ask a colleague to evaluate some of your students' work that is difficult to judge objectively (e.g., essay questions or a writing sample rather than a math problem or a multiple choice answer). Compare your colleague's evaluations with your own to see if your evaluations of particular groups of students are biased.

**4.** If you do not have teaching experience, study the way your master teacher or one or more of your professors relates to males and females and students from different ethnic backgrounds.

**5.** Interview males and females and students from different ethnic and socioeconomic backgrounds in the courses you are taking about some of the issues discussed in this chapter. What are their opinions about the origins of gender differences? Do students' opinions vary with their gender, ethnic, or socioeconomic class backgrounds?

**6.** Review the textbooks and other materials your professors assign in the courses you are taking. Are they free from gender bias? Do they deal with the gender issues inherent in the topics they cover? Do they focus exclusively or primarily on European Americans to the exclusion of other ethnic groups?

**7.** Compare your professors in terms of the time they devote to the gender issues inherent in the courses they teach. Do you find that some professors are more sensitive to, and interested in, gender issues than others?

# REFERENCES

## Origins of Gender Differences

*Biological Determinants*

The following references present evidence that some gender differences may have a biological base.

1. Archer, J. 1976. "Biological explanations of psychological sex differences." In *Exploring Sex Differences,* edited by B. B. Lloyd and J. Archer. New York: Academic Press.
2. Buffery, A. W. H., and Gray, J. A. 1972. Sex differences in the development of spatial and linguistic skills. In *Gender Differences: Their Ontogeny and Significance,* edited by C. Ounsted and D. C. Taylor. Baltimore: Williams and Wilkins.
3. Ehrhardt, A. A., and Baker, S. W. 1974. Fetal androgens, human central nervous system differentiation, and behavior sex differences. In *Sex Differences in Behavior,* edited by R. C. Friedman, R. M. Richart, and R. L. Vande Wiele. New York: Wiley.
4. Frankenhaeuser, M., von Wright, M. R., Collins, A., von Wright, J., Sedvall, G., and Swahn, C. G. 1978. Sex differences in psychoneuroendocrine reactions to examination stress. *Psychosomatic Medicine* 40 (4): 334–43.
5. Halpern, D. F. 1986. *Sex Differences in Cognitive Abilities.* Hillsdale, NJ: Erlbaum Associates.
6. Hyde, J. S. 1985. *Half the Human Experience: The Psychology of Women.* 3d ed. Lexington, MA: D. C. Heath.
7. Jacklin, C. N., Maccoby, E. E., and Doering, C. H. 1983. Neonatal sex-steroid hormones and timidity in 6–18 month-old boys and girls. *Developmental Psychobiology* 16: 163–68.
8. Jacklin, C. N., Maccoby, E. E., Doering, C. H., and King, D. R. 1984. Neonatal sex-steroid hormones and muscular strength in boys and girls in the first three years. *Developmental Psychobiology* 17: 301–10.
9. Jacklin, C. N., Wilcox, K. T., and Maccoby, E. E. 1988. Neonatal sex-steroid hormones and intellect abilities of six year old boys and girls. *Developmental Psychobiology* 21: 567–74.
10. Kimura, D. 1980. Sex differences in intrahemispheric organization of speech. *Behavior and Brain Sciences* 3: 240–41.
11. Kimura, D. 1983. Sex differences in cerebral organization for speech and praxic functions. *Canadian Journal of Psychology* 37: 19–35.
12. Kimura, D. 1985. Male brain, female brain: The hidden difference. *Psychology Today* 19: 50–58.
13. Knox, C., and Kimura, D. 1970. Cerebral processing of nonverbal sounds in boys and girls. *Neurologia* 8: 227–37.
14. Levy, J., and Gur, R. C. 1980. "Individual differences in psychoneurological organization." In *Neuropsychology of Left-Handedness,* edited by J. Herron. New York: Academic Press.
15. Levy, J., and Reid, M. 1978. Variations in cerebral organization as a function of handedness, handposture in writing, and sex. *Journal of Experimental Psychology: General* 107: 119–44.
16. Maccoby, E. E., and Jacklin, C. N. 1974. *The Psychology of Sex Differences.* Stanford, CA: Stanford University Press.
17. Maccoby, E. E., and Jacklin, C. N. 1980. Sex-differences in aggression:

A rejoinder and reprise. *Child Development* 51: 964–80.

18. Marcus, J., Maccoby, E. E., Jacklin, C. N., and Doering, C. H. 1985. Individual differences in mood: Their relation to gender and neonatal sex steroids. *Developmental Psychobiology* 18: 327–40.

19. McGlone, J. 1980. Sex differences in human brain asymmetry: A critical survey. *Behavioral and Brain Sciences* 3: 215–63.

20. McKeever, W. F. 1987. "Cerebral organization and sex: Interesting but complex." In *Language, Gender, and Sex in Comparative Perspective,* edited by S. U. Philips, S. Steele, and C. Tanz. Cambridge, England: Cambridge University Press.

21. Messent, P. R. 1976. "Female hormones and behavior." In *Exploring Sex Differences,* edited by B. B. Lloyd and J. Archer. New York: Academic Press.

22. Money, J., and Erhardt, A. A. 1972. *Man and Woman, Boy, and Girl.* Baltimore: Johns Hopkins University Press.

23. Parsons, J. E., ed. 1980. *The Psychobiology of Sex Differences and Sex Roles.* Washington, D.C.: Hemisphere Publishing.

24. Ray, W. J., Newcombe, N., Semon, J., and Cole, P. M. 1981. Spatial abilities, sex differences and EEG functioning. *Neuropsychologia* 19: 719–22.

25. Rogers, L. 1976. "Male hormones and behavior." In *Exploring Sex Differences,* edited by B. B. Lloyd and J. Archer. New York: Academic Press.

26. Seward, J. P., and Seward, G. H. 1980. *Sex Differences: Mental and Temperamental.* Lexington, MA: Lexington Books.

27. Sherman, J. A. 1971. *On the Psychology of Women.* Springfield, IL: Thomas.

28. Sherman, J. A. 1978. *Sex-Related Cognitive Differences: An Essay on Theory and Evidence.* Springfield, IL: Thomas.

29. Shucard, D. W., Shucard, J. L., and Thomas, D. G. 1987. "Sex differences in the pattern of scalp-recorded electrophysiological activity in infancy: Possible implications for language development." In *Language, Gender, and Sex in Comparative Perspective,* edited by S. U. Philips, S. Steele, and C. Tanz. Cambridge, England: Cambridge University Press.

30. Springer, S. P., and Deutsch, G. 1981. *Left Brain, Right Brain.* New York: W. H. Freeman.

31. Stafford, R. E. 1972. Heredity and environmental components of quantitative reasoning. *Review of Educational Research* 42: 183–201.

32. Susman, E. J., Inoff-Germain, G., Nottelmann, E. D., Loriaux, D. L., Cutler, G. B., and Chrousos, G. P. 1987. Hormones, emotional dispositions, and aggressive attributes in young adolescents. *Child Development* 58: 1114–34.

33. Waber, D. P. 1977. Sex differences in mental abilities, hemispheric lateralization, and rate of physical growth at adolescence. *Developmental Psychology* 13: 29–38.

34. Witelson, S. F. 1976. Sex and single hemisphere: Specialization of the right hemisphere for spatial processing. *Science* 193: 425–27.

These references deal with behavioral compatibility and opportunity to practice.

35. Eisenberg, N., Murray, E., and Hite, T. 1982. Children's reasoning

regarding sex-typed toy choices. *Child Development* 53: 81–86.

36. Huston, A. C., and Carpenter, C. J. 1985. "Gender differences in preschool classrooms: The effects of sex-typed activity choices." In *Gender Influences in Classroom Interaction*, edited by L. C. Wilkinson and C. B. Marrett. New York: Academic Press.

37. Jacklin, C. N. 1989. Female and male: Issues of gender. *American Psychologist* 44 (2): 127–33.

38. Perry, D. G., White, A. J., and Perry, L. C. 1984. Does early sex typing result from children's attempts to match their behavior to sex role stereotypes? *Child Development* 55: 2114–21.

39. Serbin, L. A., and O'Connor, J. M. 1979. Sex typing of children's play preferences and patterns of cognitive performance. *Journal of Genetic Psychology* 134: 315–16.

40. Sherman, J. A. 1967. Problems of sex differences in space perception and aspects of intellectual functioning. *Psychological Review* 74: 290–99.

*Differential Reinforcement*

The references listed next present evidence that parents reinforce children for behaving in gender-stereotypical ways.

41. Block, J. H. 1984. *Sex Role Identity and Ego Development.* San Francisco: Jossey-Bass.

42. Fagot, B. I. 1978. The influence of sex of child on parental reactions to toddler children. *Child Development* 49: 459–65.

43. Lewis, M., and Weintraub, M. 1979. Origins of early sex-role development. *Sex Roles* 5 (2): 135–53.

44. O'Brien, M., and Huston, A. C. 1985. Development of sex-typed play behavior in toddlers. *Developmental Psychology* 21 (5): 866–71.

The following references deal with the reinforcement of gender-appropriate behavior by toddlers and preschoolers.

45. Fagot, B. I. 1977. Consequences of moderate cross-gender behavior in preschool children. *Child Development* 48: 902–07.

46. Fagot, B. I. 1985. Beyond the reinforcement principle: Another step toward understanding sex roles. *Developmental Psychology* 21: 1097–04.

47. Lamb, M. E., Easterbrook, A. M., and Holden, G. W. 1980. Reinforcement and punishment among preschoolers: Characteristics, effects, and correlates. *Child Development* 51: 1230–36.

48. Lamb, M. E., and Roopnarine, J. L. 1979. Peer influences on sex-role development in preschoolers. *Child Development* 50: 1219–22.

*Cognitive Awareness of Sex-Role Differences and Modeling*

The role of cognitive awareness and modeling in the development of children's sex roles is dealt with in the following references.

49. Andersen, E. S. 1978. "Learning to Speak with Style: A Study of the Socio-Linguistic Skills of Children." Ph.D. diss., Stanford University.

50. Bem, S. L. 1981. Gender schema theory: A cognitive account of sex typing. *Psychological Review* 88 (4): 354–64.

51. Bem, S. L. 1983. Gender schema theory and its implication for child development: Raising gender

aschematic children in a gender schematic society. *Signs* 8: 598–616.

52. Bem, S. L. 1985. Androgyny and gender schema theory: A conceptual and empirical integration. In *Nebraska Symposium on Motivation: Psychology of Gender,* edited by T. B. Sonderegger. Lincoln, NE: University of Nebraska.

53. Busey, K., and Bandura, A. 1984. Influence of gender constancy and social power on sex-linked modeling. *Journal of Personality and Social Psychology* 47 (6): 1292–1302.

54. Eagly, A. H. 1987. *Sex Differences in Social Behavior: A Social-Role Interpretation.* Hillsdale, NJ: Erlbaum.

55. Fagot, B. I. 1985. Changes in thinking about early sex-role development. *Developmental Review* 5: 83–98.

56. Hargreaves, D. J., and Colley, A. M. 1987. *The Psychology of Sex Roles.* New York: Hemisphere Publishing.

57. Martin, C. L., and Halverson, C. F., Jr. 1981. A schematic processing model of sex-typing and stereotyping in young children. *Child Development* 52: 1119–34.

58. Perry, D. G., and, Bussey, K. 1979. The social learning theory of sex-differences: Imitation is alive and well. *Journal of Personality and Social Psychology* 37: 1699–1712.

59. Weintraub, M., Clemens, L. P., Sockloff, A., Ethridge, T., Gracely, E., and Myers, B. 1984. The development of sex role stereotypes in the third year: Relationships to gender labeling, gender identity, sex-typed toy preference, and family characteristics. *Child Development* 55: 1493–1503.

Research that describes the role of parents' behavior, expectations, and beliefs in fostering gender differences in students' confidence about their academic abilities and in their choice of academic courses are listed next.

60. Baker, D. P., and Entwisle, D. R. 1987. The influence of mothers on the academic expectations of young children: A longitudinal study of how gender differences arise. *Social Forces* 65: 670–94.

61. Bempechat, J. 1990. *The Role of Parent Involvement in Children's Academic Achievement: A Review of the Literature Trends and Issues No. 14.* NY: ERIC Clearinghouse on Urban Education, Institute for Urban and Minority Education.

62. Eccles, J., Adler, T. F., and Kaczala, C. M. 1982. Socialization of achievement attitudes and beliefs: Parental influences. *Child Development* 53: 310–21.

63. Eccles, J., and Jacobs, J. E. 1986. Social forces shape math attitudes and performance. *Signs* 11: 367–89.

64. Eccles, J., Kaczala, C. M., and Meese, J. L. 1982. Socialization of achievement attitudes and beliefs: Classroom influences. *Child Development* 53: 322–39.

65. Entwisle, D. R., and Baker, D. P. 1983. Gender and young children's expectations for performance in arithmetic. *Developmental Psychology* 19 (2): 200–9.

66. Entwisle, D. R., and Hayduk, L. A. 1982. *Early Schooling.* Baltimore: Johns Hopkins University Press.

67. Jacobs, J., and Eccles, J. 1985. Gender differences in math ability: The impact of media reports on parents. *Educational Researcher* 14 (3): 20–25.

68. Parsons, J. E., Adler, T. F., and Kaczala, C. M. 1982. Socialization

of achievement attitudes and beliefs: Parental influences. *Child Development* 53: 310–21.

69. Parsons, J. E., Kaczala, C. M., and Meese, J. L. 1982. Socialization of achievement attitudes and beliefs: Classroom influences. *Child Development* 53: 322–39.

70. Yee, D. K., and Eccles, J. S. 1988. Parent perceptions and attributions for children's math achievement. *Sex Roles* 19 (5/6): 317–33.

References that discuss the role of schools in the reproduction of inequities in society are listed next.

71. Anyon, J. 1979. Ideology and United States history text books. *Harvard Educational Review* 49: 361–86.

72. Apple, M. 1979. *Ideology and Curriculum* Boston: Routledge & Kegan Paul.

73. Apple, M. 1982. *Culture and Economic Reproduction in Education.* Boston: Routledge & Kegan Paul.

74. Apple, M., and Weis, L. ed. 1983. *Ideology and Practice in Schools.* Philadelphia: Temple University Press.

75. Bowles, S., and Gintes, H. 1977. *Schooling in Capitalist America.* New York: Basis Books.

76. Connell, R. W. 1989. Curriculum politics, hegemony, and strategies of social change. In *Popular Culture, Schooling and Everyday Life*, edited by H. A. Giroux and R. I. Simon. Granby, MA: Bergin & Garvey.

77. Deem, R. 1978. *Women and Schooling.* Boston: Routledge & Kegan Paul.

78. Giroux, H. A. 1981. "Hegemony, resistance, and the paradox of educational reform." In *Curriculum and Instruction: Alternatives in Educa-tion,* edited by H. A. Giroux, A. N. Penna, and W. F. Pinar. Berkeley, CA: McCutchan.

79. Giroux, H. A. 1981. *Ideology, Culture and the Process of Schooling.* Philadelphia: Temple University Press.

80. Giroux, H. A. 1983. Theories of reproduction and resistance in the new sociology of education: A critical analysis. *Harvard Educational Review* 53 (3): 257–93.

81. Giroux, H. A., and Penna, A. N. 1988. "Social education in the classroom: The dynamics of the hidden curriculum." In *Teachers as Intellectuals: Toward a Critical Pedagogy of Learning*, edited by H. A. Giroux. Granby, MA: Bergin & Garvey.

82. Grant, C. A., and Sleeter, C. E. 1988. Race, class, and gender and abandoned dreams. *Teachers College Record* 90 (1): 19–40.

83. Kelly, G., and Nihlen, A. 1982. "Schooling and the reproduction of patriarchy: Unequal workloads, unequal rewards." In *Culture and Economic Reproduction in Education,* edited by M. Apple. Boston: Routledge & Kegan Paul.

84. Valli, L. 1986. *Becoming Clerical Workers.* Boston: Routledge & Kegan Paul.

85. Weiler, K. 1988. *Women Teaching for Change: Gender, Class and Power.* Granby, MA: Bergin & Garvey.

86. Witt, S. H. 1979. "Native women in the world of work." In *Women of Color Forum: A Collection of Readings,* edited by T. Constantino. ERIC ED 191 975.

87. Wolpe, A. 1978. "Education and the sexual division of labor." In *Feminism and Materialism,* edited by A. Kuhn and A. Wolpe. Boston: Routledge & Kegan Paul.

88. Wolpe, A. 1981. "The official ideology of education for girls." In *Politics, Patriarchy and Practice,* edited by M. McDonald, R. Dale, G. Esland, and R. Fergusson. NY: Falmer Press.

The following references deal with the inadequate educational services provided to minorities and working-class students.

89. Becker, H. J. 1986. *Computer Survey Newsletter.* Baltimore, MD: Center for the Social Organization of Schools, Johns Hopkins University.

90. Center for Social Organization of Schools. 1983. *School Uses of Microcomputers: Reports from a National Survey,* No. 3. Baltimore: Johns Hopkins University Press.

91. Darling-Hammond, L. 1985. *Equality and Excellence: The Status of Black American Education.* New York: College Entrance Examination Board.

92. Furr. J. D., and Davis, T. M. 1984. Equity Issues and microcomputers: Are educators meeting the challenges? *Journal of Educational Equity and Leadership* 4: 93–97.

93. Guthrie, J. W., Kleindorfer, G. B., Levin, H. M., and Stout, R. T. 1971. *Schools and Inequality.* Cambridge, MA: MIT Press.

94. Karp, S. 1991. Rich schools, poor schools and the courts. *Rethinking Schools* 5 (2): 1–15.

95. Leacock, E. B. 1969. *Teaching and Learning in City Schools: A Comparative Study.* New York: Basic Books.

96. Moore, G. A. 1967. *Realities in the Urban Classroom.* Garden City, NY: Doubleday.

97. National Assessment of Education Progress. 1988. *Computer Competence: The First National Assessment.* Princeton, NJ: Educational Testing Service.

98. O'Brien, E. M. 1989. Texas legislators impatient to solve unfairness of school financing system. *Black Issues in Higher Education* 6 (16): 23.

99. Sexton, P. C. 1961. *Education and Income: Inequality of Opportunity in the Public Schools.* New York: Viking Press.

The following references deal with the effects of tracking and ability grouping.

100. Alexander, K. A., and McDill, E. L. 1976. Selection and allocation within schools: Some causes and consequences of curriculum placement. *American Sociological Review* 41: 969–80.

101. Alexander, K. A., Cook, M., and McDill, E. L. 1978. Curriculum tracking and educational stratification: Some further evidence. *American Sociological Review* 43: 47–66.

102. Eder, D. 1981. Ability grouping as a self-fulfilling prophecy: A microanalysis of teacher-student interaction. *Sociology of Education* 54: 151–62.

103. Gamoran, A. 1986. "The Stratification of High School Learning Opportunities." Paper presented at the annual meeting of the American Educational Research Association, San Francisco.

104. Goodlad, J. 1984. *A Place Called School.* New York: McGraw-Hill.

105. Jones, J. D., Erickson, E. L., and Crowell, R. 1972. Increasing the gap between whites and blacks. *Education and Urban Society* 4 (3): 339–49.

106. Lee, V. 1986. "The Effect of Tracking on the Social Distribution of

Achievement in Catholic and Public Secondary Schools." Paper presented at the annual meeting of the American Educational Research Association, San Francisco.

107. Oakes, J. 1983. Limiting opportunity: Student race and curricular differences in secondary vocational education. *American Journal of Education* 91: 328–55.

108. Oakes, J. 1985. *Keeping Track: How Schools Structure Inequality.* New Haven: Yale University Press.

109. Oakes, J. 1988. "Tracking in mathematics and science education: A structural contribution to unequal schooling." In *Class, Race, and Gender in American Education,* by L. Weis. Albany, New York: State University of New York Press.

110. Persell, C. H. 1977. *Education and Inequality: The Roots and Results of Stratification in American Schools.* New York: Free Press.

111. Rosenbaum, J. E. 1980. Track misperceptions and frustrated college plans: An analysis of the effects of tracks and track perceptions in the National Longitudinal Survey. *Sociology of Education* 53 (2): 74–88.

112. Shafer, W. E., and Olexa, C. 1971. *Tracking and Opportunity.* Scranton, PA: Chandler.

113. Simpson, W. 1990. "Black Male Achievement: Strategies for Ensuring Success in School." Paper presented at the annual meeting of the National Black Child Development Institute, Washington, D.C.

114. Slavin, R. 1986. *Ability Grouping in Elementary Schools: A Best Evidence Synthesis.* Baltimore: Johns Hopkins University Press.

Non-European students' success rates in community colleges are discussed in the following references.

115. Astin, A. W. 1982. *Minorities in American Higher Education.* San Francisco: Jossey-Bass.

116. Karabel, J. 1972. Community colleges and social stratification. *Harvard Educational Review* 42 (4): 521–88.

117. Moore, W. 1976. Black knight/white college. *Community and Junior College Journal* 6 (7): 18–20, 40–43.

118. Nora, A., and Rendon, L. 1988. "Hispanic student retention in community colleges: Reconciling access with outcomes." In *Class, Race, and Gender in American Education,* by L. Weis. Albany, New York: State University of New York Press.

119. Olivas, M. A. 1979. *The Dilemma of Access: Minorities in Two Year Colleges.* Washington, D.C.: Howard University Press.

120. Weis, L. 1983. Schooling and cultural production: A comparison of black and white lived cultures. In *Ideology and Practice in Schooling,* edited by M. A. Apple and L. Weis. Philadelphia: Temple University Press.

The following references deal with student resistance to school.

121. Anyon, J. 1981. Social class and school knowledge. *Curriculum Inquiry* II: 3–42.

122. Anyon, J. 1984. Intersections of gender and class: Accommodation and resistance by working class and affluent females to contradictory sex-role ideologies. *Journal of Education* 166 (1): 25–48.

123. Arnot, M. 1982. Male hegemony, social class and women's education. *Journal of Education* 164 (1): 64–89.

124. Bouie, A. 1981. *Student Perceptions of Behavior and Misbehavior in the School Setting: An Exploratory Study and Discussion.* San Francisco: Far West Laboratory for Educational Research and Development.

125. Connell, R. W., Dowsett, G. W., Kessler, S., and Aschenden, D. J. 1982. *Making the Difference.* Boston: Allen & Unwin.

126. Deem, R. ed. 1980. *Schooling for Women's Work.* Boston: Routledge & Kegan Paul.

127. Fordham, S., and Ogbu, J. U. 1986. Black students' school success: Coping with the "burden of acting white." *Urban Review* 18 (3): 176–203.

128. Fuller, M. 1980. "Black girls in a London comprehensive school." In *Schooling for Women's Work,* edited by R. Deem. Boston: Routledge & Kegan Paul.

129. Gaskell, J. 1985. Course enrollment in high school: The perspective of working class females. *Sociology of Education* 58 (1): 48–59.

130. Kessler, S., Ashenden, R., Connell, R., and Dowsett, G. 1985. Gender relations in secondary schooling. *Sociology of Education* 58 (1): 34–48.

131. Matute-Bianchi, M. E. 1986. Ethnic identities and patterns of school success and failure among Mexican-descent and Japanese-American students in a California high school: An ethnographic analysis. *American Journal of Education* 95 (1): 233–55.

132. McRobbie, A. 1978. "Working class girls and the culture of femininity." In *Women Take Issue,* Center for Contemporary Cultural Studies Women's Group. London: Hutchison.

133. Ogbu, J. U. 1974. *The Next Generation: An Ethnography of Education on an Urban Neighborhood.* New York: Academic Press.

134. Ogbu, J. U. 1978. *Minority Education and Caste: The American in Cross-Cultural Perspective.* New York: Academic Press.

135. Ogbu, J. U. 1987. Variability in minority school performance: A problem in search of an explanation. *Anthropology and Education Quarterly* 18 (4): 312–34.

136. Petroni, F. A. 1970. "Uncle Toms": White stereotypes in the Black movement. *Human Organization* 29 (4): 260–66.

137. Simon, R. 1983. But who will let you do it? Counter-hegemonic possibilities for work education. *Journal of Education* 165 (3): 235–56.

138. Thomas, C. 1980. Girls and counter-school culture. *Melbourne Working Papers.* Melbourne, Australia.

139. Weis, L. 1985. Between Two Worlds: Black Students in an Urban Community College. Boston: Routledge & Kegan Paul.

140. Weis, L. 1985. Excellence and student class, race and gender cultures. In *Excellence in Education: Perspective on Policy and Practice,* edited by P. Altbach, G. Kelly, and L. Weis. Buffalo: Prometheus Press.

141. Willis, P. 1977. *Learning to Labor: How Working Class Kids Get Working Class Jobs.* Westmead, England: Saxon House Press.

142. Willis, P. 1981. Cultural production is different from cultural re-

production is different from social reproduction is different from
production. *Interchange* 12 (2/3):
48–68.

The references listed next include suggestions for preparing students to
change both schools and society.

143. Hartsock, N. 1979. "Feminist the-
ory and the development of revo-
lutionary strategy." In *Capitalist
Patriarchy and the Case for Socialist
Feminism,* edited by Z. Eisenstein.
New York: Monthly Review Press.

144. Lather, P. 1984. Critical theory, curricular transformation and feminist mainstreaming. *Journal of
Education* 166 (1): 49–62.

The following references refer to the
authors' conclusions.

145. Halpern, D. F. 1986. *Sex Differences in Cognitive Abilities.*
Hillsdale, NJ: Erlbaum Associates.

146. Deaux, K., and Major, B. 1987. Putting gender into context: An interactive model of gender-related
behavior. *Psychological Review* 94:
369–89.

147. Hargreaves, D. J., and Colley,
A. M. 1987. *The Psychology of Sex
Roles.* New York: Hemisphere
Publishing.

**The Schools' Role**

*Fostering Gender-Stereotypical Differences
in School*

Administrative imbalance is the focus of
the following references.

148. Fennema, E., and Ayer, M. J. ed.
1984. *Women and Education: Equity
or Equality?* Berkeley, CA:
McCutchan.

149. Frazier, N., and Sadker, M. 1973.
*Sexism in School and Society.* New
York: Harper and Row.

150. Lockheed, M. E. 1984. "Sex segregation and male preeminence in
elementary classrooms." In
*Women and Education: Equity or
Equality?* edited by E. Fennema
and M. J. Ayer. Berkeley, CA:
McCutchan.

151. SUNY study finds school management still white male dominated.
1990. *Black Issues in Higher Education* 7 (5): 23.

Gender bias in curriculum materials
during the 1960s and 1970s is discussed in the following references.

152. Byers, L. 1964. Pupils' interests
and the content of primary reading texts. *The Reading Teacher*
227–33.

153. Britton, G. E., and Lumpkin,
M. C. 1977. For sale: Subliminal
bias in textbooks. *Reading Teacher*
31: 40–45.

154. Kolbe, R., and LaVoie, J. 1981. Sex-
role stereotyping in children's picture books. *Social Psychology
Quarterly* 44: 369–74.

155. Lips, H. M., and Colwill, N. L.
1978. *The Psychology of Sex Differences.* Englewood Cliffs, NJ: Prentice-Hall.

156. Roberts, E. J., ed. 1980. *Childhood
Sexual Learning: The Unwritten
Curriculum.* Cambridge, MA:
Ballinger.

157. Rupley, W. H., Garcia, J., and
Longnion, B. 1981. Sex role portrayal in reading materials: Implications for the 1980's. *Reading
Teacher* 34: 786–91.

158. Scott, K. P. 1981. Whatever hap-
pened to Jane and Dick: Sexism
in texts re-examined. *Peabody Journal of Education* 58: 135–40.

159. Stanchfield, J. M. (n.d.). Differences in Learning Patterns of Boys and Girls. Unpublished Lectures, Occidental College. As cited in Austin, D. E., Clark, V. B., and Fitchett, G. W. 1971. *Reading Rights for Boys: Sex Role in Language Experiences.* New York: Appleton-Century-Crofts.

160. Weitzman, L. J., and Rizzo, D. 1971. *Sex Role Stereotypes in Elementary School Textbooks.* New York: NOW Legal Defense and Education Fund.

161. Women on Words and Images, Dick and Jane as Victims. 1972. *Sex Stereotyping in Children's Readers.* Princeton, NJ: Women on Words and Images.

The reduction, but not elimination, of gender bias during the 1980s is documented in the following references.

162. Cooper, P. 1989. "Children's literature: The extent of sexism." In *Beyond Boundaries: Sex and Gender Diversity in Education,* edited by C. Lont and S. Friedly. Fairfax, VA: George Mason University Press.

163. Cooper, P. 1987. Sex role stereotypes of stepparents in children's literature. In *Communication, Gender and Sex Roles in Diverse Interaction Contexts,* edited by L. Stewart and S. Ting-Toomey. Norwood, NJ: Ablex.

164. Dougherty, W., and Engel, R. 1987. An 80s look for sex equality in Caldecott winners and honors books. *Reading Teacher* 40: 394–98.

165. Heinz, K. 1987. An examination of sex occupational role presentations of female characters in children's picture books. *Women's Studies in Communication* 11: 67–78.

166. Hitchcock, M. E., and Tompkins, G. E. 1987. Basis readers: Are they still sexist? *Reading Teacher* 41 (3): 288–92.

167. Nilsen, A. P. 1987. Three decades of sexism in school science materials. *School Library Journal* 34 (1): 117–22.

168. Purcell, P., and Stewart, L. 1990. Dick and Jane 1989. *Sex Roles* 22 (3/4): 177–85.

169. Tetreault, M. K. T. 1985. Phases of thinking about women in history: A report card on the textbook. *Women's Studies Quarterly* 13 (3/4): 35–47.

170. Timm, J. 1988. "Cultural Bias in Children's Storybooks: Implications for Education." Paper presented at the annual meeting of the American Educational Research Association, New Orleans.

171. Vaughn-Roberson, C., Thompkins, M., Hitchcock, M. E., and Oldham, M. 1989. Sexism in basal readers: An analysis of male main characters. *Journal of Research in Childhood Education* 4: 62–68.

172. White, H. 1986. Damsels in distress: Dependency themes in fiction for children and adolescents. *Adolescence* 21: 251–56.

173. Woodill, G. 1987. Critical issues in the use of microcomputers by young children. *International Journal of Early Childhood* 19 (1): 50–57.

These references are concerned with the harmful effects of biased curriculum materials.

174. Knell, J. A., and Winer, G. A. 1979. Effects of reading content on occupational sex role stereotypes. *Journal of Vocational Behavior* 14: 78–87.

175. Nilsen, A. P., Bosmajian, H., Gershuny, H. L., and Stanley, J. P., ed. 1977. *Sexism and Language.* Ur-

bana, IL: National Council of Teachers of English.

176. Yanico, B. J. 1978. Sex bias in career information: Effects of language on attitudes. *Journal of Vocational Behavior* 13: 26–34.


The references listed next deal with gender differences in teacher attention.

177. Becker, J. 1981. Differential treatment of males and females in mathematics classes. *Journal of Research in Mathematics Education* 12: 40–53.

178. Benz, C. R., Pfeiffer, I., and Newman, I. 1981. Sex role expectations of classroom teachers, grade 1–12. *American Educational Research Journal* 18 (3): 289–302.

179. Berk, L. E. 1971. Effects of variations in nursery school setting on environmental constraints and children's mode of adaptation. *Child Development* 42: 839–69.

180. Berk, L. E., and Lewis, N. G. 1977. Sex role and social behavior in four school environments. *Elementary School Journal* 77: 205–17.

181. Blumenfield, P., Hamilton, V., and Bossert, S. 1979. "Teacher Talk and Student Thought: Socialization into the Student Role." Paper presented at the Learning Research and Development Center Conference on Student Motivation, Pittsburgh.

182. Boudreau, F. A. 1986. "Education." In *Sex Roles and Social Patterns,* edited by F. A. Boudreau, R. S. Sennott, and M. Wilson. New York: Praeger.

183. Brophy, J. E. 1985. Interaction of male and female students with male and female teachers. In *Gender Influences in Classroom Interaction,* edited by L. C. Wilkinson

and C. B. Marrett. New York: Academic Press.

184. Brophy, J. 1986. Teaching and learning mathematics: Where research should be going. *Journal for Research in Mathematics* 17: 323–46.

185. Cherry, L. 1975. The preschool teacher-child dyad: Sex differences in verbal interaction. *Child Development* 46: 532–35.

186. Eccles, J. S., and Blumenfeld, P. 1985. Classroom experiences and student gender: Are there differences and do they matter? In *Gender Influences in Classroom Interaction,* edited by L. C. Wilkinson and C. B. Marrett. New York: Academic Press.

187. Fennema, E., and Peterson, P. L. 1985. Autonomous learning behavior: A possible explanation of gender-related differences in mathematics. In *Gender Influences in Classroom Interaction,* edited by L. C. Wilkinson and C. B. Marrett. New York: Academic Press.

188. Fennema, E., and Peterson, P. L. 1986. Teacher student interactions and sex-related differences in learning mathematics. *Teaching and Teacher Education,* 2 (1): 19–42.

189. Fennema, E., Reyes, L., Perl, T., Konsin, M., and Drakenberg, M. 1980. "Cognitive and Affective Influences on the Development of Sex-Related Difference in Mathematics." Symposium presented at the annual meeting of the American Educational Research Association, Boston.

190. Gore, D. A., and Roumagoux, D. V. 1983. Wait-time as a variable in sex-related differences during fourth-grade mathematics instruction. *Journal of Educational Research* 76 (5): 273–75.

191. Gregory, M. K. 1977. Sex bias in school referrals. *Journal of School Psychology* 5: 5–8.

192. Leinhardt, G., Seewald, A. L., and Engel, M. 1979. Learning what's taught: Sex differences in instruction. *Journal of Educational Psychology* 71 (3): 432–39.

193. Lockheed, M. 1982. "Sex Equity in Classroom Interaction Research: An Analysis of Behavior Chains." Paper presented at the annual meeting of the American Educational Research Association, New York City.

194. Minuchin, P. P., and Shapiro, E. K. 1983. "The school as a context for social development." In *Handbook of Child Psychology*, vol 4., 4th ed., edited by P. Mussen and E. M. Hetherington. New York: Wiley.

195. Morrison, T. L. 1979. Classroom structure, work involvement and social climate in elementary school classrooms. *Journal of Educational Psychology* 71: 471–77.

196. Morse, L. W., and Handley, H. M. 1985. "Listening to adolescents: Gender differences in science classroom interaction." In *Gender Influences in Classroom Interaction*, edited by L. C. Wilkinson and C. B. Marrett. New York: Academic Press.

197. Pflaum, S., Pascarella, E., Boswick, M., and Auer, C. 1980. The influence of pupil behaviors and pupil status factors on teacher behaviors during oral reading lessons. *Journal of Educational Research* 74: 99–105.

198. Putnam, S., and Self, P. A. 1988. *Social Play in Toddlers: Teacher Intrusions.* ERIC ED 319 529.

199. Serbin, L. A., O'Leary D, K., Kent, R. N., and Tonic, J. J. 1973. A comparison of teacher response to the preacademic and problem behavior of boys and girls. *Child Development* 44: 796–804.

200. Sewald, A. M., Leinhardt, G., and Engel, M. 1977. *Learning What's Taught: Sex Differences in Instruction.* ERIC ED 145 327.

201. Stake, J., and Katz, J. 1982. Teacher-pupil relationships in the elementary school classroom: Teacher gender and student gender difference. *American Educational Research Journal* 19: 465–71.

202. Stallings, J. 1979. *Factors Influencing Women's Decisions to Enroll in Advanced Mathematics Courses: Executive Summary,* Grant NIE-G-78-0024. Menlo Park, CA: SRI International.

The following references deal with gender differences in teacher feedback.

203. Adams, R. E., and Passman, R. H. 1979. Sex differences in the interaction of adults and preschool children. *Psychological Reports* 44: 115–18.

204. Dweck, C. S., Davidson, W., Nelson, S., and Enna, B. 1978. Sex differences in learned helplessness: The contingencies of evaluation feedback in the classroom, an experimental analysis. *Developmental Psychology* 14 (3): 208–76.

205. Frey, K. S. 1979. "Differential Teaching Methods Used with Girls and Boys of Moderate and High Achievement Levels." Paper presented at the annual meeting of the American Educational Research Association, Minneapolis, MN.

206. Hodes, C. L. 1985. Relative effectiveness of corrective and noncorrective feedback in computer assisted instruction on learning

and achievement. *Journal of Educational Technology Systems* 13 (4): 249–54.

207. Meece, J. L. 1987. The influence of school experiences on the development of gender schemata. *New Directions for Child Development* 38: 57–73.

208. Parsons, J. E., Kaczala, C. M., and Meese, J. L. 1982. Socialization of achievement attitudes and beliefs: Classroom influences. *Child Development* 53: 322–39.

209. Simpson, A. W., and Erickson, M. T. 1983. Teachers' verbal and nonverbal communication patterns as a function of teacher race, student gender, and student race. *American Educational Research Journal* 20: 183–98.

Gender differences in academic expectations are discussed in the following references.

210. Bem, S. 1977. On the utility of alternative procedures for assessing psychological androgyny. *Journal of Consulting and Clinical Psychology* 45: 196–205.

211. Bernard, M. 1979. Does sex role behavior influence the way teachers evaluate students? *Journal of Educational Psychology* 71: 553–62.

212. Casserly, P. L. 1975. *An Assessment of Factors Affecting Female Participation in Advanced Placement Programs in Mathematics, Chemistry, and Physics*. Washington, D.C.: National Science Foundation.

213. Dusek, J. B., and Joseph, G. 1983. The bases of teacher expectancies: A meta-analysis. *Journal of Educational Psychology* 75: 327–46.

214. Ernest, J. 1976. *Mathematics and Sex*. Santa Barbara, CA: University of California.

215. Hallinan, M. T., and Sorensen, A. B. 1987. Ability grouping and sex differences in mathematics achievement. *Sociology of Education* 60 (2): 63–72.

216. Haven, E. W. 1971. Factors associated with the selection of advanced academic mathematics courses by girls in high school. *Dissertation Abstracts International* 32: 1747A. University Microfilms No. 71–26027.

217. Luchins, E. 1976. "Women Mathematicians: A Contemporary Appraisal." Paper presented at the annual meeting of the American Association for the Advancement of Science, Boston.

218. Phillips, R. 1980. Teachers' reported expectations of children's sex-roles and evaluation of sexist teaching. *Dissertation Abstracts International* 41: 995–996-A.

Ethnic differences in the ways teachers perceive and relate to students is the focus of the following references.

219. Grant, L. 1984. Black females' "place" in desegregated classrooms. *Sociology of Education* 57: 98–110.

220. Grant, L. 1985. "Uneasy Alliances: Black Males, Teachers, and Peers in Desegregated Classrooms." Paper presented at the annual meeting of the American Educational Research Association, Chicago.

221. Pollard, D. 1979. Patterns of coping in Black school children. In *Research Directions of Black Psychologists*, edited by A. W. Boykin, A. Franklin, and F. Yates. New York: Russel Sage.

222. Washington, V. 1982. Racial differences in teacher perception of first and fourth grade pupils on

selected characteristics. *Journal of Negro Education* 51: 60–72.

The following references deal with the adverse results of gender differences in teacher attention, feedback, and expectations.

223. Brush, L. R. 1980. *Encouraging Girls in Mathematics: The Problems and the Solutions.* Boston: Abt Associates.
224. Eccles, J., Adler, T. F., Futterman, R., Goff, S. B., Kaczala, C. M., Meece, J., and Midgley, C. 1983. Expectations, values, and academic behavior. In *Perspectives on Achievement and Achievement Motivation,* edited by J. T. Spence. San Francisco: W. H. Freeman.
225. Fox, L., Brody, L. A., and Tobin, D. eds. 1980. *Women and the Mathematical Mystique.* Baltimore: Johns Hopkins University Press.
226. Fennema, E., and Sherman, J. 1977. Sex-related differences in mathematics achievement, spatial visualization, and affective factors. *American Educational Research Journal* 14: 51–71.
227. Hilton, T. L., and Berglund, G. W. 1974. Sex differences in mathematics achievement: A longitudinal study. *Journal of Educational Research* 67: 231–37.
228. Wise, L., Steel, L., and MacDonald, C. 1979. *Origins and Career Consequences of Sex Differences in High School Mathematics Achievement.* Washington, D.C.: National Institute of Education.

The following references describe how teachers and other school personnel foster sex differences in the courses and activities students choose.

229. Farris, C. 1982. *Sex Fair Knowledge, Attitudes, and Behaviors of Vocational Educators: A Research Report.* Utica, NY: SUNY College of Technology.
230. Hopkins-Best, M. 1987. The effects of students' sex and disability on counselors' agreement with postsecondary career goals. *School Counselor* 35 (1): 28–33.
231. Parmley, J. D., Welton, R. F., and Bender, M. 1980. *Opinions of Agricultural Teachers, School Administrators, Students and Parents Concerning Females as Agriculture Students, Teachers and Workers in Agriculture.* ERIC ED 209 488.
232. Schaffer, K. F. 1981. *Sex Roles and Human Behavior.* Cambridge, MA: Winthrop.
233. Stockard, J., Schmuck, P. A., Kemper, K., Williams, P., Edson, S. K., and Smith, M. A. 1980. *Sex Equity in Education.* New York: Academic Press.
234. Tanney, F., and Birk, J. 1976. Women counselors for women clients: A review of the research. *Counseling Psychologist* 6: 28–32.
235. Tavris, C., and Wade, C. 1984. *The Longest War: Sex Differences in Perspective,* 2d ed. New York: Harcourt Brace Jovanovich.

Gender segregation and separation is the focus of the following articles.

236. Guttenberg, M., and Gray, H. 1977. "Teachers as mediators of sex-role standards." In *Beyond Sex Roles,* edited by A. Sargent. St. Paul, MN: West.
237. Lockheed, M. E., and Harris A. M. 1984. Cross-sex collaborative learning in elementary classrooms. *American Educational Research Journal* 21 (2): 275–94.

The following references deal with the fact that teachers encourage different behaviors in male and female students.

238. Boudreau, F. A. 1986. "Education." In *Sex Roles and Social Patterns*, edited by F. A. Boudreau, R. S. Sennot, and M. Wilson. New York: Praeger.
239. Caplan, P. J. 1977. Sex, age, behavior, and school subject as determinants of report of learning problems. *Journal of Learning Disabilities* 10: 60–62.
240. Fagot, B. I. 1977. Consequences of moderate cross-gender behavior in preschool children. *Child Development* 48: 902–07.
241. Huffine, S., Silvern, S. B., and Brooks, D. M. 1979. Teacher responses to contextually specific sex type behaviors in kindergarten children. *Educational Research Quarterly* 4 (2): 29–35.
242. Lamb, M. E., Easterbrook, A. M., and Holden, G. W. 1980. Reinforcement and punishment among preschoolers: Characteristics, effects, and correlates. *Child Development* 51: 1230–36.
243. Levitin, T. A., and Chananie, J. D. Responses of female primary school teachers to sex-typed behaviors in male and female children. *Child Development* 43: 1309–16.
244. Levy, B. 1972. The school's role in the sex-role stereotyping of girls: A feminist review of the literature. In *Sexism and Youth*, edited by D. Gersoni. New York: Bowker.
245. Schlosser, L., and Algozzine, B. 1980. Sex behavior and teacher expectancies. *Journal of Experimental Education* 48: 231–36.

The following references detail differences in teachers' tolerance for behavior.

246. Dent, H. L. 1976. "Assessing black children for mainstream placement." In *Mainstreaming and the Minority Child*, edited by R. L. Jones. Reston, VA: Council for Exceptional Children.
247. Fagot, B. I. 1985. Beyond the reinforcement principle: Another step toward understanding sex roles. *Developmental Psychology* 21: 1097–1104.
248. Marshall, J. 1983. Developing antisexist initiatives in education. *International Journal of Political Education* 6: 113–37.
249. Wooldridge, P., and Richman, C. L. 1985. Teachers' choice of punishment as a function of a student's gender, age, race, and IQ level. *Journal of School Psychology* 23: 19–29.

Teachers' use of different management techniques with the sexes is discussed in the references next.

250. Eccles, J. S., and Blumenfeld, P. 1985. "Classroom experiences and student gender: Are there differences and do they matter?" In *Gender Influences in Classroom Interaction*, edited by C. Wilkinson and C. B. Marrett. New York: Academic Press.
251. Fagot, B. I., and Hagan, R. 1985. Aggression in toddlers: Responses to the assertive acts of boys and girls. *Sex Roles* 12 (3): 341–51.

The following references describe how teachers use different classroom management techniques with various ethnic and socioeconomic groups.

252. Barba, L. 1979. *A Survey of the Literature on the Attitudes Toward the Administration of Corporal Punishment in Schools.* ERIC ED 186 538.

253. Glackman, T., Martin, R., Hyman, I., McDowell, E., Berv, V., and Spino, P. 1980. *Corporal Punishment in the Schools As It Relates to Race, Sex, Grade Level and Suspensions.* Philadelphia: Temple University, National Center for the Study of Corporal Punishment in the Schools.

254. National Black Child Development Institute. 1990. *The Status of African American Children: Twentieth Anniversary Report.* Washington, D.C.

255. Richardson, R. C., and Evans, E. T. 1991. "Empowering Teachers to Eliminate Corporal Punishment in the Schools." Paper presented at the annual conference of the National Black Child Developmental Institute, Washington, D.C.

256. Stevens, L. B. 1983. *Suspension and Corporal Punishment of Students in the Cleveland Public Schools 1981– 1982.* Cleveland: OH: Office of School Monitoring and Community Relations.

References that indicate that males exhibit more behavior problems and get into more trouble in school than females are included next.

257. Center, D. B., and Wascom, A. M. 1987. Teacher perceptions of social behavior in behaviorally disordered and socially normal children and youth. *Behavior Disorders* 12 (3): 200–06.

258. Duke, D. L. 1978. Why don't girls misbehave more than boys in school? *Journal of Youth and Adolescence* 7 (2): 141–57.

259. Eme, R. F. 1979. Sex differences in childhood psychopathology: A review. *Psychological Bulletin* 86: 574–95.

260. Epstein, M. H., Cullinan, D., and Bursuck, W. D. 1985. Prevalence of behavior problems among learning disabled and nonhandicapped students. *Mental Retardation and Learning Disability Bulletin* 13: 30–39.

261. Ludwig, G., and Cullinan, D. 1984. Behavior problems of gifted and nongifted elementary school girls and boys. *Gifted Child Quarterly* 28 (1): 37–39.

262. National Black Child Development Institute. 1990. *The Status of African American Children: Twentieth Anniversary Report.* Washington, D.C.

263. Wadsworth, M. 1979. *Roots of Delinquency: Infancy, Adolescence and Crime.* New York: Barnes and Noble.

*Ethnic and Socioeconomic Class Bias*

The references listed below describe teachers' prejudice against various students from certain ethnic and socioeconomic backgrounds through their biased expectations for students.

264. Adams, G. 1978. Racial membership and physical attractiveness effects on preschool teachers' expectations. *Child Study Journal* 8: 29–41.

265. Adams, G., and Cohen, A. 1976. An examination of cumulative folder information used by teach-

ers in making differential judgements of children's abilities. *The Alberta Journal of Educational Research* 22: 216–25.

266. Beady, C. H., and Hansell, S. 1980. *Teacher Race and Expectations for Student Achievement.* ERIC ED 200 695.

267. Bennet, C. I. 1979. The effects of student characteristics and task performance on teacher expectations and attributions. *Dissertation Abstracts International* 40: 979-980-B.

268. Campos F. 1983. *The Attitudes and Expectations of Student Teachers and Cooperating Teachers Toward Students in Predominantly Mexican American Schools: A Qualitative Data Perspective.* ERIC ED 234 026.

269. Derlega, V., Wang, P., and Colson, W. 1981. "Racial Bias in Expectancies and Performance Attributions." Unpublished manuscript, Norfolk, VA: Old Dominion University.

270. Dusek, J. B., and Joseph, G. 1983. The bases of teacher expectancies: A meta-analysis. *Journal of Educational Psychology* 75 (3): 327–46.

271. Figueroa, R. A., and Gallegos, E. A. 1978. Ethnic differences in school behavior. *Sociology of Education* 51: 289–98.

272. Harvey, D., and Slatin, G. T. 1975. The relationship between child's SES and teacher expectations: A test of the middle-class bias hypothesis. *Social Forces* 54 (1): 140–59.

273. Henderson, E. H. 1973. *When Teachers Predict Success in First-Grade Reading.* ERIC ED 094 856.

274. Jensen, M., and Rosenfeld, L. B. 1974. Influence of mode of presentation, ethnicity and social class on teachers' evaluations of students. *Journal of Educational Psychology* 66 (4): 540–47.

275. Matute-Bianchi, M. E. 1986. Ethnic identities and patterns of school success and failure among Mexican-descent and Japanese-American students in a California high school: An ethnographic analysis. *American Journal of Education* 95 (1): 233–55.

276. Metheny, W. 1979. *The Influences of Grade and Pupil Ability Levels on Teachers' Conceptions of Reading.* ERIC ED 182 713.

277. Ogbu, J. U. 1978. *Minority Education and Caste: The American in Cross-Cultural Perspective.* New York: Academic Press.

278. Rist, R. 1973. *The Urban School: A Factory of Failure.* Cambridge, MA: MIT Press.

279. Smith, J. A. 1979. Ascribed and achieved student characteristics in teacher expectancy: Relationship of socioeconomic status to academic achievement, academic self-concept, and vocational aspirations. *Dissertation Abstracts International* 40: 959-60-B.

280. Wilkerson, M. A. 1980. The effects of sex and ethnicity upon teachers' expectations of students. *Dissertation Abstracts International* 41: 637-A.

The following references discuss bias in teachers' evaluations of students.

281. Crowl, T. K., and MacGinitie, W. H. 1974. The influence of students' speech characteristics on teachers' evaluation of oral answers. *Journal of Educational Psychology* 66: 304–08.

282. Davis, S. A. 1974. *Students' SES as Related to Teachers' Perceptions and Ability Grouping Decisions.* ERIC ED 090 487.

283. DeMeis, D., and Turner, R. 1978. Effects of students' race, physical attractiveness, and dialect on teachers' evaluations. *Contemporary Educational Psychology* 3: 77–86.

284. Eaves, R. 1975. Teacher race, student race, and the behavior problem checklist. *Journal of Abnormal Child Psychology* 3 (1): 1–9.

285. Granger, R. E., Mathews, M., Quay, L. C., and Verner, R. 1977. Teacher judgements of communication effectiveness of children using different speech patterns. *Journal of Educational Psychology* 69 (6): 793–96.

286. Marwit, K., Marwit, S., and Walker, E. 1978. Effects of student race and physical attractiveness on teachers' judgments of transgressions. *Journal of Educational Psychology* 70: 911–15.

287. Namore, R. C. 1971. Teachers' judgments of children's speech: A factor analytic study of attitudes. *Speech Monographs* 38: 17–27.

288. Pugh, L. 1974. *Teacher Attitudes and Expectations Associated with Race and Social Class.* ERIC ED 094 018.

289. Rotter, N. G. 1975. The influence of race and other variables on teachers' ratings of pupils. *Dissertation Abstracts International* 35: 7134-A.

290. Rystrom, R., and Cowart, H. 1972. Black reading "errors" or white teacher biases? *Journal of Reading* 15 (4): 273–76.

291. Stevens, G. 1980. Bias in attributions of positive and negative behavior in children by school psychologists, parents, and teachers. *Perceptual and Motor Skills* 50: 1283–90.

The perception that Black English is a deficient or undesirable form of English is found in the following references.

292. Bereiter, C. 1969. The future of individual differences. *Harvard Educational Review* 39: 162–70.

293. Bondurant, S. V. 1973. *Freedomways* 13 (2): 157–59.

294. Ferguson, A. M. 1982. A case for teaching standard English to black students. *English Journal* 71: 38–40.

295. Nash, R. L. 1970. Toward a philosophy of speech communication education for the black child. *The Speech Teacher* 19 (2): 88–97.

These references take the position that working-class dialectic English is a deficient form of English.

296. Bereiter, C. 1965. Academic instruction and preschool children. In *Language Programs for the Disadvantaged Child,* edited by R. Cobin and M. Crosby. Champaign, IL: National Council of Teachers of English.

297. Bernstein, B. 1962. Social class and linguistic development: A theory of social learning. In *Education, Economy and Society,* edited by A. H. Hasley, J. Floud, and C. A. Anderson. New York: Free Press.

298. Jansen, R. 1964. Social class and verbal learning. In *Social Class Race and Psychological Development,* edited by M. Deutsch, I. Katz, and A. R. Jensen. New York: Holt, Rinehart & Winston.

299. Klaus, R., and Gray, S. 1968. *The Early Training Project for Disadvantaged Children: A Report After Five Years*. Monographs of the Society for Research in Child Development, 33.

The following references share the perspective that Black English is a valid and effective English dialect and that teachers are biased against it.

300. Anderson, D. 1975. Language and the disadvantaged African American. *Negro Educational Review* 26 (2, 3): 85–92.

301. Armstrong, B. G., and Davis, H. 1981. The impact of teaching black English on self-image and achievement. *Western Journal of Black Studies* 5 (3): 208–18.

302. Chermak, G. D. 1976. Reviews of issues in black dialect; a proposed two-way bilingual educational approach; and considerations for the congenitally deaf child. *Psychology in the Schools* 13 (1): 101–10.

303. Cooper, G. C. 1981. Black language and holistic cognitive style. *Western Journal of Black Studies* 5 (3): 201–07.

304. Jordan, J. 1973. Black English: The politics of translation. *School Library Journal* 19 (9): 21–24.

Bias in teacher-student interactions is the focus of the following references.

305. Appleford, B., Fralick, P., and Ryan, T. J. 1976. *Teacher-Child Interactions as Related to Sex, Socio-Economic Status and Physical Attractiveness*. ERIC ED 138 869.

306. Byalick, R., and Bershoff, D. N. 1974. Reinforcement practices of black and white teachers in integrated classrooms. *Journal of Educational Psychology* 66 (4): 473–80.

307. Friedman, P. 1976. Comparison of teacher reinforcement schedules for students with different social class backgrounds. *Journal of Educational Psychology* 68: 286–93.

308. Grant, L. 1985. "Race-gender status, classroom interaction, and children's socialization in elementary school." In *Gender Influences in Classroom Interaction*, edited by L. C. Wilkinson and C. B. Marrett. New York: Academic Press.

309. Guilmet, G. M. 1979. Instructor reaction to verbal and nonverbal styles: An example of Navajo and Caucasian children. *Anthropology and Education Quarterly* 10: 254–66.

310. Hamilton, S. 1983. The social side of schooling. *Elementary School Journal* 83: 313–34.

311. Hillman, S. B., and Davenport, G. 1978. Teacher-student interactions in desegregated schools. *Journal of Educational Psychology* 70 (4): 545–53.

312. Jackson, G., and Cosca, G. 1974. The inequality of educational opportunity in the southwest: An observational study of ethnically mixed classrooms. *American Educational Research Journal* 11: 219–29.

313. McGhan, B. R. 1978. *Teachers' Use of Authority and Its Relationship to Socioeconomic Status, Race, Teacher Characteristics, and Educational Outcomes*. ERIC ED 151 329.

314. Moore, W. L., and Cooper, H. 1984. Correlations between teacher and student background and teacher perception of discipline problems and disciplinary techniques. *Psychology in the Schools* 21: 386–92.

315. Taylor, M. 1979. Race, sex and the expression of self-fulfilling prophecies in a laboratory teach-

ing situation. *Journal of Personality and Social Psychology* 37 (6): 897–912.

316. Washington, V. 1982. Racial differences in teacher perception of first and fourth grade pupils on selected characteristics. *Journal of Negro Education* 51: 60–72.

Lack of bias is treated in the following references.

317. Feldman, R., and Donohoe, L. 1978. Nonverbal communication of affect in interracial dyads. *Jour-nal of Educational Psychology* 70 (6): 979–86.

318. Weitz, S. 1972. Attitude, voice, and behavior: A repressed affect model of interracial interaction. *Journal of Personality and Social Psychology* 24: 14–21.

319. Word, C., Zanna, M., and Cooper, J. 1974. The nonverbal mediation of self-fulfilling prophecies in interracial interaction. *Journal of Experimental Social Psychology* 10: 109–20.

# ▶ Part 2

## Achieving Gender Equity in the Classroom

# ▶ 3

---

# Defining Gender Equity

Part 1 of this text identified and described three educationally relevant gender issues: gender bias in the treatment of students, gender differences in the roles for which schools prepare students, and gender disparities in educational outcomes. Part 2 describes various approaches educators can use to achieve gender equity.

## DEFINING GENDER EQUITY

What is gender equity and how can gender equity be achieved in school? Educators' opinions vary. Some equate equity with sameness. Their point of view is that gender equity is achieved when males and females participate in the *same* courses of study and extracurricular activities to the *same* degree, their achievement is the *same*, they are treated the *same* by their teachers, and they are prepared for the *same* societal roles.

Other educators define equity in terms of fairness. Assuming that there are biologically based, educationally relevant differences between male and female students, they believe equity requires each gender to be treated in accordance with their biological make-up. To them, educational equity is achieved when both genders have an opportunity to participate in whichever courses and activities they prefer and to achieve up to their different potentials, when they are treated in accordance with their needs, and when they are prepared for different societal roles.

Thus, the way teachers define gender equity in school is extremely important because it influences how they relate to their students as well as their expectations for them. This introductory section explores the issues involved in defining and achieving gender equity. It also includes self-quiz items designed to help you examine or develop your own position on these issues.

## CONTROVERSIAL AND NONCONTROVERSIAL PRACTICES

Educators may disagree about the broad issues involved in defining gender equity, but most would probably agree that certain current educational practices are unfair and should be corrected. For example, few educators would support such practices as using textbooks that only reflect the interests or contributions of one gender, or providing students of one gender less assistance when they need help. Even though educators have conflicts about the cause or causes of gender differences and different comfort levels with the status quo, most would probably agree that teachers should do the following:

1. Select textbooks, readers, and biographies that include the contributions of both males and females.
2. Pay equal attention to all students who volunteer answers or ask questions, regardless of their gender.
3. Call on male and female students equally often.
4. Provide the same kind and amount of help to all students.
5. Praise female and male students equally for high achievement, creativity, and effort.
6. Attribute the cause of students' poor performance accurately.
7. Be equally attentive to the misbehavior of males and females.
8. Avoid excessively harsh punishments with all students.
9. Discourage dependent, helpless, and excessively conforming behavior in all students.
10. Treat all students fairly, regardless of their ethnic and/or socioeconomic backgrounds.

Educators' opinions about other educational practices vary in accordance with their attitudes and opinions about the gender issues in the larger society. For example, there probably is considerable disagreement among educators about whether or not they should do the following:

1. Select textbooks and other reading materials that portray males and females fulfilling nontraditional roles.
2. Permit males and females to choose to work and play in single-sex groups.

**3.** Separate boys and girls for activities such as physical education and sex education.

**4.** Assign students to single-sex groups during class to protect females from being dominated by males.

**5.** Select male teachers for male students and female teachers for female students.

**6.** Encourage, permit, or discourage boys and girls from enrolling in courses and engaging in activities that reflect societal stereotypes.

**7.** Encourage, permit, or discourage gender differences in cooperative versus competitive behavior, assertive versus passive behavior, risk taking, politeness, conformity, and docility.

**8.** Use the same management techniques with students regardless of their gender.

**9.** Encourage students to conform to the same standards of behavior regardless of their ethnic and socioeconomic backgrounds.

**10.** Utilize the same instructional approaches and assessment procedures with all students, regardless of their ethnic and socioeconomic backgrounds.

## POSITIONS ON GENDER DIFFERENCES

Omitting practices that most educators would probably agree are unfair, the following are the four most common positions that have appeared in the literature since the 1960s regarding controversial gender issues like the ones listed above. 1. Educators should prepare males and females to fulfill different roles, 2. Schools should foster androgynous gender roles, 3. Educators have the right to decide for themselves whether to encourage students to fulfill traditional gender roles or androgynous gender roles, and 4. Students should decide what kind of gender role they prefer. As these are not mutually exclusive positions, you may find that either one or a combination is close to your own position.

**1.** Teachers do a disservice to students by treating males and females the same (2, 10, 13, 14, 15). Educators should prepare the genders to fulfill very different roles because there are natural, physiological differences between the sexes. And they should accommodate their instructional practices to existing gender differences. The following quotations are representative of this point of view and span a twenty-five year period.

> *Teachers usually value quiet, cooperative, helpful, and passive behavior. Female early childhood teachers are more comfortable with the typical girl activities, spend more time with children engaged in female sex-typical activities, and tend to punish or ignore traditional male behavior. Vehicle*

*or block play and loud behavior do not attract teacher attention or involvement; girls respond well to the more structured activities teachers tend to provide. (14, p. 50)*

The author of this statement suggests that teachers should accept and respond positively to both male and female typical behavior. Do you agree?

*School materials that induce role reversals, such as showing men as house-husbands and women as construction workers, teach false notions far from reality. (11)*

Do you agree or disagree with this statement? Do you agree with the practice currently followed by many organizations and publishers who depict males and females in more androgynous roles in the materials they prepare for use in school?

*The overriding psychological need of a woman is to love something alive. A baby fulfills this need in the lives of most women. If a baby is not available to fill that need, women search for a baby-substitute. This is the reason why women have traditionally gone into teaching and nursing careers. They are doing what comes naturally to the female psyche. The school child or the patient of any age provides an outlet for a woman to express her natural maternal need. (10, pp. 50–51)*

This statement implies that some of the gender differences in the vocational choices students make are based on biological differences that should be respected if not encouraged. Do you agree?

*Boys who rise to the top in school often resemble girls in many important ways. . . . Scholastic honor and masculinity, in other words, too often seem incompatible. . . . The feminized school simply bores many boys: but it pulls some in one of two opposite directions. If the boy absorbs school values, he may become feminized himself. If he resists, he is pushed toward school failure and rebellion. (13, pp. 13, 33)*

Do you agree that being a *real boy* is incompatible with being a good student? Do you agree that being a real boy in the sense that the term is usually used is a desirable personality characteristic? What is your opinion about the author's concern that schools feminize males?

**2.** Most gender-role differences are unnatural, outdated, and harmful. Schools should cease fostering such sex-role differences. Instead, they should prepare students for the androgynous roles that are increasingly available to them in society. In order to accomplish this, teachers should not use students' gender as a criterion for making educational decisions about them. Teachers should also encourage and prepare students to do what is necessary to transform our sexist society into a less sexist one. In short, teachers should be in the vanguard of change (1, 3–5, 6, 7, 9). The following quotes are examples of this position.

> *In American society, men are supposed to be masculine, women are supposed to be feminine, and neither sex is supposed to be much like the other. If men are independent, tough, and assertive, women should be dependent, sweet, and retiring. A womanly woman may be tender and nurturant, but no manly man may be so. . . . I have come to believe that we need a new standard of psychological health for the sexes, one that removes the burden of stereotype and allows people to feel free to express the best traits of men and women. . . .*
>
> *Traditional sextyping necessarily restricts behavior. Because people learn, during their formative years, to suppress any behavior that might be considered undesirable or inappropriate for their sex, men are afraid to do "women's work" and women are afraid to enter a "man's world." Men are reluctant to be gentle, and women to be assertive. In contrast, androgynous people are not limited by labels. They are able to do whatever they want, both in their behavior and their feelings. (4, p. 32)*

Do you agree that students should be encouraged to become androgynous? If you agree with the author, you probably favor discouraging students from accepting and acting out any gender-stereotypical roles, whatever they may be.

> *Neatness, conformity, docility, these qualities for which the young girl receives good grades and teacher's praise have little to do with active intellectual curiosity, analytic problem solving, and the ability to cope with challenging material. For good grades and teacher's praise, the grade school girl relinquishes the courage that it takes to grapple with difficult material. This naive young bargainer of seven or eight has made an exchange that will cost her dearly. (6, p. 96)*

These authors imply that neatness, conformity, and docility are qualities that interfere with the development of other personality characteristics that are more valuable and more valued by society, such as active intellectual curiosity, analytic problem solving, and the ability to cope with challenging material. Do you agree? If so, do you also agree that students, especially females, should not be encouraged to acquire the first group of habits at the expense of the second?

> *There is a compelling reason for encouraging more girls to enroll in mathematics courses. As the traditional distinctions between "men's" and "women's work" disappear, more and more often men and women compete for the same jobs. As our society becomes increasingly technical, persons with a weak background in mathematics have fewer options because more occupations are closed to them. (1, p. 11)*

The author of the above quotation appears to take the position that some gender differences, while not intrinsically undesirable, are impractical in today's world. Do you think that practicality should be a criterion for evaluating the appropriateness of gender differences?

> *At the core of any radical pedagogy must be the aim of empowering people to recognize and work for a change in the social, political, and economic structure that constitutes the ultimate source of class-based power and domination. (7, p. 427)*

Do you agree that teachers should prepare students to change society in the ways suggested by the author of this statement?

**3.** Educators should decide for themselves whether they want to prepare students to fulfill different gender roles or encourage students to fulfill similar roles. The desirability or lack of desirability of gender roles is something for the individual professional or the group to decide.

> *If we value the higher levels of aggressiveness in males, then schools should encourage aggression, competition, and assertion more in females. This might mean more emphasis on competitive athletics for girls, perhaps beginning in early elementary school, or perhaps even in the preschool years. In the academic classroom, it might mean encouraging reticent girls to speak up more forcefully in debates or to become more competitive about their success in mathematics courses. If, on the other hand, we value the low level of aggressiveness of females, we might seek to reduce the level of aggressiveness in boys, while simultaneously encouraging peaceful cooperation for them . . . We might want to de-emphasize competitive sports in favor of cooperative sports or noncompetitive ones such as jogging. In the classroom, we would avoid competitively structured learning and work toward cooperatively structured learning . . . Which of these alternatives is chosen, of course, is a matter of values. (8, pp. 64–65)*

Do you agree that gender roles are inherently neither desirable nor undesirable, but depend on the values of different individuals and societies? If so, does that mean that societies have the right to establish different expectations for their male and female members? Does it also follow that different ethnic and socioeconomic groups have the right to expect the schools to respect their freedom to bring up their children to fulfill the gender roles they believe most appropriate? Or should the greater society determine the gender roles for all the subgroups living within its boundaries?

**4.** Students themselves should be encouraged to choose whether or not they wish to conform to any particular gender-role and whether or not they prefer to be androgynous.

> *To force everyone into the new mold may violate the individual as much as to force them into the older stereotypes. . . . Freedom to choose according to individual need would seem to be the preferred way of dealing with the complex problem of man/woman roles. (12, p. 202)*

Should teachers not involve themselves in shaping their students' attitudes about gender roles? Would it be appropriate for educators to expose their students to a variety of opinions and models in order to enable them to make informed decisions about gender-role issues? In your opinion, what, if anything, should teachers do to assist their students in deciding where they stand on the kinds of gender issues raised in this book?

## LEGAL REQUIREMENTS

Educators can and do have personal opinions about how they should relate to students, how schools should be structured, and whether any particular gender difference should be encouraged or discouraged. And our laws certainly protect individual's rights to have opinions. However, in 1972, Congress passed Title IX of the Education Amendments Act, which was designed to correct the biased treatment males and females received in school. Some of the provisions of Title IX that protect students from gender bias also restrict the rights of educators to decide for themselves about how to respond to certain gender issues. Therefore, it is important to review how the law requires educators to deal with gender issues and compare these requirements to the situation as it exists today.

Title IX of the Education Amendments Act of 1972 requires schools to provide equal educational opportunities to all students regardless of gender. As it did in the 1970s and 1980s, Title IX serves as the main legal basis for

**BOX 3–1    Self-Quiz**

*Sex-Role Differences*

State whether you think each of the differences listed below should be encouraged, accepted, or discouraged. Your knowledge of the facts concerning the gender issues should help shape your conclusions about the desirability or acceptability of the sex-role differences observed in school. However, in those cases where there is little hard research data, you may have only subjective opinions rather than conclusions.

*Interpersonal Relationships*

1. Females are less competitive and more cooperative.
2. Males share less.
3. Males are less altruistic and helpful.
4. Males are less polite.
5. Males express less support for their classmates.
6. Females are less likely to deal openly with conflicts.
7. Females are less assertive.
8. Females are less aggressive.
9. In their relationships with males, females are less competitive, less assertive, less likely to perform leadership roles, and more likely to allow males to dominate the conversation.
10. Males are less compliant toward adults.
11. Males are less motivated to behave appropriately in order to obtain adults' approval.
12. Young males get their way with others by physical means; females tend to use verbal means.

13. Males are less likely to use learned helplessness to influence others.
14. Males are less likely to respond to requests and feedback from females.
15. Females are less concerned about dominance issues in group situations.

*Emotional Style*

1. Males are less willing to express weakness, fear, and anxiety.
2. Males are less likely to report that they are sad, depressed, anxious, or insecure.
3. Females express their feelings less intensely.

*Communication Style*

1. Females are more sensitive to nonverbal cues.
2. Males use less polite and more forceful language and more four-letter words.

*Moral Development*

1. Males tend to base moral decisions on impersonal principles or standards of justice and fairness. Females consider how their actions will affect the feelings and welfare of others and their relationship with them.
2. Males are described as less honest, trustworthy, empathic, and less likely to follow through on what they promise to do.
3. Females are less likely to cheat.
4. Males are less critical of themselves and are more likely to use a double standard when judging their behavior.

---

**Box 3–1** *Continued*

*Learning Style*

1. Males are less likely to delay judgment until they have the information they need.
2. Females are less likely to discard solutions to problems when they no longer fit.
3. Females react less positively to difficult and challenging situations and to the possibility of failure.
4. Males are more likely to take risks.
5. Females are less confident than males in situations that are traditionally seen as belonging to the male domain.
6. Females are more likely to inaccurately attribute their poor performance to lack of ability.
7. Males are less likely to copy what others model.
8. Males are less likely to seek the attention and assistance of adults.
9. Females are more likely to modify their opinions and judgments to conform to those of the group.
10. Females are more likely to profit from cooperative learning.

*Participation and Achievement in School*

1. Young males and females engage in different activities and play with different toys.
2. Females are less likely to engage in contact sports.
3. Females are less likely to be a president of a school organization and more likely to be a secretary.
4. Females participate less in math, science, and computer courses and such vocational courses as agriculture, electric technology, auto mechanics, and so on that are in the male domain.
5. Males are less likely to enroll in foreign language, art, and vocational courses such as home economics that are in the female domain.
6. Males score lower on tests of language arts; females score lower on tests of physical science and higher level mathematics skills.

---

efforts to eliminate gender-discriminatory educational practices. Its requirements include the following:

**1.** Students may not be denied admission to schools or subjected to discriminatory admissions practices on the basis of their gender.

**2.** Once admitted, students may not be excluded from participation in, be denied the benefits of, or be subjected to discrimination while participating in, any academic, extracurricular, research, occupational training, or other educational program or activity.

**3.** All courses and activities, except human sexuality courses, must be open to all students regardless of their gender. If offered, human sexuality courses must be available to all students, but they can be taught separately to males and females.

4. Standards for student participation in physical education activities and ability groupings within these activities must be objective and applied equally to all students regardless of gender. Separate athletic teams may be provided for males and females for contact sports or for other sports when the separation is justified by differences in skills. However, if a school has a contact sport for males only, a noncontact alternative team sport for females must be provided.

5. Dress codes must be applied equally to males and females.

6. Graduation requirements must be the same for both genders.

7. Textbooks and other instructional materials are exempted from Title IX regulations because of potential conflicts with freedom of speech rights guaranteed by the First Amendment and other legislation.

## ISSUES FOR FURTHER THOUGHT AND DISCUSSION

The following incident was reported by a school principal (16, p. 208).

> *Allen attended a parochial school where the playgrounds were segregated by gender. In one playground the girls skipped and jumped rope, in the other, the boys played football. Allen often stood on the sidelines and chatted with several other non-athletic boys. Allen's teacher was concerned and arranged privately with several of the male athletes to include Allen and his friends in the daily football game. The teacher warned that if they failed to do so, all of the boys in the class would be punished.*

How do you feel about the gender separation that existed on the playgrounds? What is your opinion about the way the teacher responded to Allen and his friends' behavior? What might have been the teacher's reason for responding in that manner? How would you have responded?

---

**BOX 3–2    Self-Quiz**

*Legal Requirements*

Title IX clearly establishes a number of legal requirements about some extremely controversial issues. Do you think educators have the right to disregard requirements that they or members of the community they work in disagree with? Do you think educators should engage in acts of civil disobedience if they disagree? Or do you think they should abide by the regulations regardless of their personal convictions or those of parents and students?

---

# REFERENCES

### Desirability of Gender Differences

The following references discuss the pros and cons of fostering gender differences in school.

1. Allen, R. H., and Chambers, D. L. 1977. *A Comparison of the Mathematics Achievement of Males and Females.* ERIC ED 159 076.
2. Austin, D., Clark, B., and Fichett, G. 1971. *Reading Rights for Boys.* New York: Appleton-Century-Crofts.
3. Becker, J. B. 1986. "Influence again: An examination of reviews and studies of gender differences in social influence." In *The Psychology of Gender,* edited by J. S. Hyde and M. C. Linn. Baltimore: Johns Hopkins University Press.
4. Bem, S. L. 1983. "Traditional sex roles are too restrictive." In *Male-Female Roles: Opposing Viewpoints,* edited by G. Leone and M. T. O'Neill. St. Paul, MN: Greenhaven Press.
5. Block, J. H. 1984. *Sex Role Identity and Ego Development.* San Francisco: Jossey-Bass.
6. Frazier, N., and Sadker, M. 1973. *Sexism in Schools and Society.* New York: Harper and Row.
7. Giroux, H. A. 1981. "Hegemony, resistance, and the paradox of educational reform." In *Curriculum and Instruction: Alternatives in Education,* edited by H. A. Giroux, A. N. Penna, and W. F. Pinar. Berkeley, CA: McCutchan.
8. Hyde, J. S. 1984. "Gender differences in aggression." In *The Psychology of Gender: Advances through Meta-Analysis,* edited by J. S. Hyde and M. C. Linn. Baltimore: Johns Hopkins University Press.
9. Jacklin, C. N. 1989. Female and male: Issues of Gender. *American Psychologist* 44 (2): 127–33.
10. Pollack, J. H. 1968. Are teachers fair to boys? *Today's Health* 46 (4): 21–25.
11. Schlafly, P. 1977. *The Power of the Positive Woman.* New York: William Morrow.
12. Schlafly, P. Personal communication, May 1989.
13. Seward, J. P., and Seward, G. H. 1980. *Sex Differences: Mental and Temperamental.* Lexington, MA: Lexington Books.
14. Sexton, P. C. 1969. *The Feminized Male.* New York: Random House.
15. Wardle, F. 1991. Are we shortchanging boys? *Child Care Information Exchange* 79: 48–51.

The incident in "Questions for Further Thought and Discussion" was included in the following reference.

16. Hebert, T. P. 1991. Meeting the affective needs of bright boys through bibliography. *Roeper Review* 13 (4): 207–12.

# ▶ 4

## Accommodating to Gender Differences

Many educators believe that students are served best when teachers match their educational approaches to gender differences in their students' learning and behavior styles. They tend to anticipate the following positive results from this approach.

**1.** Students learn more because their teachers' instructional approaches match their learning styles.

**2.** Gender disparities in educational outcomes are reduced.

**3.** Students have fewer behavior problems because their teachers' management techniques are more effective and acceptable to them.

**4.** Students experience fewer of the psychological problems that could result from possible conflicts between the gender roles they are exposed to and expected to conform to at home and in their neighborhoods and the roles their teachers expect them to fulfill.

This chapter describes the techniques that have been suggested for accommodating teaching techniques to current gender differences and the effectiveness of this approach. Teachers cannot match their teaching approaches to their students merely by treating all female students one way and all male students another way. Male and female students function too similarly to make that feasible. Even in areas where there is a gender difference, not all females and males conform to a particular gender stereotype. For example, using competitive learning strategies will not help all males; nor will using cooperative techniques suit all females. One reason is that many students, especially those from non-European American and working-class backgrounds, do not fit the prevailing generalizations about the cooperative/competitive learning styles of female and male European American middle-class students (1–33). Some male students, like Hispanic males who conform to their culture's noncompetitive learning styles for both genders and European American males who do not conform to the cultural expectation that they will be competitive, may actually experience a deterioration in achievement when exposed to competitive teaching techniques (1, 9, 13). (Also see the section entitled Cooperative Learning later in this chapter.) Thus, whether or not these anticipated benefits are actually achieved depends in part on how well teachers match their teaching approaches to their own students.

To accomplish this requires a knowledge of possible male-female differences in learning and behavior styles as they exist in specific ethnic and socioeconomic-groups as well as a procedure for determining which students do and do not conform to each stereotype. Knowledge of possible gender, ethnic, and socioeconomic stereotypes can sensitize teachers to be watchful for potential differences in learning styles, interests, and behavior patterns among students. However, stereotypes should never be used as the sole criterion for determining the best approach for a particular student. To treat all females and all males alike will not result in the benefits that proponents of accommodation expect. And it may cause problems for students who do not conform to a particular stereotype.

## FEMALE STUDENTS

While many authors have focused their educational recommendations on changing the female-typical behavior that they perceive as undesirable, self-defeating, or maladaptive, others have suggested a number of ways teachers can accommodate their instructional approaches to female learning and behavior styles that they believe are positive. These suggestions and the research evidence regarding their effectiveness are discussed in this section.

### *Cooperative Learning*

Because females typically prefer to learn in cooperative settings, some educators recommend that teachers should provide female students more cooperative learning experiences than the schools currently offer. A number of cooperative learning programs have been published and researched. Among the most widely implemented programs are Jigsaw (34, 46), Circles of Learning (39), Team Assisted Individualization (48), Student Teams Achievement Divisions (46), Teams-Games-Tournaments (36), and Group Investigation (44, 45).

In the Jigsaw approach, students are divided into several cooperative groups. Teachers provide each student in a particular learning group with only part of the information the group needs as a whole. Because each student has only one piece of the jigsaw puzzle, the students in the group have to share all their individual bits of information to complete the assigned lesson. To create cooperation between groups, students from the different groups who have the same information work in subgroups to learn the information they will have to communicate to the other members of their groups. Students' learning is evaluated individually, so this approach includes cooperative and individualistic incentives. It can also include competitive ones, if groups compete with each other for prizes.

In Circles of Learning, students are divided into heterogeneous groups based on gender, ability, and ethnic background. Teachers use a number of techniques to insure that students will function cooperatively. They assign students specific roles such as observer, recorder, summarizer/checker, and so on that require them to work as a team. Teachers evaluate students in terms of a single group product or the sum of the performances of each student in the group, so they encourage and help each other to do well. Teachers randomly call on individual members to represent the group so each represents the others as well. And they sometimes evaluate the whole group on the basis of the accomplishments of a single member.

In Team Assisted Individualization, each student works on her or his own, but team members are required to check each other's work, tutor each other, and make sure that all members of the team are ready for the test on the material they are preparing. Cooperation is encouraged by requiring team members to seek help from one another before they can seek assistance from the teacher. Individual incentives—the results of tests—are supplemented with cooperative incentives by rewarding teams whose members do well.

In Student Teams Achievement Divisions and Teams-Games-Tournaments, a large group of students is divided into smaller groups of roughly equal ability. The groups compete for prizes with all the other teams based on the total scores of their members. Members of a team are motivated to assist each other by basing the team's score on the amount each member improves.

Group Investigation is an approach in which subgroups of a large group, for example, a class, investigate different aspects of a primary topic. This organizational structure is designed to insure cooperation between members of each subgroup as well as between the subgroups themselves. There is neither competition between subgroups nor any extrinsic rewards.

These cooperative learning programs differ along several parameters: whether they include cooperative tasks and goals (students work on the same problem/task together) or individualistic tasks and goals (students in the group have their own tasks), and whether they have cooperative incentives (student reward and evaluations are based on the results of the whole group), individualistic incentives (students are evaluated and rewarded individually) or competitive incentives (groups compete for rewards and recognition).

Some proponents of cooperative learning believe that situations in which students do not work on the same project together or are evaluated separately or compete with other groups, are not truly cooperative learning. They propose that true cooperative learning involves creating situations in which students work together on the same task, can only succeed if all the members of the group succeed, and are not compared to other groups. For them, examples of cooperative learning would be a group project for which all students work on the same project and receive the same grade, or a group that continues to assist all members to learn to solve a mathematics problem until every member can succeed. Others feel that individualistic evaluations and rewards and/or competition are necessary to motivate students. They also claim that individualism and competition reflect the real world for which schools should be preparing students.

The following steps are components authors usually suggest should be included in an effective cooperative learning experience for females. These steps should be considered a list of characteristics of effective cooperative learning approaches rather than as exact steps to follow.

1. Familiarize yourself with the variety of cooperative learning techniques available to teachers. The references in the bibliography are a good source of information.
2. Select a learning situation that meets your criteria for cooperative learning.

---

**BOX 4–1    Self-Quiz**

*Cooperative Learning Environments*

What is your opinion about what is and is not cooperative learning? Do you accept the distinction between situations that supposedly only give the appearance of cooperative learning (those that also contain elements of individualistic and competitive learning) and *true* cooperative learning situations? Or do you believe that cooperative learning environments can also include other elements? Think about the various cooperative learning experiences you have been involved in recently. Which of them fit your definition of cooperative learning?

**3.** Decide whether to employ single-sex or mixed-sex group learning situations. Female students may be more likely to thrive in single-sex group settings for the reasons discussed below. However, grouping students according to sex may not satisfy the provisions of Title IX and may not be acceptable to you if you oppose gender-segregation/separation.

**4.** Inform students of the cooperative procedures they should follow and teach them how to follow them.

**5.** If you decide to utilize mixed-sex groups, prepare all students, especially female students, to assume the expert/leadership role.

**6.** Sensitize all students, especially male students who are prone to use group situations to dominate others, to the importance of allowing all students to take on all the roles available to group members.

**7.** Determine your students' learning styles. Those who have a cooperative learning style may be ready to profit from such experiences. However, you may need to prepare those who tend to do better in competitive or independent learning situations to function better in more cooperative settings before they can profit from them.

**8.** Monitor the groups closely to discourage the kinds of problems discussed above and intervene as quickly as possible when problems arise.

The positive results of cooperative learning on students' achievement, attitudes, and interpersonal relationships has been demonstrated repeatedly in research studies (5, 7, 8, 34–39). Typically, students learn more, get along better with their peers, and feel better about themselves, their peers, and school when they learn in cooperative environments. Research also indicates, however, that these results characterize only some, not all students. In general, females, African Americans, Hispanic Americans, and students who are inclined to cooperate (those who have a cooperative learning style regardless of gender or ethnicity) tend to experience the greatest academic gains from cooperative learning (1–33). But not all members of these groups demonstrate these gains.

Available research suggests that female students tend to achieve more in single-sex cooperative learning situations than in mixed-sex groups. For example, in laboratory science classes, females learn more in all-female cooperative groups than in mixed-gender groups (40, 42). Moody and Gifford believe part of the reason for this is that females participate and lead less in mixed-gender groups. They suggest that "females are forced to take leadership and responsibility in laboratory groups when working with only other females. . . . If increased female leadership and participation is desired, then grouping by gender can accomplish this objective" (42, pp. 16, 17).

There is evidence that females are often the losers in mixed-sex groups because although they tend to be the providers of assistance they are re-

When used wisely, cooperative learning can be an effective instructional technique.

jected by males when they ask for assistance (32). In addition, as noted earlier, females in mixed-sex cooperative groups often revert to a pattern of not interacting with male students, allowing males to dominate them, and viewing themselves as less helpful, less important, and less visible (2, 14, 15, 20, 21, 25, 30, 33). And there is some evidence that they may behave more competitively than they otherwise do (26). Males may actually learn more and perform better than females in cooperative mixed-sex groups because they often ignore females, contribute most of the ideas, do most of the talking, and typically function as the group leaders (4, 15, 16, 31).

Females can benefit from mixed-gender cooperative groups. They are more likely to benefit from cooperative mixed-sex groups when they have been given advanced training so they can function as expert/leader of the group and when they have had prior experience with the group task so they are familiar with what is to be learned (See the section in chapter 5 entitled Male Dominance of Mixed Gender Groups.)

Peterson and Fennema (19) point out other problems that can result in mixed-sex cooperative groups. They suggest that while girls' levels of achievement may improve in cooperative learning groups, such groups may make girls even less independent and that could further impair their already inadequate high-level thinking skills in courses such as mathematics. They are also concerned that cooperative activities may impede the higher level mathematics achievement of independent, competitive boys.

The experiences of some African American students in mixed-ethnic cooperative groups may be similar to the negative experiences of many females (20). Piel and Conwell claim that: "white children and black children may not be getting the same experience from a cooperative learning experience . . . If white children assume leadership roles and black children assume more subservient roles then the purpose for cooperative groups seems to be somewhat diminished" (20, p. 14).

Finally, there is suggestive evidence that whether or not students benefit from cooperative learning depends in part on their self-concepts (3). When students with high and low self-concepts work together, those with high self-concepts are less likely to function cooperatively, thereby thwarting the goals of the cooperative learning experiences.

For the many reasons discussed above, educators should not assume that cooperative learning benefits all students and improves the academic achievement of female students. Effective utilization of cooperative learning requires a thoughtful selection of the model to be used and a great deal of planning and preparation.

---

### BOX 4–2    Self-Quiz

*Selecting Students for Cooperative Learning Experiences*

Sharan and Shaulov note that students react to cooperative learning activities on an individual basis. They suggest that "cooperative learning should be an instructional alternative available to students who are inclined to cooperate with their peers on learning tasks . . . not all students are so inclined and they should have the option of studying with the whole class method." They go on to state that "many elementary schools, and almost all secondary schools, are still 'one-mission organizations' in terms of their instructional technology. Also, not many teachers master a range of teaching methods and employ them as circumstances and goals dictate. Most schools still behave as if there is one best way to teach" (24, p. 200).

With which students do you think cooperative learning should be used? Do you think that cooperative learning should be used primarily with those who appear to favor this type of learning, or with all students? Would you assign students to cooperative learning groups? If so, what criteria would you use to determine which students to assign to such groups? Would you allow students to choose their own learning environments?

There appear to be some advantages to same-sex teaching.

## *Same-Sex Teaching*

An individual's teaching style cannot be predicted from her or his gender alone. Many factors such as ethnic background influence teaching styles (55, 60). Research does indicate, however, that males and females tend to employ somewhat different instructional and classroom management approaches, and students react to male and female teachers' styles somewhat differently (50–61). In comparison to females, males are generally more direct with their students and more subject-centered; females are more indirect and more student-centered. Males lecture more; females ask more questions and involve themselves more often in classroom discussions. Females are more likely to praise students for answering correctly but less likely to give students feedback when their answers are wrong. Males are more likely to criticize wrong answers, offer explanations designed to help students correct their responses, and give students another chance to respond correctly.

Female teachers are more available to students during class time. They make more eye contact and maintain less distance from students. They are more sensitive to students' needs and feelings, more accepting, and less critical and harsh. When organizing students into groups, female teachers are more likely than males to assign students to specific groups while males are more likely to allow students to form their own groups.

Male teachers tend to reinforce young boys for stereotypical male behaviors more than females do. They are more tolerant of males' aggressive and disruptive behavior and less likely to send aggressive or disruptive boys to the office or to refer them to special education. But they reprimand students more than females, and do so publicly.

In general, but with many exceptions, male teachers tend to use a teaching style closer to the male learning style while females employ a teaching style that is more appropriate for females' learning styles. As a result, some educators believe females may learn more effectively when they are taught by female teachers.

Are they correct? Is same-sex teaching an effective approach with female students? Research indicates that many, but not all, females participate more actively, initiate more discussions, ask more questions, and express more ideas in classes with female instructors, even when they are coeducational (51, 53, 59, 61). Very little research has been done, though, on whether females actually learn more in classes taught by female teachers. In addition, since all females do not have the same teaching and learning styles, it does not follow that same-sex teaching will necessarily produce a good match between a particular student or group of students' learning styles and their teachers' teaching styles. There are too few female teachers to employ same-sex teaching with many students at the middle- and secondary-school levels. But even if there were sufficient teachers, Title IX would preclude such an approach. Thus, most females will continue to be taught by male as well as female teachers for the foreseeable future.

The fact that females behave differently in female instructors' classes may be enough to convince you of the efficacy of same-sex instruction. However, you may want more direct proof that it also enhances their learning before deciding that it has merit.

## Matching Teaching and Learning Styles

Some educators are not optimistic about the possibility of matching their teaching styles to the many diverse learning styles in their classrooms. In very diverse communities, it may not be feasible to adapt one's approach to each and every student's learning style. However, even in these communities, teachers can increase the likelihood that students will receive the kind of instruction that best suits them at least some of the time by varying their instructional techniques rather than employing the same ones over and over.

Because all students do not conform to stereotypes, teachers who wish to adapt their instructional styles to their students' learning styles must

**BOX 4–3   Self-Quiz**

*Teaching Style*

Does your teaching style favor one gender over another? Do you use a gender-stereotypical teaching style or is your style androgynous? Rate your teaching style in terms of the following instructional characteristics, videotape yourself, or ask a colleague to observe and rate you. You should not expect to conform to the stereotypical teaching style of your gender because these are only generalizations that do not apply to all female or male educators.

*Male Teaching Style*

- Direct with students
- Subject-centered
- Lectures a lot
- Has students discuss things strictly among themselves
- Less likely to praise students for answering correctly
- More likely to criticize wrong answers
- Offers explanations designed to help students correct their responses
- Gives students multiple chances to respond correctly
- Less sensitive to students' needs and feelings

- Positively reinforces young boys for stereotypical male behaviors
- Often reprimands students for misbehaving
- Publicly and harshly reprimands students for misbehaving
- Allows students to form their own groups

*Female Teaching Style*

- Indirect with students
- Student-centered
- Frequently asks questions
- Gets involved with students in classroom discussions
- Praises students for answering correctly
- Less likely to give students feedback when their answers are wrong
- Less likely to criticize wrong answers
- Sensitive to students' needs and feelings
- Negatively reinforces young boys for stereotypical male behaviors
- Seldom reprimands students for misbehaving
- Reprimands students privately and softly for misbehaving
- Assigns students to specific groups

begin by determining their students' individual learning styles. Learning styles can be evaluated informally. The lists of gender differences in learning and teaching styles included in chapter 1 and in this chapter can serve as checklists. Published learning and teaching style inventories are also available (62–67).

The Ramirez and Castenada Behavior Rating Scale is an example of these inventories (66). It is designed to evaluate students' preferred learning styles (whether they are field-sensitive or field-independent learners) as well as educators' teaching styles (whether they employ field-sensitive or field-independent teaching techniques). This instrument may be especially appropriate because many of the characteristics it assesses are those on which the genders differ. Many, but certainly not all females, especially African Americans and Hispanic Americans who conform to the learning styles that typify females in their cultures, tend to prefer a field-sensitive learning style (66–79). European American males, in comparison, are more field independent. The following are some of the characteristics of each type of teaching style.

### Field Independent Teachers

- Maintain formal relationships with students.
- Assume the role of the authority figure.
- Stress instructional over interpersonal objectives. Emphasize individual effort.
- Teach mathematics and science abstractly.
- Focus on facts and principles.
- Foster competition between students.
- Stress independent student functioning.

### Field-Sensitive Teachers

- Demonstrate approval and warmth toward students.
- Use personalized rewards.
- Are sensitive to students in need of help.
- Stress cooperation and group work.
- Humanize the curriculum.
- Assist students in using concepts to label their personal feelings.
- Encourage learning through modeling.
- Help students to see how concepts being learned are related to their personal experiences.

By using both the teaching and learning style sections of this instrument, teachers can determine whether their teaching style matches a particular student's learning style and so accommodate their teaching to his or her needs. The following box includes examples of items in the students' and teachers' versions.

## Single-Sex Instruction

Many educators believe that single-sex education has been shown to be a preferable alternative to mixed-sex education. They claim that single-sex

---

### The Ramirez and Castenada Behavior Rating Scale

| Field-Sensitive<br>(typically female) | Field-Independent<br>(typically male) |
|---|---|
| **Student** ||
| Likes to work with others to achieve a common goal | Prefers to work independently |
| Seeks guidance and demonstration from teacher | Likes to try new tasks without teacher's help |
| Is sensitive to feelings and opinions of others | Is task oriented; is inattentive to social environments when working |
| **Teacher** ||
| Encourages cooperation and development of group feeling; encourages class to think and work as a unit | Encourages competition between individual students |
| Humanizes curriculum; attributes human characteristics to concepts and principles | Relies on graphs, charts, and formulas |
| Is sensitive to children who are having difficulty and need help | Encourages independent student achievement; emphasizes the importance of individual effort |

---

education can provide female students with instructional approaches that suit their learning styles as well as a school environment that encourages them to participate in courses and activities usually considered to be in the male domain, as well as protect them from being dominated by males. Considerable evidence about the beneficial effects of single-sex courses and single-sex schools for females supports their position (80–92, 94–96, 98–106, 108–132).

Single-sex courses such as "math for girls/women" have been offered during the regular school day, after school, and during the summer in coeducational settings without running afoul of Title IX (88, 91, 95, 124, 128). Females perform well in such courses, and once they have succeeded in them, they are more likely to continue their studies of mathematics in regular classes during the regular academic school year (88, 95, 124, 126).

Single-sex elementary schools, high schools, and colleges are virtually complete single-sex environments (except for some male instructors that may be on their faculties). Beginning in the 1960s, the number of single-sex public elementary and secondary schools in the United States declined dramatically. However, many sectarian schools in the United States and many schools in Great Britain and Australia continue to offer students single-sex educational experiences.

The results of single-sex instruction in these schools are not completely consistent. A few studies have found that females do not fare better in single-sex schools (93, 97, 105). Most studies, however, have found that females enjoy many advantages in single-sex schools at all scholastic levels. Females attending single-sex elementary and high schools have more positive attitudes about academics, more self-confidence in their ability to do well in traditionally male domain courses, choose to enroll in more courses such as mathematics and science, and have higher academic aspirations. They spend more time on homework and achieve at higher academic levels, especially in courses traditionally perceived as being in the male domain. They have less stereotypical views about women's sex roles. They are less fearful of success and less anxious about competition. They believe they have more control over their lives, and they have better self-concepts (86, 94, 96, 98, 99, 104, 108, 117, 120, 125, 130, 132). (The research reported above on the benefits female students derive from participating in single-sex cooperative groups is further evidence of the benefits of single-sex education.)

Female students also experience significant gains in women's colleges (82, 114, 127). Female students at women's colleges are less likely to leave school before completing their degrees. They have more confidence in their intellectual ability and are more involved with the faculty and more assertive in class. They participate more in such traditionally male majors as mathematics and science and experience higher academic and professional achievement.

Results like these have led many educators to emphasize the advantages of single sex-education for females in comparison to mixed-sex education at all school levels. The following quotations are examples of their opinions.

*Mixed sex groupings constitute a disaster area for girls. (105, p. 7)*

*The recent shift toward coeducation may be disadvantageous for women, particularly for those with strong intellectual orientations. (85, p. 208)*

In contrast, educators who do not favor single-sex schooling can cite the following facts to bolster their position.

**1.** Some studies do not indicate academic advantages for single-sex education at the elementary and secondary levels (93, 97, 107).

**2.** There is evidence that an undetermined amount of the improved academic functioning in single-sex schools may actually be due to the fact that they tend to attract better prepared and better motivated students, better qualified faculty, and more resources, rather than to the fact that they are single-sex institutions (92, 107, 108).

**3.** There is also some evidence, although it is far from conclusive, that students at coeducational schools are happier, more social, and more satisfied with their peers and teachers (93, 102, 122).

Arguments against single-sex instruction that have not been researched include the following.

**1.** Separation of the sexes deprives each sex of the point of view of the other.

**2.** Lack of contact between the sexes can lead to poor communication between the sexes and to heterosexual adjustment problems later on.

**3.** Lack of interaction with, and knowledge of, the other sex fosters sex-stereotyping.

**4.** Since education exists in a male-dominated society, separate and equal single-sex schools and facilities that serve females can become separate and unequal, as they did in the case of ethnically segregated schools.

## Math, Science, and Computer Programs for Females

A number of effective programs, such as TEAM (Teacher Education and Mathematics), Operation SMART, and EQUALS, have been developed to

---

**BOX 4–4   Self-Quiz**

*Single-Sex Instruction*

What is your opinion about single-sex education? Does Title IX prohibit teachers from using single-sex instruction? Have you had any personal experiences with single-sex instruction? If so, did you find it advantageous or disadvantageous? What do you think are the advantages and disadvantages of single-sex instruction for female elementary, middle, and secondary school, and college students? Which if any of the following single-sex situations would you find acceptable for yourself or others: single-sex groups in coeducational classes, single-sex classes, single-sex elementary schools, single-sex middle schools, single-sex secondary schools, and single-sex colleges. Explain your reasoning.

Boys like to take things apart to see how they work.

assist teachers to accommodate their instructional techniques to their female students' learning and behavioral styles (133–135, 137–140). These programs are designed to reduce students' anxiety, increase their self-confidence in their abilities, improve their attitudes about math, science, and computer courses, and accommodate instructional techniques to their learning styles.

Fennema and Meyer offer the following suggestions for overcoming female students' problems with math.

> *The goal of achieving equivalent outcomes in mathematics education for males and females may require that teachers actually should treat boys and girls somewhat differently. . . . Teachers might place more stress on cooperative mathematics activities and less stress on competitive mathematics activities. Teachers need to increase their interactions with girls on high cognitive level mathematics activities, to expect girls to be able to solve the mathematics problems and then to praise them for doing so. Further, when girls respond incorrectly in mathematics class, the teacher needs to encourage divergent and independent thinking in girls by giving them hints on the mathematics strategy they might use, rather than telling them the answer or strategy. Perhaps the most important thing that a teacher can do is to expect girls to work independently. (136, p. 155)*

Some females experience an additional problem that inhibits them from enrolling or excelling in mathematics and science courses. For example, while many African American females are more likely to enroll in math and science courses than African American males, some feel inhibited about doing so. They want to do as well as they can in school. However, they do not want to outperform males, who are less likely to even enroll in these courses. These females may need help to resolve their conflicts in ways that enable them to maintain good relationships with their male peers without impeding their educational progress.

## MALE STUDENTS

For many years, some educators have been claiming that many male students earn lower grades and get into more trouble than female students because schools, especially preschools and elementary schools, are designed for students with feminine behavior and learning styles (141–46). The following quotations represent the way this point of view has been expressed.

> *There is little doubt that the character of American education is feminine, either by design or as a comfortable acceptance unintentionally adopted by the teachers and administrators developing the structure of the program. Standards of conduct, restricted environments for learning, the majority members of the instructional staff, academic and social expectations, and the physical setting for the school are all substantially feminine, with little regard for the male culture presented within the societal structure outside of the schools. (141, p. 1)*

> *Masculine virtues are usually diametrically opposite to those viewed as desirable in the typical American elementary school. The boys of our society who are labeled "little men" are aggressive—not passive. They are active and in motion rather than still. They are independent more than they are obedient. They speak out rather than keep quiet. Many of them love conflict, struggle, and a good fight rather than perpetual peace. The female code under which they operate at school is one of making as much effort as possible in studies of what is known already—what is printed in books. The male code of young boys is making the least possible effort in "book studies." They are forever satisfying their need to know by observing, listening, exploring, tearing up, putting together, trying out, and in general "just messing around." (145, p. viii)*

> *The feminized school may make it difficult for boys to see school as an appropriate masculine activity. Most teachers find the active, aggressive,*

*restless behavior of boys more difficult to accept than the behavior of girls.
. . . Emphasis is frequently placed on such qualities as neatness, conformity, excelling, and being quiet—requirements that are generally easier for
girls to meet. Schools with their female-oriented value system and female
domination have established a reward system in which success depends on
conformity to feminine values and manifestations of maleness are met with
punishment and failure. (142, p. 34)*

Educators who believe schools are too feminine have offered a number
of suggestions for defeminizing schools and accommodating instructional
strategies to the needs of male students. These suggestions include instructing males in single-sex settings, same-sex teaching, de-emphasizing personal instruction by females, and matching students' learning and teachers'
teaching styles.

## Single-Sex Education

While the research cited earlier indicates that females profit more than males
from single-sex schools, these studies also reveal that males also gain from
attending all-male elementary and secondary schools (81, 100, 118, 147–57).
They do more homework, learn more, and have better attitudes toward their
teachers and school. They feel better about themselves and have higher
self-esteem. Boys who attend all-male schools are also less stereotypical in
the courses and careers they choose and have less stereotypical views about
sex-roles. There is evidence that students at all-male colleges experience
many of the same benefits as students in all-female colleges (110, 127).

Although there has been a sharp decrease in single-sex public schools, a
number of private organizations and school districts have initiated experimental single-sex classes, schools, and programs designed to serve the needs
of African American males (80, 81, 84, 87, 100, 101, 103, 115, 116, 118, 131).
Some of them only serve African American males. However, to comply with
Title IX, others are open to both male and female students but stress the
needs of males. Some meet after school or take place off-campus.

Because many of these programs have been implemented quite recently,
it will be a while before data about their long-term effectiveness will be
available. However, a few of them have yielded impressive short-term results, including improved attendance, more acceptable behavior, reduction
in suspensions and office referrals for disciplinary problems, enhanced self-esteem, and significant gains in academic achievement measured by standardized tests and class grades (81, 100, 118).

The disadvantages that some educators attribute to single-sex educational programs for females might also apply to these African American all
male programs. Other concerns about these programs have been raised by

individuals and organizations such as the National Association for the Advancement of Colored People (NAACP) and the National Urban League (81, 111, 112). They include the following:

1. These programs may not provide the education students need to succeed in a pluralistic society.
2. They may set back the cause of desegregation.
3. They may perpetuate the myth that African American females succeed at the expense of males.
4. They may deny females access to the Afro-centered educational experiences they require.

The National Association for the Advancement of Colored People expressed the following concerns about the establishment of all-male programs for African American students: "It would legitimate the very mechanism that was used so effectively to hinder and disadvantage generations of African Americans" (111, p. 2). To date, no evidence exists regarding whether or not these supposed disadvantages actually occur in these programs.

## Same-Sex Teaching

As with female students, some individuals suggest that boys need male role models, especially in elementary school. They believe that the more boys are exposed to male teachers, the less likely they are to be feminized in school, to associate language arts and other subjects with being feminine, and to be taught in teaching styles that do not match their learning styles (141, 144, 157). Many African American educators believe African American males are especially in need of male role models and tutors in elementary schools (81). Educators who favor increasing the number of male role models suggest hiring more male teachers in elementary school and bringing more males into the school as mentors, guest speakers, and tutors.

In the 1960s and 1970s, researchers conducted a number of studies to determine whether male elementary school students learn more when taught by male or female teachers. Most, but not all, of these studies indicate that boys do not learn more in classes taught by males. However, they prefer male teachers, have better work habits, have lower absenteeism rates, have higher self-esteem, and have better attitudes toward their teachers and school, and respond better to encouragement to achieve when they are instructed by males (148–54, 156–63). Since most of these studies were done quite some time ago and concerned primarily European American males, and many individuals continue to recommend that elementary schools hire more male teachers, it would be important to return to the question once again and study the effects of same sex-teaching on both European American and non-European American students.

There is very little evidence concerning the efficacy of introducing male tutors into elementary schools. Two programs specifically designed to provide African American male with role models and tutors are Helping Hands—designed by Wake County Public Schools, Raleigh, North Carolina, which hired African American teachers to mentor youngsters after school, and Project 2000, which recruited, trained, and placed adult African American males as tutors for males in predominantly African American schools, have reported considerable success. Their results include improvements in students' attitude toward school, attendance, behavior, academic performance, and suspension rates. (81, 155). The finding that African American male tutors have a positive effect on African American male students' school performance also underlines the need to study the efficacy of same-sex teaching, especially with African American males.

## De-emphasizing Personal Instruction by Females

Some educators recommend that until female teachers are replaced by males, they should emphasize independent study, group work, television teaching, and computerized instruction in order to reduce their contact with their male students. There is almost no research regarding the effectiveness of this approach. However, some evidence suggests that certain boys learn to read more efficiently when they use programmed instruction or computerized assisted instruction than when they are taught by female teachers (164–66). Also as noted earlier in this chapter, boys are less interested in attention and feedback from teachers than girls.

## Matching Learning and Teaching Styles

Educators who believe teachers should accommodate their teaching styles to male students' learning styles offer the following suggestions for accomplishing this (144, 167, 168).

**1.** Encourage and plan for movement, free exploration, and the satisfaction of students' curiosity as long as it does not interfere with the rights of others.

> *Boys like motion, locomotion, action. Irrepressibly restless, they need learning tasks that are linked to their natural activities and interests. Manly learning calls for mastery—of self and the environment—and for the expression of outgoing and assertive impulses. It will be active rather than*

*passive and it will generate self-control rather than relying solely on the external controls that often subvert real learning. . . . Too much forced listening is passive and unmanly. . . . In small groups more children can talk, and classwork can be planned to permit more doing, participating, and independent study. (144, pp. 172, 176–77)*

**2.** Since many boys learn more effectively in competitive situations, emphasize competition to facilitate their achievement.

**3.** In the early grades, decrease the amount of reading material that contains themes that appeal primarily to females.

**4.** As much as possible, replace traditional textbooks with articles, books, and other materials that are more suitable for boys.

**5.** Establish learning laboratories made up of centers of interest that include activities and materials designed to appeal to the special interests of each sex.

**6.** Since males' fine motor coordination develops later than females, de-emphasize penmanship and handwriting with boys in the early grades.

**7.** Assign tasks that students can do on their own to boys who are field-independent learners.

The effectiveness of these techniques has not been studied. In the absence of research data, teachers must decide whether to accommodate their instructional techniques to gender differences in learning styles without the guidance of scientific information.

## Language Arts Programs for Males

The following are suggestions for accommodating instructional techniques for teaching language arts skills to males (141, 144, 169–72).

**1.** Do not pressure young students, especially working-class and African American students, who have different speech patterns to adapt the standard English used in school. To compel them to do so can attack their self-concept and cause them to become less communicative if they become concerned that their way of expressing themselves is incorrect. Instead, accept the students' language and allow them to gradually pattern their oral school language on the language they hear at school. The authors agree with the advice given by Austin, Clark, and Fichett some time ago:

*Language is an expression of personality, and the acceptance of this form of expression will greatly assist in paving the way to understanding between teacher and child . . . In many instances the language of the home or of the neighborhood is rough and frequently shocking to the middle-class teacher. It is, however, the common, out-of-school language. Teachers will need to accept this form of language until the child realizes that such speech patterns and vocabulary are not the generally used language of the school. (141, pp. 49, 52)*

**2.** Use a language experience approach to reading in the early grades with boys because boys' language and reading interests are somewhat different than the language and themes included in many basal readers.

---

### BOX 4–5   Self-Quiz

*Accommodating to Gender Differences*

State whether you would or would not be comfortable using the following techniques in your classroom for accommodating to the prevailing gender differences.

**Both Genders**

- Utilize same-sex teaching.
- Utilize single-sex instruction.

**Female Students**

- Stress cooperative learning techniques.
- Utilize field-sensitive teaching styles, including the following:
  - demonstrating approval and warmth toward students
  - using personalized rewards
  - humanizing the curriculum
  - assisting students to label their feelings
  - encouraging learning through modeling
  - relating what is to be learned to students' personal experiences

**Male Students**

- Invite male role models to participate in class activities as tutors, guest lecturers, and so on, especially at the elementary school level.
- Emphasize independent study, computer, television, and group work rather than personal instruction by female teachers.
- Stress competition.
- Employ reading material with male themes.
- Emphasize the physical sciences rather than the biological sciences.
- Utilize activity centers that encourage freedom of movement and free exploration.
- Delay or de-emphasize penmanship, handwriting, and other skills that require fine motor coordination in the early grades.
- Stress field-independent teaching techniques.

3. Teach boys language arts skills in courses they like, such as trades and sports, as part of these subjects rather than in separate reading and writing classes that they view as feminine.

4. Use male role models to strengthen males' image of reading as something manly to counteract the notion that reading is a feminine activity.

5. Reward males for participating in reading activities and provide them the additional instructional time they need to succeed.

6. Make learning to write more enjoyable for males by de-emphasizing parts of speech, proper usage, and punctuation.

7. De-emphasize penmanship and handwriting with young boys until their fine motor coordination develops sufficiently.

## DILEMMAS AND GUIDELINES

Accommodating to gender differences offers advantages and disadvantages. Accommodating to students' gender-related learning styles may produce the improvements in students' academic performances, self-concepts, and participation in nontraditional courses and careers described above. Allowing girls to act like girls (for example, to be passive and dependent and to avoid certain classes and activities) and boys to act like boys (to behave less politely and to be more active and aggressive in class) may also avoid some of the disagreements and conflicts that can occur between students and teachers when teachers try to change students' sex-stereotypical behavior and attitudes. In addition, accommodation may also avoid intrapsychic conflicts within students that can develop when they are encouraged or pressured to think, feel, and behave in one way by their teachers and an opposite way by their parents and communities.

However, accommodating to the prevailing gender stereotypes can have negative effects on students as well. Treating males and females the same may result in shortchanging the gender that requires a different approach. For example, cooperative learning groups can increase female students' learning and decrease male domination of mixed-groups. But if not employed in a well-planned manner, these approaches may result in further discouraging female students' independent behavior and lead them to act even more passively in the presence of males. Competitive, unstructured, independent learning environments may facilitate males' achievement, but they may be detrimental to female students.

Accommodating to gender stereotypes can also result in allowing, if not encouraging, females to feign helplessness in order to obtain assistance, be dominated in mixed-sex groups, and miss taking the classes that are required in order to participate in certain occupations or college courses later on. Accommodation can also encourage males to do less well in language arts and foreign languages and be assertive, aggressive, and competitive.

---

### BOX 4–6  Self-Quiz

*Critical Incidents*

While teachers, students, and parents often agree about how problems should be handled, in some situations their views may be very different. When their views and those of their students or their students' parents clash, teachers may base their classroom management decisions on their personal opinions or they may set their own views aside and respect those of students and parents. The following three incidents are examples of such conflict. In each case, the contrasting views of the teacher and the student or parent are presented. First describe how you think the teacher involved should handle each of the following critical incidents. Then disregard the description of the teacher. Instead, put yourself in the teacher's place, imagine what your point of view would be, and state how you would deal with the problem.

**1.** A parent who is representing the parents of all six of the Chinese American students in a class asks the teacher not to require their children to express their opinions in class because they are in school to learn what the teacher knows, not to discuss their personal views about things of which they have little knowledge. The teacher understands and appreciates the cultural reasons for the parent's request but also believes

students should be participants in the learning process, not merely banks into which teachers deposit information.

**2.** One of a teacher's best math students, an eighth grade Hispanic American female, informs the teacher that she is not going to enroll in algebra the following year because she is not planning to go to college. When the teacher asks why, she replies that college is for boys. She says her plans are to finish high school, work at a job for a while, get married, and then stay home. The teacher feels that college is appropriate for females as it is for males.

**3.** A ninth grade student in a predominantly working-class neighborhood school complains that his teacher is too tough on him. He accuses the teacher of being insensitive to the students in the class because the teacher gives them too much homework. And he maintains that he should not be marked down every time he does not complete an assignment because he has to work after school to earn money for his family. The teacher realizes that the student is telling the truth but also feels that teachers in urban schools should expect as much from their students as teachers in more affluent schools do. In the teacher's opinion, to expect less of students is to condemn them to life as second-class citizens.

---

Since many techniques that at first sight appear to offer great advantages may also involve potential disadvantages, especially if not implemented correctly, educators should consider the possible positive and negative effects of accommodating to a particular gender difference. They should weigh and balance the anticipated positive and negative results of each course of action. And whatever actions they choose, they should develop a plan for their effective application and attempt to minimize the likelihood of negative results.

## SUMMARY

Many educators believe that students learn more, behave better, and develop better attitudes toward their teachers and school when teachers accommodate their approaches to the different needs of the two genders. They claim that some approaches such as matching teaching and learning styles, single-sex instruction, and same-sex instruction are appropriate for both genders. They feel cooperative learning and field-sensitive teaching techniques are especially appropriate for females. Approaches they recommend for males include defeminizing schools, introducing more male tutors into elementary school classrooms, emphasizing active learning, and stressing field-independent teaching techniques.

Research indicates that some of these suggestions have merit; most remain untested. Title IX may make the implementation of certain recommended approaches illegal or at least difficult. Because accommodating to gender stereotypes can have negative as well as positive results, educators should consider both possibilities before choosing a course of action.

## ACTIVITIES

1. Use the list of male and female teaching style characteristics to rate the teaching styles of a few of your professors. Compare the results for male and female professors to determine whether your results are similar to the differences between the genders reported by researchers. If you are a practicing teacher, ask some colleagues to rate themselves on the items and compare the results for males and females.

2. Divide the courses you have taken in the past few years into two groups: those you were satisfied with and those with which you were dissatisfied. Then divide the courses into two other groups: those that stressed cooperative learning and those that stressed competitive learning. Do you prefer one type of learning environment over the other? If so, does your preference fit the gender stereotypes reported in this chapter?

3. Ask your colleagues or peers who attended single-sex schools or classes to describe their experiences to you.

4. Ask a few of your colleagues or fellow students to respond to the three critical incidents described in this chapter. Examine their responses for areas of agreement and disagreement. Also look for possible gender differences in their responses.

# REFERENCES

Gender and ethnic differences in reactions to competition and cooperation are discussed in the following references.

1. Bryant, B., and Meadow, A. 1976. School-related problems of Mexican-American adolescents. *Journal of School Psychology* 14 (2): 139–50.
2. Chalesworth, W. R., and LaFrenier, P. 1983. Dominance, friendship utilization and resource utilization in preschool children's groups. *Ethology and Sociobiology* 4: 175–86.
3. DeVoe, M. W. 1977. Cooperation as a function of self-concept, sex and race. *Educational Research Quarterly* 2 (2): 3–8.
4. DeVries, D. K., and Edwards, K. J. 1974. Student teams and learning games: Their effects on cross-race and cross-sex interaction. *Journal of Educational Psychology* 66 (5): 741–49.
5. DeVries, D. K., Edwards, K. J., and Slavin, R. 1978. Biracial learning teams and race relations in the classroom: Four field experiences using Teams-Games-Tournament. *Journal of Educational Psychology* 70: 356–62.
6. Fennema, E. H., and Peterson, P. L. 1985. "Autonomous learning behavior: A possible explanation of gender-related differences in mathematics." In *Gender Influences in Classroom Interaction*, edited by L. C. Wilkinson and C. B. Marrett. New York: Academic Press.
7. Johnson, R. T., and Johnson, D. W. 1981. Effects of cooperative and individualistic learning experiences on interethnic interaction. *Journal of Educational Psychology* 73: 444–49.
8. Johnson, R. T., Johnson, D. W., Scott, L. E., and Ramolae, B. A. 1985. Effects of single-sex and mixed-sex cooperative interaction on science achievement and attitudes and cross-handicap and cross-sex relationships. *Journal of Research in Science Teaching* 22 (3): 207–20.
9. Kagan, S. 1980. "Cooperation-competition, culture, and structural bias in classrooms." In *Cooperation in Education*, edited by S. Sharan, P. Hare, C. D. Webb, and R. Hertz-Lazarowitz. Provo, UT: Brigham Young University Press.
10. Kagan, S. 1986. "Cooperative learning and sociocultural factors in schooling." In *Beyond Language: Social and Cultural Factors in Schooling Language Minority Students: Evaluation, Dissemination, and Assessment*. Los Angeles: California State University.
11. Kagan, S., Zahn, G., Widaman, K., Schwarzwald, J., and Tyrrell, G. 1985. Classroom structural bias impact of cooperative and competitive classroom structure on cooperative and competitive individuals and groups. In *Learning to Cooperate, Cooperating to Learn*, edited by R. Slavin, S. Sharan, S. Kagan, R. Hertz-Lazarowitz, C. Webb, and R. Schmuck. New York: Plenum Press.
12. Kinney, J. H. 1989. *A Study of the Effects of a Cooperative Learning Program on the Achievement of Ninth Grade Multi-Cultural Biology Classes.* ERIC ED 309 096.
13. Knight, G. P. 1979. "Cooperative-Competitive Social Orientation and the School Achievement of Anglo-American and Mexican-American Children." Paper presented at the annual meeting of the Western Psychological Association, San Diego.

14. Lockheed, M. E. 1977. Cognitive style effects on sex status in student work groups. *Journal of Educational Psychology* 69: 158–65.

15. Lockheed, M. E., and Harris, A. M. 1984. Cross-sex collaborative learning in elementary classrooms. *American Educational Research Journal* 21 (2): 275–94.

16. Lockheed, M. E., Harris, A. M., and Nemceff, W. P. 1983. Sex and social influence: Does sex function as a status characteristic in mixed-sex groups of children? *Journal of Educational Psychology* 75: 877–88.

17. Lucker, G. W., Rosenfield, D., Sikes, J., and Aronson, E. 1976. Performance in the interdependent classroom: A field study. *American Educational Research Journal* 13: 115–23.

18. Masden, M. C., and Shapira, A. 1970. Cooperative and competitive behavior of urban Afro-American, Anglo-American, Mexican-American, and Mexican village children. *Developmental Psychology* 3: 16–20.

19. Peterson, P., and Fennema, E. 1985. Effective teaching, student engagement in classroom activities, and sex-related differences in learning mathematics. *American Educational Research Journal* 22 (3): 309–34.

20. Piel, J. A., and Conwell, C. R. 1989. *Differences in Perceptions between Afro-American and Anglo-American Males and Females in Cooperative Learning Groups.* ERIC ED 307 348.

21. Powlishta, K. 1987. "The Social Context of Cross-Sex Interactions." Paper presented at the biennial meetings of the Society for Research in Child Development, Baltimore.

22. Schniedewind, N. 1983. "Feminist values: Guidelines for teaching methodology in women's studies." In *Learning Our Way: Essays in Feminist Education,* edited by C. Bunch and S. Pollack. Trumanburg, NY: Crossing Press.

23. Sharan, S. ed. 1990. *Cooperative Learning: Theory and Research.* New York: Praeger.

24. Sharan, S., and Shaulov, A. 1990. Cooperative learning, motivation to learn, and academic achievement. In *Cooperative Learning: Theory and Research,* edited by S. Sharan. New York: Praeger.

25. Siann, G., and Macleod, H. 1986. Computers and children of primary school age: Issues and questions. *British Journal of Educational Technology* 17: 133–44.

26. Skarin, K., and Moely, B. E. 1974. *Sex Differences in Competition-Cooperation Behavior of Eight-Year Old Children.* ERIC ED 096 015.

27. Slavin, R. E. 1977. *Student Learning Team Techniques: Narrowing the Achievement Gap between the Races.* Baltimore: Center for Social Organization of Schools, Johns Hopkins University, Report No. 228.

28. Slavin, R. E. 1983. *Cooperative Learning.* New York: Longman.

29. Slavin, R. E., and Oickle, E. 1981. Effects of cooperative learning teams on student achievement and race relations: Treatment by race interactions. *Sociology of Education* 54: 174–80.

30. Underwood, G., McCaffrey, M., and Underwood, J. 1990. Gender differences in a cooperative computer-based language task. *Educational Research* 32 (1): 44–49.

31. Webb, N. 1984. Microcomputer learning in small groups: Cognitive requirements and group pro-

cesses. *Journal of Educational Psychology* 76 (6): 1076–88.

32. Webb, N. M., and Kenderski, C. M. 1985. "Gender differences in small-group interaction and achievement in high- and low-achieving classes." In *Gender Influences in Classroom Interaction*, edited by L. C. Wilkinson and C. B. Marrett. New York: Academic Press.

33. Wilkinson, L. C., Lindow, J., and Chiang, C. P. 1985. "Sex differences and sex segregation in students' small-group communication." In *Gender Influences in Classroom Interaction*, edited by L. C. Wilkinson and C. B. Marrett. New York: Academic Press.

Various cooperative learning programs and the effects of cooperative learning are discussed in the following references.

34. Aronson, E., Blaney, N., Sikes, J., and Snapp, M. 1978. *The Jigsaw Classroom.* Beverly Hills, CA: Sage.

35. Asher, C. 1986. *Cooperative Learning in the Urban Classroom.* ERIC Digest, 30.

36. DeVries, D., and Slavin, R. E. 1978. Teams-Games-Tournaments: A research review. *Journal of Research and Development in Education* 12: 28–38.

37. Humphreys, B., Johson, R. T., and Johnson, D. W. 1982. Effects of cooperative, competitive and individualistic learning on students' achievement in science class. *Journal of Research in Science Teaching* 19 (5): 351–56.

38. Johnson, D. W., Johnson, R. T., Holubec, E. J., and Roy, P. 1984. *Circles of Learning.* Alexandria, VA: Association for Supervision and Curriculum Development.

39. Johnson, D. W., Maruyama, G., Johnson, R., Nelson, D., and Skon, L. 1981. Effects of cooperative, competitive, and individualistic goal structures on achievement: A meta analysis. *Psychological Bulletin* 89: 47–62.

40. Kahle, J. B., and Lakes, M. K. 1983. The myth of equality in science classrooms. *Journal of Research in Science Teaching* 20: 131–40.

41. Lazarowitz, R., and Karesenty, G. 1990. Cooperative learning and students' academic achievement, process skills, learning environment, and self-esteem in tenth-grade biology classrooms. In *Cooperative Learning: Theory and Research,* edited by S. Sharan. New York: Praeger.

42. Moody, J. D., and Gifford, V. D. 1990. *The Effect of Grouping by Formal Reasoning Ability, Formal Reasoning Ability Levels, Group Size, and Gender on Achievement in Laboratory Chemistry.* ERIC ED 326 443.

43. Sharan, S. 1980. Cooperative learning in small groups: Recent methods and effects on achievement, attitudes, and ethnic relations. *Review of Educational Research* 50: 241–71.

44. Sharan, S., and Hertz-Lazarowitz, R. 1980. A group-investigation method of cooperative learning in the classroom. In *Cooperation in Education,* edited by S. Sharan, P. Hare, C. D. Webb, and R. Hertz-Lazarowitz. Provo, UT: Brigham Young University.

45. Sharan, S., Kussell P., Hertz-Lazarowitz, R., Bejarano, Y., Raviv, S., and Sharan, Y. 1984. *Cooperative Learning in the Classroom: Research in Desegregated Schools.* Hillsdale, NJ: Erlbaum Associates.

46. Slavin, R. E. 1980. Student team learning: A manual for teachers. In *Cooperation in Education,* edited by S. Sharan, P. Hare, C. D. Webb, and R. Hertz-Lazarowitz. Provo, UT: Brigham Young University.

47. Slavin, R. E. 1983. *Cooperative Learning.* New York: Longman.

48. Slavin, R. E. 1985. "Team assisted individualization: Combining cooperative learning and individualized instruction in mathematics." In *Learning to Cooperate, Cooperating to Learn,* edited by R. Slavin, S. Sharan, S. Kagan, R. Hertz-Lazarowitz, C. Webb, and R. Schmuck. New York: Plenum Press.

49. Tudge, J. 1986. *Collaboration, Conflict, and Cognitive Development: The Efficacy of Joint Problem Solving.* ERIC ED 274 424.

The following references are concerned with differences between male and female instructional and management styles and students' reactions to male and female teachers.

50. Allen, J. L., O'Mara, J., and Long, K. M. 1987. *The Effects of Communication Avoidance, Learning Styles and Gender upon Classroom Achievement.* ERIC ED 291 111.

51. Brophy, J. 1985. "Interaction of male and female students with male and female teachers." In *Gender Influences in Classroom Interaction,* edited by L. C. Wilkinson and C. B. Marrett. New York: Academic Press.

52. Etaugh, C., Collins, G., and Gerson, A. 1975. Reinforcement of sex-typed behaviors of two-year-old children in a nursery school setting. *Developmental Psychology* 11: 255.

53. Kajander, C. 1976. The effects of instructor and student sex on verbal behavior in college classrooms. *Dissertation Abstracts International* 37 (5-A): 2743–2744.

54. Karp, D., and Yoels, W. 1976. The college classroom: Some observations on the meanings of student participation. *Sociology and Social Research* 60: 421–39.

55. Lubeck, S. 1988. Nested Contexts. In *Class, Race, and Gender in American Education,* edited by L. Weis. Albany, NY: State University of New York Press.

56. McIntyre, L. L. 1988. Teacher gender: A predictor of special education referral? *Journal of Learning Disabilities* 21 (60): 382–83.

57. Pratt, D. L. 1985. Responsibility for student success/failure and observed verbal behavior among secondary science and mathematics teachers. *Journal of Research in Science Teaching* 22 (9): 807–16.

58. Richardson, L., Cook, J., and Macke, A. 1981. Classroom management strategies of male and female university professors. In *Issues in Sex, Gender, and Society,* edited by L. Richardson and V. Taylor. Lexington, MA: Heath.

59. Stake, J., and Katz, J. 1982. Teacher-pupil relationships in the elementary school classroom: Teacher-gender and pupil-gender differences. *American Educational Research Journal* 19: 465–71.

60. Simpson, A., and Erickson, M. 1983. Teachers' verbal and nonverbal communication patterns as a function of teacher race, student gender, and student race. *American Educational Research Journal* 20: 183–98.

61. Sternglanz, S., and Lyberger-Ficek, S. 1977. Sex differences in student-teacher interactions in the college classroom. *Sex Roles* 3: 345–52.

Instruments for evaluating students' learning styles are listed and discussed in the following references.

62. Dunn, R., and Dunn, K. 1978. *Teaching Students Through Their Individual Learning Styles: A Practical Approach.* Reston, VA: Reston Publishing Company.
63. Keefe, J. 1979. "Learning style: An overview." In *Student Learning Styles: Diagnosing and Prescribing Programs.* Reston, VA: National Association of Secondary School Principals.
64. McCarthy, B. 1980. *The 4 Mat System: Teaching to Learning Styles with Right/Left Mode Techniques.* Oak Brook, IL: Excel.
65. Perrin J. 1982. *Learning Style Inventory: Primary Version.* Jamaica, NY: St. John's University.
66. Ramirez, M., and Castaneda, A. 1974. *Cultural Democracy, Bicognitive Development and Education.* New York: Academic Press.
67. Renzulli, J., and Smith, L. 1978. *The Learning Style Inventory: A Measure of Student Preference for Instructional Techniques.* Mansfield Center, CT: Creative Learning Press.

These references discuss gender and ethnic differences in field sensitivity and field independency.

68. Buriel, R. 1975. Cognitive styles among three generations of Mexican-American children. *Journal of Cross-Cultural Psychology* 6 (4): 417–29.

69. Dixon, C. N. 1977. *Matching Reading Instruction to Cognitive Style for Mexican-American Children.* ERIC ED 158 269.
70. Gitter, A. G., Black, H., and Mostofsky, D. 1972. Race and sex in the perception of emotion. *Journal of Social Issues* 28: 63–78.
71. Hsi, V., and Lin, V. 1977. *A Summary of Selected Research on Cognitive and Perceptual Variables.* ERIC ED 145 003.
72. Kagan, S., and Zahn, L. C. 1975. Field dependence and the school achievement gap between Anglo-American and Mexican-American children. *Journal of Educational Psychology* 67 (5): 643–50.
73. Knight, G. P., Kagan, S., Nelson, W., and Gumbiner, J. 1978. Acculturation of second-and third generation Mexican-American children: Field independence, locus of control, self-esteem and school achievement. *Journal of Cross-Cultural Psychology* 9 (1): 87–97.
74. Perney, V. 1976. Effects of race and sex on field dependence-independence in children. *Perceptual Motor Skills* 42: 975–80.
75. Ramirez, M., Castaneda, A., and Herold, P. L. 1974. The relation of acculturation to cognitive style among Mexican Americans. *Journal of Cross-Cultural Psychology* 5 (4): 424–33.
76. Ramirez, M., and Price Williams, D. 1974. Cognitive styles of children of three ethnic groups in the United States. *Journal of Cross-Cultural Psychology* 55: 212–19.
77. Robbins, H. A. 1976. *"A Comparison Study of Cognitive Styles Across Educational Levels, Race and Sex."* Ph.D.

diss., East Texas State University, Commerce, TX.

78. Schratz, M. 1976. "A Developmental Investigation of Sex Differences in Perceptual Differentiation and Mathematic Reasoning in Two Ethnic Groups." Ph.D. diss., Fordham University, New York, NY.

79. Shade, B. J. 1979. *Racial Preference in Psychological Differentiation: An Alternative Explanation to Group Differences.* ERIC ED 179 672.

The following articles deal with single-sex educational experiences.

80. African American Male Task Force, Milwaukee Public Schools, 1990. *Educating African American Males: A Dream Deferred.* Milwaukee.

81. Ascher, C. 1991. *School Programs for African American Male Students.* Trends and Issues No. 15. New York, NY: ERIC Clearinghouse on Urban Education, Institute for Urban and Minority Education.

82. Astin, A. E. 1977. Four Critical Years: Effects of College on Beliefs, Attitudes, and Knowledge. San Francisco: Jossey-Bass.

83. Astin, A. E., and Panos, R. J. 1969. *The Educational and Vocational Development of College Students.* Washington, D.C.: American Council on Education.

84. Berger, J. 1991. New York Board backs school for minority men. *New York Times,* January 10, pp. A1, B7.

85. Block, J. H. 1984. *Sex Role Identity and Ego Development.* San Francisco: Jossey-Bass.

86. Bone, A. 1983. *Girls and Girls Only Schools: A Review of the Evidence.* Manchester, England: Equal Opportunities Commission.

87. Bradley, A. 1991. New York City Board backs new school geared toward black and Hispanic males. *Education Week,* January 15, p. 5.

88. Brody, L., and Fox, L. H. 1980. "An accelerative intervention program for mathematically gifted girls." In *Women and the Mathematical Mystique,* edited by L. H. Fox, L. Brody, and D. Tobin. Baltimore: Johns Hopkins University Press.

89. Conciatore, J., and Hughes, M. 1990. The race between education and catastrophe. *Black Issues in Higher Education* 7 (17): 6–7.

90. Detroit Public Schools. 1991. *Male Academy Implementation Document.* Detroit.

91. Downie, D., Slesnick, T., and Stenmark, J. K. 1981. *Math for Girls and Other Problem Solvers.* Berkeley: University of California.

92. Equal Opportunities Commission. 1981. *Education for Girls.* London: Equal Opportunities Commission.

93. Feather, N. T. 1974. Coeducation, values and satisfaction with school. *Journal of Educational Psychology* 66: 317–19.

94. Finn, J. 1980. Sex difference in educational outcomes: A cross national study. *Sex Roles* 6: 9–15.

95. Fox, L. H. 1976. "Sex differences in mathematical precocity: Bridging the gap." In *Intellectual Talent: Research and Development,* edited by D. P. Keating. Baltimore: Johns Hopkins University Press.

96. Harding, J. 1980. "Sex differences in performance in science examinations." In *Schooling for Women's Work,* edited by R. Deem. London: Routledge & Kegan Paul.

97. Harvey, T. J. 1985. Science in single-sex and mixed-sex groups. *Educational Research* 27 (3): 179–82.

98. Harvey, J. T., and Stables, A. 1984. Gender differences in subject preferences and perception of subject importance among third year secondary school pupils in single-sex and mixed comprehensive schools. *Educational Studies* 10: 243–53.

99. Harvey, J. T., and Stables, A. 1986. Gender differences in attitudes to science for third-year pupils: An argument for single-sex teaching groups in mixed schools. *Research in Science and Technological Education* 4 (2): 163–70.

100. Inroads/Wisconsin. 1990. *Investing in Our Nation—A Link to Economic Prosperity: The African American Male.* Milwaukee: Inroads Wisconsin Youth Leadership Academy.

101. Johnson, D. 1990. Milwaukee creating 2 schools just for black boys. *New York Times,* September 30, pp. A1, 26.

102. Jones, J. C., Shallcross, J., and Dennis, C. L. 1972. Coeducation and adolescent values. *Journal of Educational Psychology* 63: 334–41.

103. Lawton, M. 1990. Two schools aimed for black males set in Milwaukee. *Education Week,* October 10: pp. 1, 12.

104. Lee, V. R., and Bryk, A. S. 1986. Effects of single-sex secondary schools on student achievement and attitudes. *Journal of Educational Psychology* 78: 381–95.

105. Mahony, P. 1985. *Schools for Boys? Co-Education Reassessed.* London: Hutchinson.

106. Marland, M., ed. 1983. *Sex Differentiation and Schooling.* London: Heinemann.

107. Marsh, H. W. 1989. Effects of attending single-sex and coeducational high schools on achievement, attitudes, behaviors, and sex differences. *Journal of Educational Psychology* 81 (1): 70–85.

108. Marsh, H. W., Relich, J., and Smith, I. D. 1981. *Self-Concept: The New Validity of the Self Description Questionnaire.* ERIC ED 210 306.

109. Martini, R. 1982. *Sex Differences and Achievement, Research and Statistics.* RS 823/82. London: ILEA.

110. Mattfeld, J. 1980. "The Impact of the Feminist Movement on Women in Higher Education: Women's Colleges Versus Coeducational Institutions." Unpublished paper, University of California at Berkeley.

111. NAACP Legal Defense and Education Fund Inc. (1991). *Reflections on Proposals for Separate Schools for African American Male Pupils.* New York.

112. National Urban League Education Department. 1991. Schooling for African American Males? New York.

113. Newby, R. G., and Scott, N. J. 1982. "Single-Sex Schooling and Sex-Role Socialization." Paper presented at the annual meeting of the American Educational Research Association, New York.

114. Oates, M. J., and Williamson, S. 1978. Women's colleges and achievement. *Signs* 3: 795–806.

115. Omolade, B. 1991. Give Ujamma a real chance. *New York Newsday,* February 21, pp. 60, 102.

116. Pike, C. L. 1990. "Fulton Academics and Athletics Magnet School, San Diego City Schools: An Effective Elementary School Model with Special Emphasis on the Pilot Project 'Improving the Achievement of African American

Males.' " Paper presented at the National Conference on Educating Black Children, Los Angeles.

117. Price, J., and Talbot, B. 1984. Girls and physical science at Ellis Guilford School. *School Science Review* 66 (234): 7–11.

118. Rasberry, W. 1989. Dade educator proved the case for male teachers in all boys classes. *Miami Times*, September 21.

119. Rennie, L. J., and Parker, L. H. 1987. Detecting and accounting for gender differences in mixed-sex and single-sex groupings in science lessons. *Educational Review* 39 (1): 65–73.

120. Riordan, C. 1985. Public and Catholic schooling: The effects of gender context policy. *American Journal of Education* 93 (4): 518–40.

121. Riordan, C. 1990. *Girls and Boys in School: Together or Separate?* New York: Teachers College Press.

122. Rowe, K. J. 1988. Single-sex and mixed-sex classes: The effects of class type on student achievement, confidence and participation in mathematics. *Australian Journal of Education* 32 (2): 180–202.

123. Schneider, F. W., and Coutts, L. M. 1982. High school environment: A comparison of coeducation and single-sex schools. *Journal of Educational Psychology* 74: 898–906.

124. Stage, E, K., Kreinberg, N., Eccles (Parsons), J. E., and Becker, J. R. 1985. Increasing the participation and achievement of girls and women in mathematics, science, and engineering. In *Handbook for Achieving Sex Equity through Education,* edited by S. S. Klein. Baltimore: Johns Hopkins University Press.

125. Steedman, J. 1984. *Examination Results in Mixed and Single-Sex Schools: Findings from the National Child Development Study.* Manchester, England: Equal Opportunities Commission.

126. Subotnik, R., and Strauss, S. 1990. "Gender Differences in Achievement and Classroom Participation: An Experiment Involving Advanced Placement Calculus Classes." Paper presented at the annual meeting of the American Educational Research Association, Boston.

127. Tidball, M. E., and Kistiakowsky, V. 1976. Baccalaureate origins of American scientists and scholars. *Science* 193: 646–52.

128. Tobias, S. 1978. *Overcoming Math Anxiety.* New York: Norton.

129. Trickett, E. J., Castro, J. J., Trickett, P. K., and Shaffner, P. 1982. The independent school experience: Aspects of the normative environments of single-sex and coed secondary schools. *Journal of Educational Research* 74: 374–81.

130. Willis, S., and Kenway, J. 1986. On overcoming sexism in schooling: To marginalize or mainstream. *Australian Journal of Education* 30 (2): 132–49.

131. Wright, W. J. (n.d.). *The At Risk Endangered Species: The Black Male Child.* Miami: Dade County Public Schools.

132. Young, D. J., and Fraser, B. J. 1990. Science achievement of girls in single-sex and co-educational schools. *Research in Science and Technological Education* 8 (1): 5–20.

These references discuss special mathematics, science, and computer programs for females.

133. Chapline, R., and Newman, C. 1984. *Teacher Education and Mathe-*

*matics (TEAM): A Course to Reduce Math Anxiety and Sex Role Stereotyping in Elementary Education.* New York: Women's Equity Act Program, Queens College of the University of New York.

134. Chapline, R., Newman, C., Denker, E., and Tittle, C. K. 1980. *Final Report: Teacher Education and Mathematics Project.* New York: Queens College of the City University of New York.

135. Cook, N., and Kersh, M. E. 1980. "Improving teachers' ability to visualize mathematics." In *Proceedings of the Fourth International Conference for the Psychology of Mathematics Education,* edited by R. Karplus. Berkeley: University of California.

136. Fennema, E., and Meyer, M. R. 1989. Gender, equity, and mathematics. In *Equity in Education,* edited by W. G. Secada. New York: Falmer Press.

137. Fraser, S. 1982. *SPACES: Solving Problems of Access to Careers in Engineering and Science.* Berkeley: University of California.

138. Girls Club of America. 1986. *Operation SMART: A Program to Encourage Every Girl in Science, Math, and Relevant Technology.* New York.

139. Kaseberg, A., Kreinberg, N., and Downie, D. 1980. *Use EQUALS to Promote the Participation of Women in Mathematics.* Berkeley: University of California.

140. Kreinberg, N. 1981. 1,000 teachers Later: Women, mathematics, and the components of change. *Public Affairs Report* 22 (4): 1–7.

*Males*

The following references discuss the position that schools are too feminine and staffed by too many female teachers.

141. Austin, D. E., Clark, V. B., and Fitchett, G. W. 1971. *Reading Rights for Boys: Sex Role in Language Experiences.* New York: Appleton-Century-Crofts.

142. Firester, L., and Firester, J. 1974. Wanted: A new deal for boys. *Elementary School Journal* 75 (1): 28–36.

143. Guttenberg, M., and Bray, H. 1976. *Undoing Sex Stereotypes: Research and Resources for Educators.* New York: McGraw-Hill.

144. Sexton, P. C. 1969. *The Feminized Male.* New York: Random House.

145. Van Allen, R. 1971. "Forward." In *Reading Rights for Boys: Sex Roles in Language Experience,* edited by D. Austin, V. Clark, and G. Fitchett. New York: Appleton-Century-Crofts.

146. Wardle, F. 1991. Are we shortchanging boys? *Child Care Information Exchange* 79: 48–51.

The advantages of same-sex teaching for males is the subject of the following references.

147. Asher, S. R., and Gottman, J. M. 1973. Sex of teacher and student reading achievement. *Journal of Educational Psychology* 65: 168–71.

148. Bennett, D. A. 1966. *A Comparison of the Achievement of Fifth Grade Pupils Having Male Teachers with Those Having Female Teachers.* Ph.D. diss., University of Colorado, Denver. University Microfilms No. 67-3940.

149. Clapp, R. C. 1967. "The Relationship of Teacher Sex to Fifth Grade Boys' Achievement Gains and Attitudes toward School." Ph.D.

diss., Stanford University, Stanford, CA. University Microfilms No. 67-17553.

150. Doolittle, W. 1968. "Teacher plays 'big daddy' successfully in Newark." *Education* 3: 9.

151. Farkas, G., Grobe, R. P., Sheenan, D., and Shuan, Y. 1990. Cultural resources and school success: Gender, ethnicity, and poverty groups within an urban school district. *American Sociological Review* 55: 127–42.

152. Forslund, M. A., and Hull, R. E. 1974. Teacher sex and achievement among elementary school pupils. *Education* 95: 87–89.

153. Halperin, M. S. 1977. Sex differences in children's responses to adult pressure for achievement. *Journal of Educational Psychology* 69 (2): 96–100.

154. Lahaderne, H. M., and Cohen, S. 1972. "Freedom and Fairness: A Comparison of Male and Female Teachers in Elementary Classrooms." Paper presented at the annual conference of the American Educational Research Association, Chicago.

155. Mitchell, Travis, E. 1990. Project 2000: Gateway to success for some Black males. *Black Issues in Higher Education* 7 (18): 49–50.

156. Scheiner, L. 1969. *A Pilot Study to Assess the Academic Progress of Disadvantaged First Graders Assigned to Class by Sex and Taught by a Teacher of the Same Sex.* ERIC ED 035 462.

157. Smith, D. F. 1971. "A Study of the Relationship of Teacher Sex to Fifth Grade Boys' Sex Role Preference, General Self-Concept, and Scholastic Achievement in Science and Mathematics." Ph.D. diss., University of Miami, Coral Gables, Florida. Microfilms No. 71-4312.

158. Shinedling, M. M., and Pedersen, D. M. 1971. Effects of sex of teacher and student on children's gain in quantitative and verbal performance. *Journal of Psychology* 76: 79–84.

159. Sweeny, H. D. 1969. "The Effect of the Male Elementary School Teacher on Children's Self-Concept." Ph.D. diss., University of Maryland, College Park. University Microfilms No. 70-16034.

160. Triplett, L. 1968. Elementary education—a man's world? *The Instructor* 78 (3): 50–52.

161. Vroegh, K. 1973. "The Relationship of Sex of Teacher and Father Presence-Absence to Academic Achievement." Ph.D. diss., Northwestern University, Evanston, IL. University Microfilms No. 73-10310.

162. Vroegh, K. 1976. Sex of teacher and academic achievement: A review of research. *Elementary School Journal* 76 (7): 389–405.

163. Willis, S., and Kenway, 1986. On overcoming sexism in schooling: To marginalize or mainstream. *Australian Journal of Education* 30: 132–49.

De-emphasizing the role of female teachers through programmed instruction and computer assisted instruction is discussed in the following references.

164. Hativa, N., and Shorer, D. 1989. Socioeconomic status, aptitude, and gender differences in CAI gains of arithmetic. *Journal of Educational Research* 83 (1): 11–21.

165. McNeil, J. D. 1964. Programmed instruction versus usual classroom procedures in teaching boys

to read. *American Educational Research Journal* 1: 113–19.

166. Walker, E., and Azumi, J. E. 1985. *The Impact of Computer Assisted Instruction on Mathematics Learning Gains of Elementary and Secondary Students.* ERIC ED 275 487.

The following references are concerned with matching teaching and learning styles.

167. Best, R. 1983. *We've All Got Scars: What Boys and Girls Learn in Elementary School.* Bloomington, IN: Indiana University Press.
168. Stanchfield, J. M. (undated). "Differences in Learning Patterns of Boys and Girls." Unpublished manuscript as cited in Austin, D. E., Clark, V. B., and Fitchett, G. W. 1971. *Reading Rights for Boys: Sex Role in Language Experiences.* New York: Appleton-Century-Crofts.

Special approaches to improve male students' language arts skills are the focus of the following references.

169. Dwyer, C. A. 1974. Influence of children's sex role standards on reading and arithmetic achievement. *Journal of Educational Psychology* 66: 811–16.
170. Leinhart, G., Seewald, A. M., and Engel, M. 1979. Learning what's taught: Sex Differences in instruction. *Journal of Educational Psychology* 71: 432–39.
171. Scott, K. P., Dwyer, C. A., and Lieb-Brilhart, B. 1985. Sex equity in reading and communication skills. In *Handbook for Achieving Sex Equity through Education,* edited by S. S. Klein. Baltimore: Johns Hopkins University Press.
172. Skolnick, J. Langbort, C., and Day, L. 1982. *How to Encourage Girls in Math and Science.* Englewood Cliffs, NJ: Prentice-Hall.

# ► 5

## Reducing Gender-Stereotypical Behavior

This chapter describes techniques teachers have been using to reduce students' gender-stereotypical behavior and the research findings regarding their effectiveness. The techniques include eliminating educators' stereotypical behavior; correcting students' stereotypical beliefs about gender roles, courses, and careers; expanding students' restricted gender-stereotypical learning styles; discouraging gender-stereotypical relations and communication patterns between the genders; and increasing cross-gender interactions.

### ELIMINATING EDUCATORS' STEREOTYPICAL PERCEPTIONS AND BEHAVIOR

As noted, many teachers foster gender-stereotypical behavior by modeling such behavior themselves, communicating stereotypical expectations to their students, and rewarding them for behaving in stereotypical ways. Thus, if you wish to eliminate your students' stereotypical behavior, first examine your own behavior for possible gender bias and correct any that you may discover (1, 2). As Lockheed and Klein suggest: "Teachers should monitor their own behavior to be sure that they praise or reward male and female students for engaging in the same activities and exhibiting the same characteristics, punish and reprimand students of both sexes in a similar

To gain self-insight, discuss relations between you and students with your colleagues.

manner, and communicate similar expectations and evaluations to both male and female students" (1, pp. 212–13).

Many of the previous exercises are designed to enhance awareness of your attitudes about gender-role differences and the ways, if any, you encourage gender differences in your classroom. Reading the material and completing the self-quizzes and activities in this chapter should provide you with additional insight. Remember, research indicates that educators can modify their gender and ethnic stereotypes (3–8).

Becoming aware of your own gender-stereotypical perceptions and behavior is a necessary first step in changing them. But self-insight alone is insufficient, especially since the very structure of society supports gender bias. Because behavioral change requires determined effort over time, you might consider working with another teacher on changing a few behaviors or attitudes each month, forming a support group with other colleagues, or asking your school to provide in-service training in gender equity.

In-service training has proven to be an effective way to reduce teachers' gender and ethnic stereotypes and prepare them to use nonsexist approaches in their classrooms (3–8). Programs such as GESA—Gender Expectations and Student Achievement have successfully reduced teachers' general gender stereotypes (4–6). In addition, programs designed to reduce gender bias among teachers in specific subject areas have also proven successful. For example, programs for elementary school teachers and secondary school science teachers have had both a direct effect on their attitudes and behavior and an indirect effect on the students they taught. Specifically, teachers developed less stereotypical attitudes, used more nonbiased materials, and called on females more frequently. Female students' attitudes about science became less stereotypical, they participated more and on a more equal basis in class, and they engaged in more active, less passive learning. (3, 7, 8).

## CORRECTING STUDENTS' STEREOTYPICAL BELIEFS ABOUT GENDER ROLES

The following are suggestions for modifying students' stereotypical attitudes about gender roles, courses, and careers.

***Reward students at as early an age as possible for playing with nontraditional materials and engaging in nontraditional activities***
Many educators advise teachers to use praise, teacher-attention, gold stars, food, and the like to reward preschool and primary grade students for

In-service training can be extremely valuable.

interacting with both sexes, playing with toys, and engaging in activities that are usually considered appropriate only for the opposite sex. They recommend starting early with students because they believe students are most malleable when they are young.

Research done in the 1970s indicates that rewarding very young children for behaving in nontraditional ways has been fairly effective in the short run with young girls, but relatively ineffective with young boys (10, 12, 15, 16). In addition, most of the changes in boys' behavior and a significant amount of the changes in girls' behavior quickly disappear, and the children revert to their original stereotypical ways as soon as teachers stop actively encouraging students to behave in nonsexist ways.

There are a number of explanations for why teachers' attempts to modify the sex-role behavior of young children are not very effective.

**1.** Short-term intervention may produce only short-term change even in girls. Long-term, continuous intervention may be necessary to achieve more lasting results.

**2.** Young children may receive more positive reinforcement for behaving in stereotypical ways *out of school* than they receive *in school* for nonstereotypical behavior.

**3.** Rewards alone may be insufficient. Efforts to modify young children's sex-role stereotypes need to be comprehensive to be effective.

**4.** Students are more likely to modify their gender stereotypes when they have acquired the cognitive skills necessary to think about and make rational decisions concerning gender roles. As will be seen below, attempts to modify the gender stereotypes of older students have been much more successful.

Why boys' stereotypical behavior is especially resistant to change is unclear. Two explanations appear particularly plausible.

**1.** Rewarding individuals for behaving in nonstereotypical ways may be an ineffective approach. Since boys reward each other for complying with gender stereotypical behavior and punish each other for behaving in ways that do not conform to these stereotypes (9, 11, 13, 14, 18 ), it may be necessary to change boys' peer culture values before it is possible to modify an individual's behavior. "Much evidence indicates that it would be extremely hard to alter boys' definition of masculinity by simply changing the nature of the school. This self-definition develops very early, largely through interactions in the home and with other children" (17, p. 72).

**2.** Teachers may be using the wrong rewards to motivate boys to change. Since most preschool and primary grade teachers are females and boys are less responsive to females, teachers may have to rely on impersonal, material rewards rather than interpersonal rewards to motivate them.

Whatever the explanation, during the 1970s attempts to modify very young students' stereotypical behavior by merely rewarding them for changing were not very effective. This does not mean that children's stereotypical views cannot be changed. As will be shown below, the opposite is the case. What it does mean is that educators should not employ rewards as their *only* strategy. Rewards should be used as one aspect of a more comprehensive approach that includes the other strategies discussed throughout this chapter.

When employing rewards as part of a comprehensive program, the following suggestions may make your rewards more effective.

**1.** Commit to a long range approach, one that involves the full academic year.

**2.** Model the behavior you want your students to adopt.

**3.** Give equal attention to modifying students' peer cultures and modifying individual student's attitudes and behavior.

**4.** Select a mix of reinforcers that are likely to be effective with both males and females. Stress interpersonal rewards with field-sensitive students and impersonal rewards with field-independent students.

**5.** If possible, convince your colleagues to continue your program with your students after they leave you, and to model nonsexist behavior themselves.

### Expose students to nonsexist roles

Some students, especially those who come from environments in which traditional views of sex-roles hold sway, may profit from being exposed to nonsexist points of view (19–29). Teachers can do this as part of their regular classroom activities by expressing their opinions about gender issues and organizing group discussions. They can include published materials, modules, and exercises that appear to have some ability to correct students stereotypical perceptions of male and female roles in their daily curriculum (21–23, 26, 29). It is also possible to offer women's studies courses for secondary school students or to encourage students to enroll in such courses if they are already being offered (30, 35). The effectiveness of these courses, however, has not been researched.

In addition to exposing students to nonsexist roles, it is helpful to show them how to behave in nonstereotypical ways and encourage them to practice such behavior. For example, assertiveness training techniques designed to help students decide to stand up for their rights, express their feelings,

Expose students to nonsexist nonstereotypical role models.

participate more fully in mixed-gender groups, and so on have made unassertive females more assertive (28).

### Expose students to nonsexist instructional and counseling materials

One of the most commonly used techniques for modifying students' gender-stereotypical perceptions and behavior is to replace instructional and counseling materials that portray males and females in a stereotypical fashion and with nonsexist materials. Although materials can be biased against either gender, they are commonly biased against females. Educators who wish to eliminate students' stereotypes should be especially alert to the following types of sex bias against females (38, 47, 56).

1. Invisibility in instructional materials—omitting women, especially minority women, altogether or underrepresenting them
2. Stereotyping in instructional material—presenting females in stereotypical roles at work and play, attributing stereotypical personality characteristics to them, assigning them traditional and stereotypical roles that imply that they have limited abilities and potential
3. Selectivity and imbalance—omitting the roles of women in history, their contributions to science, and so on, and presenting only a male perspective on such issues as family planning and abortion, subsidized child care, and equity in the work place

**4.** Superficiality in instructional materials—glossing over or ignoring such controversial or troublesome issues as single parent families, bias in employment and salaries, and the like that involve or are relevant to women

**5.** Isolation in instructional materials—setting women off in boxes away from the main body of the text, which remains biased and one-sided

**6.** Linguistic bias—using male terminology such as mankind and forefathers to represent humankind and always mentioning the male pronoun first, e.g., *him* or *her, he* and *she.*

Teachers have access to a considerable amount of published nonsexist instructional and counseling material suitable for classroom use at the elementary, middle, and high school levels. Lists of specific nonsexist materials and publishers of such material are also available (30–38). As a result, teachers can substitute nonsexist materials for much of the sexist materials currently in use.

It is important to avoid tokenism when incorporating these materials into the curriculum. As Scott and Schau advise: "Presenting just a few token females and males engaged in nontraditional activities will not influence pupils' sex role attitudes, knowledge, or behavior beyond the examples presented. Pupils need exposure to a sufficient quantity of sex equitable materials to allow them to incorporate nontraditional role behavior and attitudes into their cognitive schema" (36, pp. 225–26).

At present, not enough commercially prepared nonsexist materials exist for use in all courses and activities at all levels. As a result, you may not always be able to substitute published unbiased materials for biased ones. When unbiased materials are unavailable or you do not have the final say about textbooks and other materials, you can add teacher-prepared materials to your curriculum and correct the bias in the textbooks and other materials you are required to use. The following advice has considerable merit.

> *It is important to confront this bias rather than to ignore it. . . . Level with your students. . . . Acknowledge that texts are not always perfect. . . . Engage your students in a discussion about textbook omission and stereotyping . . . It is critical that you go beyond simply calling attention to omission, stereotyping, and other forms of bias. . . . It will be up to you to supply the information that has been omitted from or distorted in your classroom text. (47, pp. 87–88)*

Most, but not all, of the studies on the effectiveness of nonsexist materials have found that they have considerable effect on student attitudes, especially girls, in the short run (12, 39–59). Whether they have long-term effects and change students' behavior has not been adequately researched. In general, the authors agree with the following conclusions:

*(1) exposure to sexist materials may increase sex-typed attitudes, especially among young children. (2) exposure to sex-equitable materials and to same-sex characters results in decreased sex-typed attitudes in students from 3 to 22 years of age; (3) the effects of sex-equitable materials do not usually generalize to areas not specifically covered in the materials, especially for preschool and elementary-aged students, although there may be some generalization for older students, especially those who initially are more sex-typed; and (4) attitude change toward equity increases with increased exposure. . . . Thus, it is very clear that use of sex-equitable materials in schools helps students develop more flexible sex role attitudes, which allows them to make educational and career choices based on their own interests rather than on preconceived notions of what is "right" for a female or male. (36, p. 221)*

## MODIFYING STUDENTS' STEREOTYPICAL BELIEFS ABOUT COURSES AND CAREERS

Teachers have used a variety of approaches to encourage students to change their gender-stereotypical attitudes and behavior about courses and careers. Some of them have been quite helpful.

***Use Nonstereotypical Role Models for Guest Speakers, Tutors, and Mentors***
The severe shortage of female science and math teachers and male English and art teachers gives students little reason to question their gender-stereotypical notions. To counteract students' stereotypical points of view about these subjects, teachers can invite male guest speakers, tutors, and mentors to participate in courses that are traditionally seen as feminine, e.g., male artists and females to participate in courses seen as male, such as female physicians and scientists. It is very important to include African American and Hispanic American male and female role models because of their serious underrepresentation among school faculty (61, 63). The limited research about the effectiveness of this approach shows that exposing students to same-sex models improves girls' participation in math and boys' academic achievement in a variety of courses (60, 62, 64).

***Recruit Nontraditional Students into Courses that are Viewed in Stereotypical Ways***
As noted, there are numerous forces that dissuade many female students from enrolling in mathematics, computer, and science courses. Their parents often do not expect them to do well in these classes (see chapter 2). They have less confidence than boys in their mathematics, computer, and science

Encourage all students to enroll in computer courses.

ability (see chapter 1). They believe these courses are less valuable to them (74, 89) (see chapter 1). And they are anxious about taking such courses (66, 71, 81).

Teachers can do many things to counteract these forces. The following advice offered a number of years ago to teachers who want to encourage females to participate more fully in math programs is still relevant.

*Teachers of elementary mathematics (K-6) should be as concerned about their students' attitude toward mathematics as they are about achievement. Elementary school teachers should also make their students aware of the role of mathematics in careers, even if this is done only in a very general way. They should also work in a positive way to counter sex-role stereotypes which develop in young children and which identify mathematics and mathematics related topics as primarily male domains. Secondary school teachers of mathematics frequently will have to work with students who already have formed negative feelings about mathematics. These attitudes may be (1) that mathematics is not important, (2) that mathematics is unpleasant, (3) that mathematics is more appropriate for boys. . . . Teachers should identify students having one or more of these attitudes and work to create a more positive orientation toward mathematics on the part of the student. . . . It is also important that they stress the role of mathematics as a "critical filter" in the sense that a lack of mathematical preparation will eliminate many college and career choices. (65, p. 7)*

Special mathematics and science courses such as Math without Fear or Girls Into Science and Technology that are designed for female students who are anxious about enrolling in regular mathematics and science courses, lack confidence in their ability to do well in such courses, or believe these courses are not relevant to them have proven helpful to both female and male students (76, 90–92). Typically they begin by accommodating to students' anxieties, concerns, and learning styles, but by the end they change students' attitudes and prepare them to succeed in regular courses.

Enrichment programs designed to accommodate existing courses to the needs of female students, such as the Math Bridge Program, Southeastern Consortium for Minorities in Engineering (SECME), and the Computer Equity Training Project have also succeeded in increasing females' participation and achievement in mathematics, science, and computer courses (78, 86, 87). By introducing women role models as guest speakers, providing staff development training in equity to reduce gender bias, eliminating sexist materials, and highlighting the relevancy of mathematics for various careers, Math Bridge Program significantly increased females' participation in mathematics courses (87). The SECME was particularly effective in increasing African American females' educational aspirations and interest in science and engineering courses and careers. The Computer Equity Training Project raised the participation of females in computer courses by 144 percent (77, 78).

Changing the climate of the school so that it does not foster the idea that courses belong in the domain of a particular gender can also have a positive effect on the achievement of females (77, 78).

Programs that are offered outside the regular school have also proven effective. *Multiplying Options and Subtracting Biases* is a typical example of such programs. It is a comprehensive approach that involves students, teachers, counselors, and parents whose attitudes can affect students' perceptions of mathematics. Designed to improve female students' attitudes and self-confidence about mathematics and modify their parents', teachers', and counselors' beliefs about the relevancy of mathematics for females, the program includes four workshops built around videotapes prepared for the four target audiences. Results of these workshops have shown that it is effective with each of the four groups. It changes female students' attitudes about the usefulness of math, reduces their tendency to attribute their lack of success to lack of ability, and increases their enrollment in mathematics courses (72, 73).

Other effective programs such as SPACES (Solving Problems of Access to Careers in Engineering and Science), COMET (Career-Oriented Modules for Exploring Topics in Science), and Expanding Your Horizons in Math and Science, and Futures Unlimited: Expanding Choices in Nontraditional Careers have improved female students' basic skills in these areas and increased their knowledge of, and interest in, nontraditional courses and careers. (68, 73, 75, 79, 80, 84, 85).

After reviewing 136 precollege programs that had received funds in order to increase female and minority participation in science, mathematics, and engineering, Malcolm, et al. concluded that the programs typically achieve their objectives. They described exemplary programs as follows: "Successful intervention programs are those that have strong leadership, highly trained and highly committed teachers, parent support and involvement, clearly defined goals, adequate resources, follow-up, and evaluation. For the positive effects to be sustained, these programs must eventually be institutionalized, that is made part of the educational system" (79, p. viii).

Special programs are often unnecessary. A single teacher can often have a real impact on a student's attitudes and behavior (67, 86). This is especially true when teachers "provide active encouragement to females in the form of (1) exposure to role models, (2) sincere praise for high ability and high performance, and (3) explicit advice regarding the value of math and its potential utility for high-paying jobs" (86, p. 243).

Techniques that individual teachers have used successfully with female students in classrooms include the following (93–103):

1. Reducing memorization of procedures and rules in favor of understanding and problem-solving through estimations
2. Using manipulatives, visual aids, and small group and recreational activities
3. Emphasizing cooperation
4. Providing female role models
5. Using nonbiased materials designed to interest girls
6. Connecting the subjects to the real world
7. Having students speak the language of these subjects in class
8. Correcting students' stereotypical attitudes about their imagined inabilities
9. Using relaxation, assertiveness, and anxiety control training
10. Teaching students to think logically about math and science
11. Providing students the additional instruction time, help, and tutoring they need to dispel their anticipation of failure

Even though the forces that discourage females from enrolling in science, computer, and mathematics courses are powerful, educators who want females to enroll in nontraditional courses have much to be optimistic about. And regardless of how it is accomplished, through formal programs, informally through individual teacher's efforts, or through other means, females who believe courses such as math and science are not in the male domain and females who have confidence in their ability to do well in these courses do achieve more (82, 83, 88). Likewise, getting students to participate in computer courses and activities makes dramatic changes in their subsequent attitudes, interests, and enrollment patterns (69, 70).

### Encourage Students to Consider Nontraditional Careers and Occupations

Also encourage them to make a career choice based on their abilities, interests, and values. Inform them about their employment rights and current antidiscrimination laws. And help them understand the changing role of males and females in the family and work place.

Many teachers believe that students are not ready to discuss and explore career and vocational issues until they are in high school. However, evidence confirms that students do profit from dealing with such issues at a much earlier age. Sex-equitable programs and materials that can help change students' stereotypical attitudes about, and choices of, vocational courses are available for inclusion in the regular curriculum at both the elementary and secondary school levels (104, 106–110). Exposing students to role models engaged in nontraditional occupations and careers can change their stereotypical views (112). Actively recruiting students into nontraditional vocational courses during the regular school year and into special introductory summer courses has worked with some students (104, 196). Requiring students to take coeducational classes of vocationally oriented courses that have been traditionally viewed as in the domain of the opposite sex has heightened their interests in these nontraditional areas and proven to be another effective way of changing students' stereotypical beliefs (109). Providing even a single-day workshop can alter the career plans of many students (111).

These kinds of interventions may be more important for female students from working-class backgrounds than females from middle- and upper-class backgrounds and for Hispanic American and Vietnamese American females than for African American, European American, and Filipino American females. They are the ones who are more likely to be expected to fulfill traditional female vocational and career roles and whose career choices are the most stereotypical (113–16) (see chapter 1).

As noted in chapter 1, the type of counseling that is culturally appropriate for different groups of ethnically diverse females depends on their ethnic backgrounds. Southeast Asian American, African American, Hispanic

In recent years, students have become less stereotypical.

American, and European American students do not respond to the same kinds of counseling techniques. Since the studies cited above did not include significant numbers of minority students, it is unclear whether these interventions can be effective with students from non-European American backgrounds.

Those who wish to modify students' gender stereotypical career/occupational attitudes and choices can be optimistic. While many students' views of their future occupational roles still reflect society's stereotypes, over the years children's and especially adolescents' career aspirations and choices have become less stereotypical (105, 112). In fact, they appear to become less stereotypical with age. In addition, educators have developed a variety of techniques to achieve their goals. Research indicates that these techniques do modify students' stereotypical career and vocational beliefs and attitudes, at least those of the European American students with whom they have been used. However, because researchers typically have not studied the long-range effects of these techniques, more research is needed to establish that they also change students' career and vocational choices and their actual enrollment in career and vocational courses (108).

## EXPANDING STUDENTS' RESTRICTED GENDER-STEREOTYPICAL LEARNING STYLES

Educators have offered the following recommendations for modifying and expanding students' gender-stereotypical learning styles. Many of them are merely good instructional approaches that can benefit most students.

### Discourage Stereotypical Language Patterns

1. Encourage females to express themselves more directly and assertively and males to be more communicative about themselves and their feelings.

2. Reward students for breaking with stereotypical communication patterns.

**3.** Help students learn to identify linguistic bias in the materials they read, the programs they view on television, and the language they and others use (117, 120, 121, 124). And encourage them to use nonsexist language. For example, help them avoid using male-centered pronouns such as *he,* when the gender of a person or animal is unknown and masculine terms such as fisherman or policeman for all people who perform a particular activity or function (118, 119, 123).

**4.** Use published materials such as *Changing Words in a Changing World* and *Decisions about Language,* which are designed to make students aware of their gender-stereotypical language patterns and help them decide to modify their communication patterns (118, 119, 122).

### Improve Female Students' Self-Confidence
The following are techniques for increasing students' confidence in their capacity to achieve their goals.

**1.** Correct any stereotypical ideas female students have about their inability in the male domains by using techniques such as exposing them to nonsexist points of view and nonstereotypical role models in the form of guest speakers, tutors, and mentors.

**2.** Insure that students succeed by individualizing instructional techniques to their strengths and weaknesses, selecting work at their ability levels, and providing assistance as needed.

**3.** Counteract students' pessimistic self-perceptions by pointing out the strengths and skills they bring to each task and expressing confidence in their ability to succeed.

**4.** Use one of the many published structured self-concept enhancement programs that have proven to be effective (125–27, 131, 132).

Do not expect your efforts to produce immediate results. Research shows that teachers can improve students' self-confidence, but it takes time (125, 126, 128–31).

### Reduce Students' Tendency to Inaccurately Attribute their Poor Performance to Lack of Ability
Help students determine when the cause of their poor performance is lack of ability and when it is lack of effort or motivation by pointing out the reasons they have not done as well as they might and teaching them to examine for themselves the causes of their poor performance.

### Help Males to be More Cooperative and Concerned about Others
Although it is important to be able to function independently, people should be able to work cooperatively and to be concerned about the needs and feelings of others. You can foster students' cooperative spirit and sensitivity

to the needs of others in many ways (133–34). For example, it may be possible to increase some students' cooperative behavior merely by providing them with opportunities to accomplish more in cooperative groups than they could working independently. Other students, at least at the beginning, may require an extrinsic reward for behaving cooperatively and responding positively to others' needs. Very self-centered students may first have to learn to care about others before they can be responsive to their needs and to work cooperatively with them. A number of techniques are available for helping these hard-to-reach students (135–38).

***Encourage females to be competitive when necessary, function more independently in appropriate situations, and maintain their opinions and attitudes when they believe they are right and others are wrong***
Some female students purposely perform poorly in competitive situations when their performance will be compared to others, especially males. They may also find it difficult to maintain their own opinions and points of view when others disagree. This stems from the belief that some female students have that it is not feminine or polite to openly disagree with others or hold out against their opinions or wishes. These students may require a change in attitude before they can change their behavior. These techniques may be helpful.

**1.** Explain why such norms for female behavior are stereotypical and self-defeating.
**2.** Expose students to female models of more competitive, self-assertive behavior.
**3.** If you are a female, model the desirable behavior yourself.
**4.** Reinforce students when they behave in ways you believe are more appropriate or desirable.
**5.** Point out the positive results that occur from behaving more assertively and competitively as they occur.

## ELIMINATING STEREOTYPICAL RELATIONSHIPS

Educators have been using many different techniques to change the stereotypical ways students relate to the opposite gender and increase cross-gender interaction in elementary and middle schools. As will be seen below, their efforts have met with mixed results.

### Male Dominance of Mixed-Sex Groups

The following are techniques teachers can use to reduce male dominance of females who act passively in mixed-gender situations (139–45). However, they may not be equally appropriate for females from different ethnic backgrounds. As noted above, not all ethnic groups expect males to dominate mixed-gender groups. For example, African American, Filipino American, and American Indian females are not dominated by males as are females from other ethnic backgrounds. "Feminists who see themselves as victims of a male-dominated society cannot assume that Indian societies are male-dominated in the same way as their own nor that the system of rewards for being a wife and mother is the same in Indian society as it is in the dominant society" (139, abstract).

**1.** Teach students that all members of a group should have the opportunity to participate equally.

You can do this with young students by describing the rights and obligations of group members. With older students, involve them in guided discussions that elicit acceptable guidelines for how the groups should function from the students themselves.

**2.** Reward students for behaving in nonstereotypical ways.

This may include rewarding females for participating more actively and assertively and males for allowing females to participate more equally.

**3.** Use cooperative learning activities.

Female students profit from participating in cooperative group activities when teachers make a conscious effort to facilitate desirable change by assigning girls leadership roles or training them to be the group's experts at solving the problems the group confronts (142, 143).

As noted earlier in the introduction to part 2 and in chapter 4, merely involving students in mixed-sex unstructured cooperative learning situations or groups without adequate preparation is not enough to bring about a more egalitarian relationship between the sexes. The results in unprepared groups may be that boys ignore girls, contribute most of the ideas, do most of the talking, and are perceived by the group members as the leaders and contributors of the best ideas. In addition, overusing cooperative learning situations could cause girls to become even less independent in their thinking and could be detrimental to those boys who learn better in competitive situations.

## Cross-Gender Interaction

When given the chance to form their own groups, children as young as two or three will form same-gender groups. Until high school, the older they are, the more pronounced is this tendency (1, 18, 147–49, 153, 155, 156, 159–62).

Young children tend to form same-gender groups.


Educators have used many techniques to encourage students to form mixed-gender groups, including the following:

1. Labeling all play and learning activities as appropriate for both genders
2. Discussing the importance of cross-gender grouping and play with students
3. Reinforcing students when they engage in cross-gender play
4. Praising children's positive cross-gender communication
5. Using mixed-gender groupings when assigning students to seats, lines, teams, discussion groups, group projects, and so on
6. Intervening to reduce cross-gender exclusion, dominance, cruelty, or teasing (1, 16, 95, 146, 151, 152, 154, 156–59, 163)

Because ethnic and socioeconomic groups bring up children to relate to the opposite gender differently (see previous sections of the text), teachers should take these dissimilarities into account when attempting to increase cross-sex interaction. For example, many Hispanic American adolescents are not expected to be involved in certain cross-gender interactions that are quite acceptable to European American students. Religion can also be a factor because some religious groups strongly support single-sex education.

There is very little research on the effectiveness of these approaches. Assigning students to cross-gender cooperative learning groups and rewarding them for cross-gender interactions increases cross-gender interaction, helping behavior, and friendships in the short run (16, 146, 150, 152, 154). Using a combination of techniques has also brought about change (1,152, 154, 158). For example, a combination of techniques, including discussing the reasons why students avoided interacting with the opposite gender, pointing out how their stereotypical behavior limits their options, suggesting ways they can interact more, and rewarding them for doing so made fourth graders feel more at ease in cross-gender interactions and led to less cross-gender teasing (154). A similar combination of techniques increased students' voluntary cross-gender interaction

---

### BOX 5–1    Self-Quiz

*Critical Incidents*

First describe how you think the teacher involved should handle each of the following critical incidents. Then disregard the description of the teacher. Instead, put yourself in the teacher's place, imagine what your point of view would be, and state how you would deal with the problem.

1. The father of a Hispanic American preschool student comes to school irate because his son told him that the teacher encouraged him to play in the housekeeping/doll house area. He tells the teacher he does not want his son to play with "girl things." The teacher believes that doll and housekeeping play are important for all children because they foster caring and nurturing qualities in children.

2. A group of second grade boys does not want some of the girls to join in their game on the schoolyard. The teacher believes students should

learn to get along with both genders. The teacher also wants to encourage students to participate in nontraditional activities.

3. A fourth grade student suggests that the class should have a spelling bee with the boys against the girls, like some other fourth grade classes. The teacher believes in bringing the genders together rather than separating them in competing groups. The teacher also feels the students are already too competitive and wants them to learn to be more cooperative.

4. After hearing a sixth grade student tell his classmate that he would "get him" after school, the teacher tells the two students they should settle their arguments without fighting, reminds them that fighting is against the rules, and warns them that if they fight after school they will get into trouble. The student who did the threatening answers that his parents expect him to stand up for himself, especially when someone threatens him or says something derogatory about his family.

on the playground, in the cafeteria, and in classes, especially in elementary school (152). More research is needed to determine whether the changes produced by these techniques continue after the intervention programs have ended and whether they carry over to students' after-school relationships.

---

**BOX 5–2   Self Quiz**

*Eliminating Gender-Stereotypical Behavior*

Teachers have used many techniques to eliminate the prevailing gender stereotypes. State whether you would be comfortable doing the following in your own classroom. Explain your reasoning.

**1.** Rewarding students for playing with nontraditional materials and engaging in nontraditional activities
**2.** Labeling all play and learning activities as appropriate for both genders
**3.** Exposing students to nonsexist perspectives on social roles
**4.** Exposing students to nonsexist instructional and counseling materials
**5.** Discussing the gender biases in the materials students read
**6.** Including nonstereotypical role models as guest speakers, mentors, and tutors
**7.** Encouraging females to enroll in math and science courses and males to enroll in English, foreign language, and art courses
**8.** Encouraging students to consider nontraditional careers and occupations
**9.** Discouraging gender-stereotypical language patterns

**10.** Improving males' ability to delay judgment
**11.** Improving females' self-confidence
**12.** Reducing females' tendency to incorrectly attribute the cause of their poor performance to lack of ability
**13.** Helping males to be more cooperative and concerned about the needs and feelings of others
**14.** Encouraging females to be more competitive in appropriate situations
**15.** Encouraging females to be more independent in situations that require independent functioning
**16.** Encouraging females to maintain their opinions and attitudes instead of conforming to those of others
**17.** Discussing the importance of cross-gender grouping and play
**18.** Structuring and preparing mixed-gender groups in ways that decrease male dominance
**19.** Rewarding students for interacting with the opposite gender
**20.** Assigning students to mixed-gender activity, study, and play groups
**21.** Assigning both genders to leadership positions
**22.** Intervening to reduce cross-gender dominance, exclusion, cruelty, or teasing

## FOSTERING RESISTANCE TO STRUCTURAL REPRODUCTIVE FORCES

As noted in chapter 2, many authors believe that because schools and society exert such a powerful influence on the gender-stereotypical behavior of students, teachers will be unable to eliminate gender biases in school until the structure of schools and society is changed. These authors believe that teachers should work toward bringing about these changes and encourage and prepare their students to do the same. If you agree with their position, you may find the suggestions included in the articles and books listed in chapter 2 helpful.

## REALISTIC EXPECTATIONS

A number of obstacles stand in the path of teachers who believe males and females have different needs and should be treated differently. What they may want to do may not fit Title IX regulations. They may have to convince students to accept different classroom management techniques, instructional approaches, reading materials, and so on for males and females. Some students have preferences in these areas that teachers feel are more appropriate for the opposite sex. And it may be difficult to simultaneously treat both sexes differently.

Other factors make it difficult to change students' behavior. Society-at-large, through the media, language, and the like exerts an almost constant countervailing pressure on students to maintain gender-specific behavior. Children, especially boys, begin to pressure each other to conform to gender stereotypes while still in preschool. Parents transmit their sex-role expectations for their children often without even being aware of it. Many working-class parents and non-European American parents have sex-role expectations that vary widely from those of European American middle-class parents, and they often pressure their children to maintain their traditional values in the face of teachers' attempts to change them.

Despite these forces, however, research clearly indicates that teachers can make a considerable contribution toward eliminating gender-stereotypical behavior in school if they choose to do so. Merely ceasing to encourage sex-role differences among students probably helps. But actively attempting to discourage stereotypical attitudes and behavior in the ways described in this chapter helps even more.

Until more research becomes available, there will continue to be room for disagreement about the probable outcome of any attempts to modify gender-stereotypical behavior. Opinions on this question range from complete optimism to the opposite. Tavris and Wade exemplify the optimistic point of view. They believe that:

*If children can learn sex roles in school, they should be able to unlearn them there, too. Even one math teacher can inspire a girl to be interested in math if the teacher gives sincere praise for good work and explicit advice about the usefulness of math in high-paying, high-status jobs. And nothing about children's classroom behavior is impervious to change. Using praise and attention as rewards, preschool teachers can get girls to be more independent and both sexes to play more with each other and select both boys' and girls' toys. The effects are surprisingly rapid; simply by moving into a particular area and giving attention to a particular type of play, a teacher, within minutes, can eliminate sex differences in play patterns that were "obvious" all semester. When the teacher withdraws attention or praise, children tend to revert rapidly to their previous sex-typed behavior. Still the fact that such behavior can be eliminated quickly shows the enormous impact of the environment—including the teacher—on children's day-to-day conformity to sex roles. (166, pp. 226–27)*

At the other end of the continuum, Schlafly claims that "teachers used to believe they were doing a good thing by trying to make left-handed children right-handed. We now know that is unwise. Likewise, it is unwise to ignore gender identity and try to teach gender neutrality. Gender differences cannot be eradicated, and mixed-up children are the results of those who try" (165).

Brophy represents a midpoint between these extremes. He has concluded that "though gradual change can be expected, drastic change is unlikely. . . . Schools as institutions are inherently conservative, and most teachers come from conservative home backgrounds. Yet things are changing. Teachers of both sexes are less traditional than in the past and more sensitized to sexism issues" (164, p. 139).

## DILEMMAS AND GUIDELINES

Attempts to eliminate students gender-stereotypical beliefs and behavior can have both positive and negative results. Convincing girls that they can do well in math, science, and computer courses or convincing boys to enroll

---

**BOX 5–3    Self-Quiz**

*Expected Outcomes of Attempts to Eliminate Gender Differences in School*

What is your opinion about the likely outcome of efforts to reduce or eliminate students' gender-stereotypical attitudes and behavior? Are you optimistic, pessimistic, or do you stand somewhere in the middle? Why?

in language arts, drama, and other *feminine* courses and to be more open about their feelings can be very beneficial to them. But pressuring girls to take courses they feel they can not do well in or compete with boys when they are uncomfortable about doing so, or trying to get boys to take home economics courses or expose their feelings when they are not ready, can create, not solve, problems. For this reason, teachers should use their power to try to change students sex-role behavior in a thoughtful way. At times the wise, compassionate educator will choose to respect students' values, wishes, and fears rather than *improve* their behavior.

Clashes in cultural values present another dilemma. Teachers, parents, and students often have equally strong but very different beliefs about sex-roles. In a pluralistic society, educators' values do not always reflect those of their students or their parents. When students', parents', and teachers' values clash, it is unclear that educators have the right to impose their values on the others.

In such cases, there are important differences between merely *exposing* students to particular points of view and ways of behaving, encouraging students to accept these points of view and to behave in these ways, rewarding them for doing so, and pressuring them to do so. Merely exposing students may be the least effective way to bring about change, but it is the approach that is least likely to put students in conflict situations between their values, their parents' values, and those of their teachers. It may also be the most democratic and fair approach. Encouraging and rewarding students seem to be the most effective ways to bring about change, but it can actually place students in between their teachers' desires and the conflicting expectations of their families and communities.

Pressuring students to modify their behavior is probably an ineffective way to bring about real change; it is certainly unfair to students. And only a fine line separates encouraging students to change from pressuring them to do so. What a teacher thinks is encouragement, students can interpret as pressure. Therefore, exposing students to alternative models of behavior, points of view, values, and so on without encouraging, expecting, rewarding, or pressuring them to change may be the best way to relate to students whose beliefs and attitudes about sex-role stereotypes are different from what teachers prefer.

## SUMMARY

There is good reason for educators who want to reduce gender-stereotypical behavior in school to be optimistic. To accomplish their goals, educators should begin by examining their own beliefs, attitudes, and behavior for possible gender bias. Once they have corrected their own stereotypical behavior, their efforts to modify their students' attitudes and behavior will be more effective.

Many techniques have been suggested for expanding students' gen-der-stereotypical learning styles, beliefs about gender roles, and limited views on choices of courses and careers. Techniques that discourage gender-stereotypical relations and communication patterns between males and females and increase cross-gender interactions are also avail-able. Research indicates that these techniques do reduce students' gen-der-stereotypical behavior.

Techniques for changing students' stereotypical beliefs and behavior can also have negative effects if they are not used in a thoughtful way. Thus, exposing students to alternative models of behavior, points of view, values, and so on without expecting, rewarding, or pressuring them to change may prove to be the best way to relate to students whose beliefs and attitudes about gender-role stereotypes are different from what teachers prefer them to be.

## ACTIVITIES

**1.** Ask a colleague or fellow student to examine your instructional and classroom management approaches at the beginning of the school year for gender, ethnic, or socioeconomic bias. Establish specific self-improve-ment goals. Have the same person evaluate you later in the year and report to you on the extent to which you have, or have not, achieved your goals.

**2.** Examine your students' behavior at the beginning of the school year for indications of gender-stereotypical behavior. List the realistic changes you expect to achieve during the time they will be with you. Work on achieving your objectives and reevaluate their behavior after a suitable period of time.

**3.** Read the material included in the text and references about the educa-tionally relevant cultural characteristics of one of the following ethnic groups: American Indians, Asian/Pacific Island Americans, African Ameri-cans, Hispanic Americans. Describe the group's cultural characteristics that teachers should take into account when they attempt to modify students' gender-stereotypical attitudes and behavior. Be sure to state which tech-niques you believe are likely to be culturally appropriate.

**4.** Ask a few of your colleagues or fellow students to respond to the four critical incidents included in this chapter. Examine their responses for areas of agreement and disagreement. Look for possible gender differences in their responses.

# REFERENCES

The following articles discuss the importance of reducing teachers' gender-stereotypical perceptions and behavior.

1. Lockheed, M. E., and Klein, S. S. 1985. "Sex equity in classroom organization and climate." In *Handbook for Achieving Sex Equity Through Education*, edited by S. Klein. Baltimore: Johns Hopkins University Press.

2. Rennie, L. J., and Parker, L. H. 1987. Detecting and accounting for gender differences in mixed-sex and single-sex groupings in science lessons. *Educational Review* 39 (1): 65–73.

Materials and programs for identifying and changing teachers' gender-stereotypical behavior are listed below.

3. Chevalier, Z. W., Roark, Calnek, S., and Strahan, D. B. 1982. *Responsive Evaluation of an Indian Heritage Studies Program: Analyzing Boundary Definition in a Suburban School Context.* ERIC ED 220 226.

4. Grayson, D. A. 1985. "Implementing the Gender Expectations and Student Achievement (GESA) Teacher Training Program." Paper presented at the annual meeting of the American Educational Research Association, Chicago.

5. Grayson, D. A. 1987. *Evaluating the Impact of the Gender Expectations and Student Achievement (GESA) Program.* ERIC ED 283 881.

6. Grayson, D. A. and Martin, M. 1984. "Gender Expectation and Student Achievement: A Teacher Training Program Addressing Gender Disparity in the Classroom." Paper presented at the annual meeting of the American Educational Research Association, New Orleans.

7. Rennie, L. J., Parker, L. H., and Hutchinson, P. E. 1985. *The Effect of In-service Training on Teacher Attitudes and Primary School Science Classroom Climates.* Research Report Number 12. ERIC ED 280 867.

8. Weiss, I. R. 1984. *Development and Evaluation of the Science Careers Program.* ERIC ED 254 402.

The following references deal with rewarding students' nonstereotypical behavior.

9. Fagot, B. I. 1977. Consequences of moderate cross-gender behavior in preschool children. *Child Development* 48: 902–07.

10. Fagot, B. I. 1978. "The Socialization of Sex Differences in Early Childhood." Paper presented at the annual meeting of the Oregon Psychological Association, Eugene, Oregon.

11. Fagot, B. I. 1985. Beyond the reinforcement principle: Another step toward understanding sex roles. *Developmental Psychology* 21: 1097–1104.

12. Flerx, V. C., Fidler, D. S., and Rogers, R. W. 1976. Sex role stereotypes: Developmental aspects and early intervention. *Child Development* 47: 998–1007.

13. Lamb, M. E., Easterbrook, A. M., and Holden G. W. 1980. Reinforcement and punishment among preschoolers: Characteristics, effects, and correlates. *Child Development* 1230–36.

14. Schofield, J. W. 1981. Complementary and conflicting identities: Images of interaction in an interracial school. In *The Development of Chil-*

*dren's Friendships,* edited by S. A. Asher and J. M. Gottman. New York: Cambridge University Press.

15. Serbin, L. A., Connor, J. H., Burchardt, C. J., and Citron, C. C. 1979. Effects of peer presence on sex typing of childrens play behavior. *Journal of Experimental Child Psychology* 27: 303–09.

16. Serbin, L. A., Tonick, I. J., and Sternglanz, S. H., 1977. Shaping cooperative cross-sex play. *Child Development* 48: 924–29.

17. Stockard, J., Schmuck, P. A., Kemper, K., Williams, P., Edson, S. K., and Smith, M. A. 1980. *Sex Equity in Education.* New York: Academic Press.

18. Thorne, B. 1986. "Girls and boys together, but mostly apart." In *Relationship and Development,* edited by W. W. Hartup and Z. Rubin. Hillsdale, NJ: Erlbaum.

Teaching nonsexist views of male and female roles is the focus of the following references.

19. Ahlum, C., and Fralley, J. 1976. *High School Feminist Studies.* Westbury, NY: Feminist Press.

20. Cain, M. A. 1980. *Boys and Girls Together: Nonsexist Activities for Elementary School.* Holmes Beach, FL: Learning Publications.

21. Eyler, J. 1974. Classroom strategies: Teaching about justice for women. *Law in American Society* 3: 40–45.

22. Gillespie, P. H. 1973. Boy things, girl things. *Instructor* 83: 62–66.

23. Guttentag, M., and Bray, H. 1976. *Undoing Sex Stereotypes: Research and Resources for Educators.* New York: McGraw-Hill.

24. Kaub, S. J. 1984. Women's studies at the secondary school level. In *Women and Education,* edited by

E. Fennema and M. J. Ayer. Berkeley, CA: McCutchan.

25. Kampelman, M. 1973. *WAEL K-12 Education Kit.* Washington, DC: Women's Equity Action League.

26. Sadker, M. P., and Sadker, D. M. 1982. *Sex Equity Handbook for Schools.* New York: Longman.

27. Sheridan, M. ed. 1982. *Sex Stereotyping and Reading: Research and Strategies.* Newark, DE: International Reading Association.

28. Stewart, C. G., and Lewis, W. A. 1986. Effects of assertiveness training on the self-esteem of black high school students. *Journal of Counseling and Development* 64: 638–41.

29. Tiedt, I. M. 1976. *Sexism in Education.* Morristown, NJ: General Learning Press.

The following references list various sex-equitable instructional materials and publishers of such materials.

30. Froschl, M., and Sprung, B. 1988. *Resources for Educational Equity: A Guide for Grades Pre-Kindergarten-12.* New York: Garland.

31. Guttenberg, M., and Bray, H. 1976. *Undoing Sex Stereotypes: Research and Resources for Educators.* New York: McGraw-Hill.

32. Hahn, C. L., and Bernard-Powers, J. 1985. Sex equity in social studies. In *Handbook for Achieving Sex Equity through Education,* edited by S. S. Klein. Baltimore: Johns Hopkins University Press.

33. National Women's History Project. 1990. *Women's History Resources.* Windsor, CA.

34. Olsen, L. 1977. *Nonsexist Curricular Materials for Elementary Schools.* Westbury, NY: Feminist Press.

35. Rosenfelt, D. S. 1976. *Strong Woman: An Annotated Bibliography for the High School Classroom.* Westbury, NY: Feminist Press.

36. Scott, K. P., and Schau, C. G. 1985. "Sex equity and sex bias in instructional materials." In *Handbook for Achieving Sex Equity through Education*, edited by S. S. Klein. Baltimore: Johns Hopkins University Press.

37. Shafer, S., and Gordon, B. 1982. "A resource directory for sex equity in education." In *Sex Equity Handbook for Schools*, edited by M. P. Sadker and D. M. Sadker. New York: Longman.

38. Stitt, B. A. 1988. *Building Gender Fairness in Schools.* Carbondale, IL: Southern Ilinois University.

The following references discuss the effectiveness of exposing students to sex-equitable instructional materials.

39. Ashby, M. S., and Wittmaier, B. C. 1978. Attitude changes in children after exposure to stories about women in traditional or nontraditional occupations. *Journal of Educational Psychology* 70: 945–49.

40. Barclay, L. K. 1974. The emergence of vocational expectations in preschool children. *Journal of Vocational Behavior* 4: 1–14.

41. Bem, S. L., and Bem, D. L. 1973. Does sex-biased job advertising "aid and abet" sex discrimination? *Journal of Applied Social Psychology* 3: 6–18.

42. Berg-Cross, L., and Berg-Cross, G. 1978. Listening to stories may change children's attitudes. *Reading Teacher* 31: 659–63.

43. Cornillin, S. K. ed. 1974. *Images of Women in Fiction: Feminist Perspectives.* Bowling Green, OH: Bowling Green University Press.

44. Costello, E. M. 1979. The impact of language in job advertising on fair practices in hiring: A research note. *Journal of Applied Social Psychology* 9: 323–25.

45. Davidson, E. E., Yasuna, A., and Tower, A. 1979. The effects of television cartoons on sex-role stereotyping in young girls. *Child Development* 50: 596–600.

46. Franzoni, J. B. 1980. "Childrens Reactions to Gender-Biased Materials in Career Education." Paper presented at the annual meeting of the American Psychological Association, Montreal.

47. Gollnick, D., Sadker, M., and Sadker, D. 1982. "Beyond the Dick and Jane syndrome: Confronting sex bias in instructional materials." In *Sex Equity Handbook for Schools*, edited by M. P. Sadker and D. M. Sadker. New York: Longman.

48. Greene, A. L., Sullivan, H. J., and Beyard-Tyler, K. 1982. Attitudinal effects of the use of role models in information about sex-typed careers. *Journal of Educational Psychology* 74: 393–98.

49. Johnson, J., Ettma, J., and Davidson, T. 1980. *An Evaluation of Freestyle: A Television Series to Reduce Sex-Role Stereotypes.* Ann Arbor: University of Michigan.

50. Lutes-Dunckley, C. J. 1978. Sex-role preferences as a function of sex of storyteller and story content. *Journal of Psychology* 100: 151–58.

51. National Council of Teachers of English. 1976. *Responses to Sexism: Class Practices in Teaching English 1976–1977.* Urbana, IL: NCTE.

52. Pingree, S. 1978. The effects of nonsexist television commercials and

perceptions of reality on children's attitudes about women. *Psychology of Women Quarterly* 2: 262–77.

53. Rosenfelt, D. S. ed. 1976. *Strong Women.* Old Westbury, NY: Feminist Press.

54. Schau, C. G. 1978. "Evaluating the Use of Sex-Role Reversed Stories for Changing Children's Stereotypes." Paper presented at the annual meeting of the American Educational Research Association, Toronto.

55. Schau, C. G., Kahn, L., and Tremaine, L. 1976. "Effects of Stories on Elementary School Children's Gender Stereotyped Attitudes toward Adult Occupations." Unpublished manuscript, University of New Mexico, Albuquerque.

56. Schmitz, B. 1984. Guidelines for reviewing foreign language textbooks for sex bias. *Women's Studies Quarterly* 12 (3): 7–9.

57. Scott, K. P. 1986. Effects of sex-fair reading materials on pupils' attitudes, comprehension and interest. *American Educational Research Journal* 23: 105–16.

58. Scott, K. P., and Feldman-Summers, S. 1979. Children's reactions to textbook stories in which females are portrayed in traditionally male roles. *Journal of Educational Psychology* 71: 396–402.

59. Showalter, E. ed. 1974. *Women's Liberation and Literature.* NY: Harcourt Brace Jovanovich.

The following references deal with the effectiveness of exposing students to nontraditional role models.

60. Brody, J., and Fox, L. H. 1980. "An accelerative intervention program for mathematically gifted girls." In *Women and the Mathematical Mys-*

*tique,* edited by L. H. Fox, L. Brody, and D. Tobin. Baltimore: Johns Hopkins University Press.

61. Concciatore, J. 1990. Shortage of minority teachers leads some to look to majority. *Black Issues in Higher Education* 7 (10): 8.

62. Mitchell, T. 1990. Project 2000 gateway to success for some black males. *Black Issues in Higher Education* 7 (18): 49–50.

63. *Resegregation of Public Schools: The Third Generation.* 1989. Portland, OR: Northwest Regional Educational Laboratory.

64. Tobin, D., and Fox, L. 1980. "Career interests and career education: A key to change." In *Women and the Mathematical Mystique,* edited by L. H. Fox, L. Brody, and D. Tobin. Baltimore: Johns Hopkins University Press.

The following references are concerned with encouraging students to consider and enroll in nontraditional courses.

65. Allen, R. H., and Chambers, D. L. 1977. *A Comparison of the Mathematics Achievement of Males and Females.* ERIC ED 159 076.

66. Brush, L. 1978. A validation study of the mathematics anxiety rating scale (MARS). *Educational and Psychological Measurements* 38: 485–490.

67. Casserly, P. L. 1979. "The Advanced Placement Teacher as the Critical Factor in High School Women's Decisions to Persist in the Study of Mathematics." Paper presented at the annual meeting of the American Educational Research Association, San Francisco.

68. Chasek, A. S. 1985. *Futures Unlimited: Expanding Choices in Nontraditional Careers.* New Brunswick, NJ:

Consortium for Educational Equity, Rutgers, The State University.

69. Chen, M. 1985. *Gender and Computers: The Beneficial Effects of Experience on Attitudes.* ERIC ED 265 848.

70. Eastman, S. T., and Krendl, K. A. 1984. *Computer and Gender: Differential Effects of Electronic Search on Students' Achievement and Attitudes.* ERIC ED 258 827.

71. Eccles, J., Adler, T. F., and Meece, J. L. 1984. Sex differences in achievement: A test of alternate theories. *Journal of Personality and Social Psychology* 46: 26–43.

72. Fennema, E., and Ayer, M. J. 1984. *Women and Education: Equity or Equality.* Berkeley, CA: McCutchan.

73. Fennema, E., Wolleat, P. L., Pedro, J. D., and Becker, A. D. 1981. Increasing women's participation in mathematics: An intervention study. *Journal of Research in Mathematics* 12 (1): 3–14.

74. Fox, L. H., Tobin, D., and Brody, L. 1979. "Sex-role socialization and achievement in mathematics." In *Sex-Related Differences in Cognitive Functioning: Developmental Issues,* edited by M. S. Witting and A. C. Petersen. New York: Academic Press.

75. Fraser, S. 1982. *SPACES: Solving Problems of Access to Careers in Education and Science.* Berkeley, CA: University of California.

76. Kelly, A. 1985. Changing schools and changing society: Some reflections on the Girls into Science and Technology project. In *Race and Gender: Equal Opportunities Policies in Education,* edited by M. Arnot. NY: Pergamon Press.

77. Lockheed, M. E., Thorpe, M., Brooks-Gunn, J., Casserly, P., and McAloon, A. 1985. *Understanding Sex/Ethnic Related Differences in Mathematics, Science and Computer Science for Students in Grades Four to Eight.* Princeton, NJ: Educational Testing Service.

78. Lockheed, M. E., Thorpe, M., Brooks-Gunn, J., Casserly, P., and McAloon, A. 1985. *Sex and Ethnic Differences in Middle School Mathematics, Science, and Computer Science: What Do We Know: A Report.* ERIC ED 303 353.

79. Malcolm, S. M., Aldrich, M., Hall, P. Q., Boulware, P., and Stern, V. 1984. *Equity and Excellence: Compatible Goals. An Assessment of Programs That Facilitate Increased Access and Achievement of Females and Minorities in K-12 Mathematics and Science Education.* ERIC ED 257 884.

80. Mallow, J. V. 1986. *Science Anxiety: Fear of Science and How to Overcome It.* Clearwater, FL: H & H Publishing.

81. Meece, J. L. 1981. "Sex Differences in Achievement-Related Affect." Paper presented at the annual meeting of the American Educational Research Association, Los Angeles.

82. Oliver, J. S., and Simpson, R. D. 1985. "Affective Influences on Commitment to Science." Paper presented at the 60th annual meeting of the National Association for Research in Science Teaching, Washington, D.C.

83. Simpson, R. D., and Oliver, J. S. 1985. Attitude toward science and achievement motivation profiles of male and female science students in grades six through ten. *Science Education* 69 (4): 511–26.

84. Smith, W. S. 1986. *Making Science Useful: COMETS Workshop Leader's Guide.* Lawrence KS: University of Kansas.

85. Smith, W. S., Molitor, L. L., Nelson, B. J., and Mathew, C. E. 1982. *Career Oriented Modules to Explore Topics in Science.* Lawrence: University of Kansas.

86. Stage, E. K., Kreinberg, J. E., Eccles (Parson), J., and Becker, J. R. 1985. "Increasing the participation and achievement of girls and women in mathematics, science, and engineering." In *Handbook for Achieving Sex Equity through Education,* edited by S. S. Klein. Baltimore: Johns Hopkins University Press.

87. Taylor, R. 1982. "Equity in Mathematics: A Case Study." Paper presented at the core conference of the National Council of Teachers of Mathematics, Reston, VA.

88. Travis, K. J., and McKnight, C. C. 1985. Mathematics achievement in U.S. schools: Preliminary findings from the second IEA Mathematics Study. *Phi Delta Kappa* 66: 407–13.

89. Wise, L., Steel, L., and MacDonald, C. 1979. "Origins and Career Consequences of Sex Differences in High School Mathematics Achievement." Washington, DC: National Institute of Education.

The following references deal with the efficacy of special courses.

90. Davis, B. G., and Stage, E. K. 1980. *Evaluation Report for a Math Learning Center with Microcomputers.* Berkeley: University of California.

91. Gale, D., Frances, S., Friel, M., and Gruber, M. 1978. *Building Math Confidence in Women* (Report of 1977–1978 innovative grant). Humboldt, CA: Humboldt State University.

92. Resnek, D., and Rupley, W. H. 1980. Combatting "mathophobia" with a conceptual approach to mathematics. *Educational Studies in Mathematics* 11: 423–41.

The references listed below describe techniques for improving female students' academic achievement.

93. Afflack, R. 1982. *Beyond EQUALS: To Encourage the Participation of Women in Mathematics.* Oakland, CA: Math/Science Network.

94. Brush, L. R. 1980. *Encouraging Girls in Mathematics: The Problem and the Solution.* Cambridge, MA: Abt Books.

95. Burger, C. F. 1982. Attainment of skill in using science processes. I. Instrumentation, methodology, and analyses. *Journal of Research in Science Teaching* 19: 249–60.

96. Cheek, H. N. ed. 1984. *Handbook for Conducting Equity Activities in Mathematics Education.* Reston, VA: National Council of Teachers of Mathematics.

97. Downie, D., Slesnick, T., and Stenmark, J. K. 1981. *Math for Girls and Other Problem Solvers.* Berkeley: University of California.

98. Fennema, E. 1981. *Multiplying Options and Subtraction Bias.* Reston, VA: National Council of Teachers of Mathematics.

99. Perl, T. H., and Manning, J. M. *Women, Numbers, and Dreams.* Santa Rosa, CA: Women's History Project. Undated.

100. Skolnick, J., Langbort, C., and Day, L. 1982. *How to Encourage Girls in Math and Science.* Englewood Cliffs, NJ: Prentice-Hall.

101. Tobias, S. 1980. *Paths to Programs for Intervention: Math Anxiety, Math Avoidance, and Reentry Mathematics.* Washington D.C.: Institute for the Study of Anxiety in Learning.

102. Wallace, J. M. 1986. Nurturing an "I can" attitude in mathematics. *Equity and Choice* Winter: 35–40.

103. Wallace, J. M. 1988. "Mathematics." In *Resources for Educational Equity: A Guide for Grades Pre-Kindergarten-12,* edited by M. Froschl and B. Sprung. New York: Garland.

These references are concerned with encouraging students to consider nontraditional careers and occupations.

104. American Institutes for Research 1979. *The Vocational Education Equity Study, Vol. 3: Case Studies and Promising Approaches.* Palo Alto, California.

105. Archer, C. J. 1984. Children's attitudes toward sex-role division in adult occupational roles. *Sex Roles* 10 (1/2): 1–10.

106. Becker, W. J., and Cole, J. M. 1980. *Reduction of Sex Stereotyping in Vocational Education Programs.* (July 1979–June 30, 1980). Gainesville, FL: University of Florida.

107. Farmer, H. S. 1981. *Career Motivation Achievement Planning: C-MAP.* Champaign, IL: University of Illinois.

108. Farmer, H. S., and Sidney, J. S. 1985. Sex equity in career and vocational education. In *Handbook for Achieving Sex Equity through Education,* edited by S. S. Klein. Baltimore: Johns Hopkins University Press.

109. Harrison, L. 1980. "Sex-stereotyping programs." In *Programs to Combat Stereotyping in Career Choice,* American Institutes for Research. Washington, D.C.: U.S. Office of Education.

110. Johnson, J., and Ettema J. 1982. *Positive Images: Breaking Stereotypes with Children's Television.* Beverly Hills: Sage.

111. Kerr, B. A. 1983. Raising the career aspirations of gifted girls. *Vocational Guidance Quarterly* 32 (1): 37–43.

112. Sandell, A. C., and Burge, P. L. 1988. Profiles of secondary vocational students enrolled in programs nontraditional for their sex. *Journal of Vocational Education Research* 13 (4): 16–32.

These references deal with socioeconomic class differences in students' stereotypical perceptions of careers and occupations.

113. Franken, M. W. 1983. Sex role expectations in children's vocational aspirations and perceptions of occupations. *Psychology of Women Quarterly* 8 (1): 59–68.

114. Hannah, J. S., and Kahn, S. E. 1989. The relationship of socioeconomic status and gender to the occupational choices of grade 12 students. *Journal of Vocational Behavior* 34 (2): 161–78.

115. Lyson, T. A. 1977. *Career Plans and Regional Context: A Study of Rural Youth in Two Appalachian Settings.* ERIC ED 142 345.

116. Scholssberg, N. K., and Goodman, J. A. 1972. A woman's place: Children's sex stereotyping of occupations. *Vocational Guidance Quarterly* 20: 266–70.

The following references concern reducing gender stereotypical language patterns.

117. Adams, K., and Ware, N. C. 1984. "Sexism and the English language: The linguistic implications of being a woman." In *Women: A Feminist Perspective.* 3d ed., edited

by J. Freeman. Palo Alto, CA: Mayfield.

118. Florida State University 1983. *Decisions about Language. Teacher's Guide. Fair Play: Developing Self-Concept and Decision-Making Skills in Middle School.* ERIC ED 238 518.

119. Florida State University 1983. *Decisions about Language. Student Guide. Fair Play: Developing Self-Concept and Decision-Making Skills in Middle School.* ERIC ED 238 519.

120. Graddol, D., and Swann, J. 1989. *Gender Voices.* Oxford, England: Basil Blackwell.

121. Hill, A. O. 1986. *Mother Tongue, Father Time. A Decade of Linguistic Revolt.* Bloomington: Indiana University Press.

122. Nilsen, A. P. 1980. *Changing Words in A Changing World.* Washington, D.C.: Women's Educational Equity Program, U.S. Department of Education.

123. Sheldon, A. 1990. "Kings are royaler than queens": Language and socialization. *Young Children* 45: 4–9.

124. Thorne, B., Kramarae, C., and Henley, N. ed. 1983. *Language, Gender, and Society.* Rowley, MA: Newbury House.

These references deal with improving students' self-concepts.

125. Canfield, J., and Wells, J. C. 1976. *100 Ways to Enhance Self-Concept in the Classroom.* Englewood Cliffs, NJ: Prentice-Hall.

126. De Charms, R. 1976. *Enhancing Motivation.* New York: Harper & Row.

127. Felker, D. W. 1974. *Building Positive Self-Concepts.* Minneapolis: Burgess.

128. Hauserman, N., Mitler, J. S., and Bond, F. T. 1976. A behavioral approach to changing self-concept in elementary school children. *Psychological Record* 26: 111–16.

129. Lane, J., and Muller, D. 1977. The effect of altering self-descriptive behavior on self-concept and classroom behavior. *Journal of Psychology* 97: 115–25.

130. Scheier, M. A., and Kraut, R. E. 1979. Increasing educational achievement via self-concept change. *Review of Educational Research* 49: 131–49.

131. Schulman, J. L., Ford, R. C., and Busk, P. 1973. A classroom program to improve self-concept. *Psychology in the Schools* 10: 481–87.

132. Simmons, C. H., and Parsons, R. J. 1983. Developing internality and perceived competence: The empowerment of adolescent girls. *Adolescence* 18 (72): 917–22.

Cooperative learning activities are described in the following references.

133. Lyman, L., and Foyle, H. C. 1990. *Cooperative Grouping for Interactive Learning: Students, Teachers, and Administrators.* Washington, DC: National Education Association.

134. Slavin, R. 1990. *Cooperative Learning: Theory, Research, and Practice.* Englewood Cliffs, NJ: Prentice-Hall.

Increasing caring behavior is the focus of the following articles.

135. Lickona, T. 1977. Creating the just community with children. *Theory into Practice* 16 (2): 103.

136. McPhail, P. 1975. *Learning to Care.* Niles, IL: Argus Communications.

137. Newman, F. 1975. *Education for Citizen Action: Challenges for Secon-*

*dary Curriculum.* Berkeley, CA: McCutchan.

138. Newman, F., Bertocci, T. A., and Landsness, R. M. 1977. *Skills in Citizen Action.* Skokie, IL: National Textbook.

These references deal with lessening male dominance and female passivity in mixed-gender groups.

139. Kidwell, C. S. 1975. *American Indian Women: Problems of Communicating a Cultural/Sexual Identity.* ERIC ED 172 289.

140. Lockheed, M. E. 1976. *The Modification of Female Leadership Behavior in the Presence of Males.* ERIC ED 160 628.

141. Lockheed, M. E., and Hall, K. P. 1976. Conceptualizing sex as a status characteristic: Application to leadership training strategies. *Journal of Social Issues* 32 (3): 111–19.

142. Scott, K. P. 1982. Teaching about sex differences in language. *Clearing House* 55: 410–13.

143. Scott, K. P., Dwyer, C. A., and Lieb-Brilhart, B. 1985. Sex equity in reading and communication. In *Handbook for Achieving Sex Equity through Education,* edited by S. S. Klein. Baltimore: Johns Hopkins University Press.

144. Webb, N. 1982. "Interaction Patterns: Powerful Predictors of Achievement in Cooperative Small Groups." Paper presented at the annual meeting of the American Educational Research Association, New York.

145. Women's Educational Equity Program. 1983. *Fair Play: Developing Self-Concept and Decision-Making Skills in the Middle School.* Newton, MA: Education Development Center.

Increasing cross-gender interaction is the focus of the following references.

146. Best, R. 1983. *We've All Got Scars: What Boys and Girls Learn in Elementary Schools.* Bloomington: Indiana University Press.

147. Edwards, C. P., and Whiting, B. B. 1988. *Children of Different Worlds.* Cambridge, MA: Harvard University Press.

148. Grant, L. 1982. "Sex-Roles and Statuses in Peer Interactions in Elementary Schools." Paper presented at the annual meeting of the American Educational Research Association, New York.

149. Hallinan, M. T., and Tuma, N. B. 1978. Classroom effects on change in children's friendships. *Sociology of Education* 51: 270–82.

150. Hansell, S. 1982. "Cooperative Group Learning and the Racial and Sexual Integration of Peer Friendships." Paper presented at the Second International Conference on Cooperative Education at Brigham Young University, Provo, Utah.

151. Harris, A. M., and Lockheed, M. E. 1982. "Individual and Group Problem Solving Performance for Boys and Girls." Paper presented at the annual meeting of the American Educational Research Association, New York.

152. Hutchison, B. 1981. *Lincoln County National Demonstration Project.* Portland, OR: Northwest Regional Educational Laboratory.

153. Jacklin, C. N., and Maccoby, E. E. 1978. Social behavior at 33 months in same-sex and mixed-sex dyads. *Child Development* 49: 557–69.

154. Karkau, K. 1973. *Sexism in the Fourth Grade.* Pittsburg: KNOW.

155. LaFreniere, P., Strayer, F. F., and Gauthier, R. 1984. The emergence of same-sex preference among preschool peers: A developmental ethological perspective. *Child Development* 55: 1958–65.

156. Lockheed, M. E., Finkelstein, K. J., and Harris, A. M. 1979. *Curriculum and the Search for Equality: Model Data Package.* Princeton: Educational Testing Service.

157. Lockheed, M. E., and Harris, A. M. 1982. Classroom interaction and opportunities for cross-sex peer learning in science. *Journal of Early Adolescence* 2 (2): 135–43.

158. Lockheed, M. E., Harris, A. M., and Finkelstein, K. J. 1979. *Curriculum and Research for Equity: A Training Manual for Promoting Sex Equity in the Classroom.* Princeton, NJ: Educational Testing Service.

159. Luria, Z., and Herzog, E. 1985. "Gender Segregation Across and Within Settings." Paper presented at the biennial meeting of the Society for Research in Child Development, Toronto, Canada.

160. Maccoby, E. E. 1988. Gender as a social category. *Developmental Psychology* 24 (6): 755–65.

161. Maccoby, E. E., and Jacklin, C. N. 1987. "Gender segregation in childhood." In *Advances in Child Development and Behavior* vol. 20, edited by E. H. Reese. New York: Academic Press.

162. Raviv, S. 1982. "The Effects of Three Teaching Methods on the Cross-Sex Cooperative and Competitive Behaviors of Students in Ethnically-Mixed Seventh Grade Classes." Paper presented at the Second International Conference on Cooperative Education at Brigham Young University, Provo, Utah.

163. Scott, K. P. 1984. *Teaching Social Interaction Skills: Perspectives on Cross-Sex Communication.* ERIC ED 252 445.

References that deal with realistic expectations are listed below.

164. Brophy, J. E. 1985. "Interaction of male and female students with male and female teachers." In *Gender Influences in Classroom Interaction,* edited by L. C. Wilkinson and C. B. Marrett. New York: Academic Press.

165. Schlafly, P. 1989. Personal Communication, May 1989.

166. Tavris, C., and Wade, C. 1984. *The Longest War: Sex Differences in Perspective.* 2d. ed. New York: Harcourt Brace Jovanovich.

# Index